KING RICHARD III

SHAKESPEARE AT STRATFORD

Published by The Arden Shakespeare in association with
The Shakespeare Birthplace Trust

General Editor: Robert Smallwood, The Shakespeare Centre

Associate Editors: Susan Brock, The Shakespeare Centre Library
Russell Jackson, The Shakespeare Institute

KING RICHARD III   *Gillian Day*
THE MERCHANT OF VENICE   *Miriam Gilbert*
THE WINTER'S TALE   *Patricia E. Tatspaugh*

Forthcoming titles:
ROMEO AND JULIET   *Russell Jackson*
THE TEMPEST   *David Lindley*
AS YOU LIKE IT   *Robert Smallwood*

KING RICHARD III

GILLIAN DAY

The Arden website is at
http://www.ardenshakespeare.com

Shakespeare at Stratford: *King Richard III*
first published 2002 by The Arden Shakespeare
in association with the Shakespeare Birthplace Trust

© 2002 Gillian Day

Arden Shakespeare is an imprint of Thomson Learning

Thomson Learning
Berkshire House
168-173 High Holborn
London WC1V 7AA

Typeset by LaserScript, Mitcham, Surrey

Printed by Zrinski in Croatia

British Library Cataloguing in Publication Data
A catalogue record for this book is available from the British Library

Library of Congress Cataloguing in Publication Data
A catalogue record has been applied for

ISBN 1-903436-12-5 (pbk)
NPN 9 8 7 6 5 4 3 2 1

THE AUTHOR

Gillian Day is a Senior Lecturer in English Literature at the University of Central England in Birmingham. She studied at the University of London and took her master's degree and doctorate at the Shakespeare Institute of the University of Birmingham. She has taught English and Drama in secondary and higher education in Britain, North America and Scandinavia, and has held visiting lectureships at the Universities of Helsinki and Düsseldorf. She is also a visiting academic at the Shakespeare Centre in Stratford-upon-Avon, lecturing to university groups from Europe and North America on Text and Theatre.

FOR

MY PARENTS

CONTENTS

LIST OF ILLUSTRATIONS

SOURCES
Joe Cocks Studio: The Joe Cocks Studio Collection, The Shakespeare Centre Library, Stratford-upon-Avon
Malcolm Davies: The Shakespeare Centre Library, Stratford-upon-Avon
Thomas Holte: The Tom Holte Theatre Photographic Collection, The Shakespeare Centre Library, Stratford-upon-Avon
Gordon Goode, Angus McBean and Reg Wilson: The Royal Shakespeare Company Collection, The Shakespeare Centre Library, Stratford-upon-Avon
Central Press Photos: The Hulton Archive
Manuel Harlan: EPO Online on behalf of the Royal Shakespeare Company
John Bunting
Ivan Kyncl
Michael Le Poer Trench
Richard Mildenhall

Every effort has been made to contact copyright holders and the publishers will be pleased to include further acknowledgements.

GENERAL EDITOR'S PREFACE

The theatre archive housed in the Shakespeare Centre Library here in Stratford-upon-Avon is among the most important in the world; for the study of the performance history of Shakespeare's plays in the twentieth century it is unsurpassed. It covers the entire period from the opening of Stratford's first Shakespeare Memorial Theatre in 1879, through its replacement, following the fire of 1926, by the present 1932 building (renamed the Royal Shakespeare Theatre in 1961) and the addition of the studio theatre (The Other Place) in 1974 and of the Swan Theatre in 1986, and it becomes fuller as the years go by. The archive's collection of promptbooks, press reviews, photographs in their hundreds of thousands, and, over the last couple of decades, archival video recordings, as well as theatre programmes, costume designs, stage managers' performance reports, and a whole range of related material, provides the Shakespeare theatre historian with a remarkably rich and concentrated body of material. The wealth and accessibility of this collection have sometimes tended to give general performance histories of Shakespeare's plays an unintentional Stratford bias; the aim of the Shakespeare at Stratford series is to exploit, and indeed revel in, the archive's riches.

Each volume in the series covers the Stratford performance history of a Shakespeare play since World War II. The record of performances at Stratford's various theatres through this period unquestionably offers a wider, fuller and more various range of productions than is provided by any other single theatre company. It may fairly be said, therefore, that a study of the Stratford productions since 1945 of any Shakespeare play provides a representative cross-section of the main trends in its theatrical interpretation in the second half of the twentieth century. Each volume in the Shakespeare at Stratford series will, however, begin with an introduction that sets this Stratford half-century in the wider context of the main trends of its play's performance history before this period and of significant productions elsewhere during it.

The organization of individual volumes is, of course, the responsibility of their authors, though within the general aim of the series to avoid mere chronicling. No volume in the series will therefore offer a chronological account of the Stratford productions of its play: some will group together for consideration and analysis productions of similar or comparable style or approach; others will examine individual aspects or sections of their plays across the whole range of the half-century of Stratford productions' treatment of them. Illustrations are chosen for what they demonstrate about a particular production choice, a decision that, on some occasions, may be more important than photographic quality. Given the frequency with which individual plays return, in entirely new productions, to the Stratford repertoire, most volumes in the series will have some ten or even a dozen productions' approaches and choices to consider and contrast, a range that will provide a vivid sense of the extraordinary theatrical diversity and adaptability of Shakespeare's plays.

The conception and planning of this series would not have been possible without the support and enthusiasm of Sylvia Morris and Marian Pringle of the Shakespeare Centre Library, Kathy Elgin, Head of Publications at the Royal Shakespeare Company, Jessica Hodge and her colleagues at the Arden Shakespeare, and, above all, my two Associate Editors, Susan Brock of the Shakespeare Centre Library and Russell Jackson of the Shakespeare Institute. To all of them I am deeply grateful.

ROBERT SMALLWOOD

The Shakespeare Centre, Stratford-upon-Avon

ACKNOWLEDGEMENTS

This book would not have been possible without the theatre archive of the Shakespeare Centre in Stratford-upon-Avon, and the professional knowledge, skill and kindness of those librarians and archivists who maintain the collection. I owe a particular debt to Joanna Lockhart, Senior Library Assistant, for her extensive knowledge of the photograph collection, and to Roger Howells, former Production Manager at the RSC, for his acute recollection of production details. Working in the Shakespeare Centre Library reading room continues to be one of the greatest pleasures of research. My thanks, especially for their patience, go to the Arden editorial team of Jessica Hodge, Hannah Hyam and Linden Stafford, and to the School of English of the University of Central England for study leave in which to begin research. The General Editor and originator of the series, Robert Smallwood, invited me to write this book and has been a mainstay throughout. I am fortunate in the many friends who have encouraged this project, and am particularly indebted to Jenifer Waite, and to Rebecca Brown, Lecturer in Shakespeare Studies at the Shakespeare Centre, whose intelligence, perception and kindness have been invaluable. To her above all, my thanks.

GILLIAN DAY
Birmingham, June 2001

INTRODUCTION

RICHARD
> Come, cousin, canst thou quake and change thy colour,
> Murder thy breath in middle of a word,
> And then again begin, and stop again,
> As if thou wert distraught and mad with terror?

BUCKINGHAM
> Tut, I can counterfeit the deep tragedian,
> Speak, and look back, and pry on every side,
> Tremble and start at wagging of a straw,
> Intending deep suspicion.

(3.5.1–8)

Midway through *Richard III*, Richard and Buckingham compare ways of feigning fear on stage: one would ham it with tragic gestures, the other would simply hint it with a pause. A similar discussion precedes modern revivals of the play, usually at the point when the director and the actor playing Richard match interpretative approach to acting style. And their choice falls somewhere between the same extremes – theatrical melodrama or psychological realism – spanned by the performance history of *Richard III*. Over the last hundred years interpretations of Richard's villainy have ranged from the imposing Vice-figures of Frank Benson and Baliol Holloway to the naturalistic schemer of Ian Holm, and his shape has shifted from twisted crookbacks to smaller, boyishly realistic and seemingly vulnerable figures, the offspring of a family, and more like someone we might know.

This book examines the theatrical shaping of Richard III and his history in the twelve productions of *Richard III* at Stratford since 1945. It seeks to provide theatregoers who are interested in performance and stage history, including students of theatrical interpretation, with a detailed comparative analysis of different approaches to the play, and to introduce them to some of the methods by which future performances might be read. The chapter structure responds to the particular challenges that *Richard III* poses. Unlike some of Shakespeare's other histories, it offers few convenient divisions for comparative analysis; there are no plot/subplot categories or generic 'worlds', it does not focus for long on family or factional opposition, nor, beyond the court/ battlefield contrast, does it create significantly different locations. The figure of Richard dominates almost two-thirds of the action, and other major characters are identified largely in relation to him. Moreover, and in spite of this tight-knit dramatic structure, the play has been so variously adapted in the last half-century, both as a solo drama and as part of a history cycle with the *Henry VI* plays, that a scene-by-scene, or sectional, comparison of twelve productions not only complicates but is actually unhelpful to an understanding of the overall reading that each adaptation offers.

The twelve productions are therefore discussed in three chapter divisions – political, psycho-social and metatheatrical – each of which broadly defines a major directorial approach to the play over the last fifty years. All three sections reflect responses not only to the central figure but also to the nature, and meaning, of evil since World War II. Inevitably some productions match their definition more exactly than do others, with certain aspects of interpretation crossing categories, as will be clear from the discussions that follow. Richard rarely settles for a single shape, as directors, adapters and actors at Stratford and elsewhere have found. This introduction offers some discussion of approaches not represented in the volume, as well as placing the twelve

Stratford productions within the wider performance history of the play.

As the Royal Shakespeare Company's record of four productions in the last decade reveals, *Richard III* is still one of Shakespeare's most popular plays, at least in the UK. Indeed its central figure has become so much part of popular perception that the image of the historical Richard III in people's minds is almost always Shakespeare's. Rarely off the stage since the late 1590s, the play was so much in demand in Shakespeare's lifetime that five reprints of the 1597 quarto text were required, and records of performances throughout the eighteenth and nineteenth centuries confirm one of the longest uninterrupted stage histories in the Shakespeare canon. Yet, as these productions testify, it remains a record and a public image sustained by constant adaptation of the play.

Probably the most famous, certainly the longest-lasting and most influential, adaptation was that of Colley Cibber in 1700, who cut the text and added lines from *Richard II*, *Henry V* and parts of *Henry VI*, as well as his own pastiche verse, to 'improve' the original for his Restoration audience. Cibber's adaptation dominated stage productions for almost two centuries. One reason for this was its clarity: streamlining the play's increasingly obscure historical background eased some of its problems for audiences less familiar than we suppose the Elizabethans to have been with 'the history so far'. Another reason was its realism, especially since, after the Restoration, there was a diminishing awareness of the non-realist narrative and theatrical conventions to which Shakespeare's play alludes. Cibber's text reined Richard in. It reduced the figure's metadramatic and symbolic status by developing the man, giving him motivation bound up with personality and rooted in social relationships, and shaped a character who was in most respects the same as those who watched him. David Garrick, who made his acting début as Cibber's Richard in 1741, played the role as if it were Hamlet or Macbeth.

The influence of Cibber's structure survived long after the theatre returned to Shakespeare's original, and indeed helped to create the binary focus that dominated twentieth-century productions of the play. Henry Irving's much vaunted restoration of Shakespeare's text in 1877 actually tailored it to Cibber's frame. He diminished every character but Richard, and then performed the role himself so realistically that F.A. Marshall detected leadership potential in the 'audacious criminality ... [of] ... a splendid ruler of men' (Irving and Marshall, 13–14). When the figure's criminal power declined, Irving displayed an underlying moral sensitivity and vulnerability even more characteristic of Cibber's Richard than of Shakespeare's. On awaking from the ghost-filled dream, he held up a crucifix and declared, 'No creature loves me' (5.3.201), neatly ending the scene there so that no self-recrimination followed. The image was repeated at the final curtain, when the dying Richard held high the cross-hilt of his sword; and this time nothing of Richmond's epilogue spoiled the pathos.

Irving was not alone, however, in reviving Shakespeare's text; Samuel Phelps had returned briefly to it in 1845, as had Charles Calvert in 1870. As Calvert's announcement shows, his 'Grand Historical Revival of *The Life and Death of Richard III* ... perfect in correctness of detail and accuracy of mis-en-scène' took full advantage of the historical context that Cibber and Irving cut from the original. But then his staging was a direct response to historic events – the anticipated invasion of Britain by Napoleon III in the autumn of 1870. Calvert even announced his forthcoming production on Bastille Day.

Calvert staged *Richard III* as history, and Irving played it as pathetic tragedy, each making Richard a figure of the time; the political enemy without or the psychological threat within. And this divide, with its common human denominator, dominated twentieth-century productions on the English stage. Cibber's focus on Richard was subsumed into Shakespeare's play, assisted by adaptation which either echoed Cibber's structure or reflected his rationalizing, humanizing intent. And the reasons for this were remarkably similar to those that applied in 1700, as post-Enlightenment scepticism of providential patterning, alongside trust in a self-determined psycho-social state, continued to foster interest in the complex mentality of a realistic Richard within a recognizable, material world.

The year 1945 marks a watershed for productions of the play. For, at the close of that eventful year, Laurence Olivier was playing Richard III at the New Theatre, London, in an interpretation – later expanded into his 1955 film – that some consider definitive, and which probably remains the most widely known. Every production in this volume exists to an extent in Olivier's shadow. And, even half a century on, critics still make comparison; just as in 1945 they had measured Olivier against the legendary Irving. In fact, Olivier's film retained some of the central features of the Cibber/Irving tradition, particularly in its exclusive focus on Richard and its unhistorical emphasis – this last acknowledged in the opening sequence, which speaks of preserving Richard's story as a legend, not as history.

From 1945 to the late 1950s, Olivier seemed, unfairly, to dominate the play; but in the event his monopoly of one interpretation became a catalyst for innovative, alternative readings, particularly ones which opened up aspects of the text excluded by the Cibber/Irving approach. The first chapter of this book discusses three productions, from the early 1960s to the late 1980s, which explored the play's historical context in terms of contemporary political debate. In the Cold War Europe of the 1960s, directors such as William Gaskill (1961) and Peter Hall (1963) looked back to a parallel period of unease in the wake of World War I, and found inspiration in the Berlin theatre productions of Leopold Jessner and Bertolt Brecht. During the 1920s and 1930s, German theatregoers had seen explicitly topical productions of the play. Jessner's *Richard III*, for example, at Berlin's Staatliches Schauspielhaus in 1920 (and then in repertoire), used the play didactically. Aiming to present 'the idea behind the story' (Jessner, 40), he portrayed history as a grand staircase whose blood-soaked steps marked the mounting ambition of each new tyrant, Richard being the most cruel; a frighteningly real product of the power-struggle mechanism of history. Gaskill's 1961 production used Brecht's symmetrical counterpoint to uncover similar patterns in the play. Then, in *The Wars of the Roses* (1963), Peter Hall and John Barton extended the patterning back through the *Henry VI* plays to reveal Richard's political acts as the cumulative result of internecine conflict and power struggles which pre-dated his arrival on the scene.

This line of interpretation, illuminating the darker ages of English history by the light of twentieth-century politics, was taken up in two further trilogy adaptations: Michael Bogdanov's 1988 production for the English Shakespeare Company (also called *The Wars of the Roses*) and, in the same year, Adrian Noble's RSC production *The Plantagenets*. They were quite different stagings, but both invited audiences to view past conflicts as popular chronicles of the time.

These political responses to the play regarded man as essentially an animal whose wilder instincts are kept in check by a rationally structured society. However, the psycho-social interpretations, discussed in chapter 2, saw instincts and emotions as potentially civilizing forces, but open to corruption from social structures and taboos. The first to take this approach, and to present Richard as a vulnerable protagonist, was Glen Byam Shaw, in the first post-war production of the play at Stratford (1953). Like his successor, Terry Hands, who directed *Richard III* in 1970 and 1980, Byam Shaw expanded aspects of the Irving/Olivier inheritance into a consideration of the social context that had shaped Richard's psychological flaws. All three stagings therefore mapped out the social landscape of the play. The chapter sets these beside Elijah Moshinsky's more recent attempt (1998) to combine a psycho-social reading with a commercial production structure such as Stratford would have known before the war.

In the event, however, these commercial imperatives precluded the sort of detailed attention to characterization, text and business that a realization of the play's social context requires.

It was Peter Hall's strategic alteration of the theatre organization at Stratford from just such a commercial, star-focused structure to a subsidized ensemble – the Royal Shakespeare Company – in 1961 that allowed directors the artistic and financial freedom to explore less conventional interpretations of the plays. In fact Hall's landmark 1963 cycle, *The Wars of the Roses*, was partly devised to support the RSC's claim for a larger Arts Council subsidy that would allow it to develop the sort of artistic autonomy that Brecht's Berliner Ensemble enjoyed: 'These productions ... were Peter's last chance; he sank or swam by them, and the fortunes of the company depended upon them' (Sir Fordham Flower, quoted in Addenbrooke, 269). Hall's production of *Richard III*, discussed in chapter 1, illustrates the links between his democratic vision for the company and his political interpretation of the play.

Since then, history cycles have featured significantly in the history of the RSC, as the epitome of its ensemble philosophy, and the affirmation of its national significance. Productions of both tetralogies marked the quatercentenary of Shakespeare's birth in 1964, and the turn of the millennium in 2001. Productions of both parts of *Henry IV* opened London's Barbican theatre in 1982, and Adrian Noble made his mark on the company as the new Artistic Director with the *Plantagenets* trilogy in 1988. Indeed it would be true to say that renewed theatrical interest in the *Henry VI* plays has resulted in large measure from their various Royal Shakespeare Company and English Shakespeare Company revivals. But, whereas performance as a history cycle is seen to enhance the theatrical effectiveness of these relatively less well-known early histories, it can appear to modify that of *Richard III* to a degree that conflicts with the drama's reputation in theatre history. Even when all four texts are performed as a tetralogy, as in Michael Boyd's 2001 production, *Richard III* seems slightly out of step with the preceding plays. One reason for this is the requirement that the separate parts of the cycle coalesce. In over nine hours of performance, the interests of clarity demand continuity and coherence, which adaptation imposes through textual and visual patterning; historical detail is rationalized into causation and effect, so that events develop logically and characters psychologically. The broad tapestry of figures and action in the *Henry VI* plays gives directors the freedom to identify themes and issues for the audience through cutting and conflation, and in the staging of events.

Richard III, however, presents a different form of dramatic conflict. Verbal encounters replace the physical confrontation of the earlier histories, and most of the violence remains off stage. The text is less adaptable because the physical and dramatic landscapes are more circumscribed than in the earlier plays, and the plot structure more unitary. There is also a greater imbalance between roles, which in turn makes cutting difficult, because Richard not only dominates the narrative but frames two-thirds of it through soliloquy and aside, or in staged scenes. As presenter, therefore, Richard takes over part of the narrative function intended by the adapter's patterns in the earlier texts. This creates a divided perspective, foregrounding *Richard III*'s dramatic structure in a way not seen in *Henry VI*. The result is a metatheatrical frame of reference, which can be either diminished by adaptation to create a realistic reading, as in 1963, or subsumed into the overall staging, as in 1988 and 2001. Such modifications are an understandable attempt by directors to avoid frustrating expectations set up by the earlier plays. Yet the final play can still be something of an anticlimax, largely because each cycle seeks a uniformity of voice and structure that *Richard III*'s dialogic inconsistencies seem to qualify. This is also complicated by the possibility that the play's theatrical reputation and audience pulling-power, earned as a solo drama, prevent too radical an alteration. In all the trilogy adaptations so far, *Richard III* has been the least cut, and the least added to, of the four texts.

Chapter 3 discusses the recent Stratford productions that have explored this metatheatrical dimension, and opened up the ironic interplay of dramatic forms suppressed in realist accounts. A characteristic of these metatheatrical responses is their use of performance space, often inspired by the limitations of small-cast touring, and, in some cases, the experimental techniques of French, German and Eastern European theatre. In its combination of various forms of performance, including clowning and mime, the Rustaveli Company's *Richard III* directed by Robert Strurua, which played at the Edinburgh Festival in 1979, showed some of this experimentation. Richmond (in white) and Margaret (in black) remained onstage throughout, representing the moral extremes of the action, with Margaret speaking stage directions at key moments, especially to those about to die. By intercutting events and repeating speeches, Strurua highlighted the drama's morality-play ancestry, particularly in Richard's Vice-figure relationship with his encircling audience. Jane Howells's full-text productions of *Richard III* (and *Henry VI*) for BBC Television in 1983 also staged the play in a circle, this time in a version of an open-air children's playground with wooden climbing frames and a circular fence, while Jon Pope (1988) brought actors and audience on to the small stage of Glasgow's Citizens' Theatre (which was undergoing renovation at the time), where flies and traps added vertical reinforcement to the play's morality dimension. In 1994 Barrie Rutter toured his Yorkshire-accented account of the play for Northern Broadsides (1992–4), in which clog-dancing folk-ritual supported a gutsy exploration of class distinction – the aspiring Richard, sporting one clog and one shoe, making it unclear which represented his disability. The production visited various non-theatrical venues, including the Tower of London, a transport warehouse in Barrow-in-Furness and a yacht repair shed in Hull.

Three of Stratford's five metatheatrical productions were staged in The Other Place and Swan theatres, where the relationship between audience and playing space is more flexible and intimate than in the Royal Shakespeare Theatre. But even the two main-house productions, directed by Bill Alexander (1984) and Steven Pimlott (1995), successfully exploited the so-called limitations of the pictorial stage to expose the way in which the play's conscious theatricality draws on its dramatic inheritance. Indeed the theatrical bravura of each production, particularly the perfor-mances of Antony Sher (1984) and David Troughton (1995), was thought to hark back to the barnstorming Richards of Baliol Holloway (1920s), Donald Wolfit (1930s) and, to some degree, Laurence Olivier (1945/1955). But, as chapter 3 explains, the framework and setting of each production made it clear that Sher's spider-Richard and Troughton's Punch-Richard alluded to rather than revived the melodramatic villain.

Most of this theatrical allusion reveals that a complicating consequence of the play's lengthy popularity has been its incorporation into the myth-history that it ironizes. Four hundred years on it must be acknowledged that a range of external dramatic and historical references, accrued through the play's interpretative history, now supplements the narrative frames of reference within the text. Olivier's film recognized this paradox by defining the drama as legend, not history, and by underlining its artifice in the framing of events. And then Olivier's interpretation became part of the myth.

Richard Eyre's 1991 National Theatre production, on which Richard Loncraine's 1996 film of *Richard III* was based, developed this dialogue, using allusions to stage and celluloid versions of Shakespeare's Richard, as well as to the artistic imaging of other villain-figures, to set the play's role in history alongside history's role in the play. Staging Baynard's Castle (3.7) as a propaganda rally was nothing new, but this time the performance was defined in cinematic terms. The auditorium audience was not a citizen crowd but cinema spectators, with Ian McKellen's Hitler-Richard – a figure drawn from newsreel and propaganda footage – playing not to them but to cameras and television monitors set on the circle front. It was a double frame, which reinforced the fact that theatrical parallels between Richard and Hitler are themselves drawn from historical image-making – images whose instant recognition depends on their repeated transmission through the lens of recorded account. Richard Loncraine's film adaptation did something of the same, although it underpinned the Richard/ Hitler story with allusions to the cinematic conventions of fictional gangster movies rather than newsreel and newspaper report. Also missing from the film was the ironic allusion in Ian McKellen's stage performance to Edward VIII as Hitler-Richard, which, by playing on newly publicized doubts about the Duke of Windsor's wartime loyalty, constructed a fascist King of England from archive footage, to flesh out what has become, in retrospect, another monstrous fear. Thus, by inviting the audience to recognize an archetypal pattern in the performance of its villain-hero's tale on stage and screen, Eyre's interpretation alerted its audience to that pattern. And it went on to identify the play's place in the myth-making process, by drawing attention to the media-focalized potential for representing modern history as myth, and myth as material history.

Stratford's twelve post-war productions of *Richard III* can therefore be said to represent a comprehensive cross-section of theatrical responses to the play in the second half of the twentieth century – a range undoubtedly enhanced by the variety of Stratford's playing spaces. *Richard III* is one of the few Shakespeare plays to have been staged in all three venues – the Royal Shakespeare Theatre, the Swan and The Other Place – and each has challenged the play's scale and dynamic, as have the different production structures: ensemble, touring, repertoire, low-budget and star-spectacle.

The unusual concentration of this range of responses in one place is particularly interesting to the performance historian because of the extensive theatre archive held in Stratford at the Shakespeare Centre Library. Most of the following discussion is based on the Library's RSC collection. My analysis of the first six productions (1953, 1961, 1963, 1970, 1975 and 1980), none of which I saw, draws heavily on theatre promptbooks, production records and photographs, published reviews and, where possible, discussions with directors and members of the cast, stage managers, and others who remember the performances. Discussions of the 1984, 1988, 1992, 1995, 1998 and 2001 productions are supplemented by my own record and recollection of seeing each at Stratford, or in Stratford and London, at least twice, by video recordings of all post-1982 productions, made either at Stratford or following the London transfer, and, where available, by audio recordings of the London transfers held by the National Sound Archive at the British Library. These recordings (detailed in Appendix 1) provide an important record of action and the delivery of lines, although their account sometimes contradicts the promptbook, especially when the staging has been reworked for the London transfer. My discussions of both trilogy adaptations – *The Wars of the Roses* (1963) and *The Plantagenets* (1988) – focus on the detailed textual alterations as initial guides to each interpretation. Published versions of both adaptations exist, with introductions by the directors, although these can differ from the promptbook text. In the case of the 1963 trilogy cycle, the production was further adapted for BBC Television in 1965, and a copy of the film is held in the archive. Any details drawn from this film are indicated in the text.

Each chapter draws as widely as possible on this range of resources in order to illustrate their role in the attempted reconstruction and analysis of performance. Within this, the selection of moments or scenes from individual productions depends, to a large extent, on the areas of the play emphasized by each approach, as well as on the availability of accurate information. For example, the political responses use detailed adaptation and stage business to define relationships between individuals and factions, whereas the metatheatrical interpretations focus attention on Richard's interaction as a performer with the onstage and theatre audiences, and on the structural patterning of the play. If no video or audio record exists, Richard's many soliloquies, and lengthy scenes with only two active figures on stage – as in Richard's wooing of Anne (1.2) and of Elizabeth (4.4) – can be difficult to reconstruct because movement is not always noted in the promptbook. In contrast, the detailed treatment of the short citizens' scene (2.3) in textual adaptation and staging from 1963 onwards testifies to its increased importance in interpreting the play. There is no detailed discussion of 1.4, the scene of Clarence's murder, chiefly because promptbook accounts are either very limited, with few specific clues as to the delivery of the murderers' comic debate or of Clarence's dream speech (just as there are frustratingly few accounts of Richard's nightmare soliloquy), or so full that it is difficult to draw clear conclusions about individual moves, particularly when Clarence begins to fight for life. None of the productions omits the scene or extensively adapts it. The necessarily selective evidence of different areas of emphasis, and of adaptation, is a consequence of the range of responses among the twelve productions discussed.

Although the promptbook detail for the 1953 and 1961 productions is relatively thin, the increasing thoroughness of annotations for subsequent productions acknowledges the fact of longer runs, with transfers and sometimes tours, during which stage management responsibility changes hands. Even so, video recordings, reviews and actors' recollections can still contradict promptbook detail; the death of Richard in the 1970 production (discussed in chapter 2) is a case in point. Unfortunately some moments resist even minimal reconstruction, as promptbook lacunae and the absence of photographs, video and sound recordings, fading memories, the lack of detailed reviews and other records make it frustratingly impossible to discover exactly how a line, a speech or a scene was directed.

A generous range of photographs from the RSC archive extends the description and analysis, although the earliest of these, particularly those by Angus McBean, were posed and lit for the photographer and cannot therefore be taken as wholly representative of stage action. Later photographs capture the energy and immediacy of performance. The difficulty of showing stage settings arises from this, because different lighting is required to photograph the set, and frequently no specific record exists. For the 1963 production, therefore, I have shown the set model for *Richard III*. When the action is lit atmospherically, as by Terry Hands in 1980, photographs replicate the chiaroscuro that the director intended on stage.

Individual production details are given in Appendix 1; full references to reviews (abbreviated in the text), including informative commentaries not directly mentioned, are provided in Appendix 2; and abbreviations used are listed in Appendix 3. Since most reviews are written for a specific readership, the possible preconceptions, and expectations, of reviewers must be borne in mind, as must the performance tradition against which a particular interpretation is measured – a background which, in the case of *Richard III*, has changed considerably over the past half-century.

The cast lists and production details given in Appendix 1 follow the Arden edition, with added figures such as the Lord Mayor's Wife (1963), Jane Shore (1970, 1975, 1980, 1995), Princess Elizabeth (1963, 1970, 1980) and extra ghosts (2001). This enables actors' names to be kept to a minimum in the text itself. The cast lists reveal that several actors, particularly women, have played in more than one production; including Cherry Morris, who understudied Peggy Ashcroft's Queen Margaret in 1963, and went on to play the role in the very different productions of 1992 and 1995; Penny Downie, who moved from Lady Anne in 1984 to Queen Margaret in *The Plantagenets* (1988); Brenda Bruce, who was Queen Elizabeth in 1970 and Queen Margaret in 1975; Marjorie Yates, who was the Duchess of York in 1980 and 1988; and Ian Richardson, who was a notable Catesby in 1961, and then played Buckingham in 1970, and Richard himself in 1975. Some of those playing lesser parts are now better known: Penelope Keith (the Lord Mayor's Wife in 1963), Ben Kingsley (Ratcliffe in 1970), Charles Dance (Catesby in 1975) and Ralph Fiennes (the Ghost of Henry VI in 1988).

The programmes, from which most of the production details are taken, offer a range of character groupings: some begin with Margaret and then identify figures according to family loyalties (the psycho-social approaches), or factional and class loyalties (the political approaches); others name them in the order of appearance, so that Richard leads the company. Only in 1961 were the female figures listed separately and following the men. All the programmes follow Byam Shaw's initiative and include a family tree, to which the 1988 programme added actors' photographs to assist identification across the three *Plantagenet* plays. Programme notes began, in 1961, with the director, William Gaskill, briefly detailing the play's political and historical background, followed in 1963 with six pages of extracts and essays – including 'The Grand Mechanism' and a piece by Peter Hall entitled 'Blood will have Blood' – each piece focused, like the production, on the play's contemporary political relevance. Extracts in the 1970 and 1980 programmes supported Terry Hands's interest in the play's mythical and ritualistic rather than its political elements. From 1984, academic essays on 'Shakespeare's Histories' (Stanley Wells, 1995, 1998), 'History and Power' (Alan Sinfield, 1988), 'History, Chronicle and Myth' (Rosemary Horrox, 1998) and 'Shadows in the Sun' (Graham Holderness, 1998) took the place of directors' notes (some of them reprinted in several programmes). The 1995 programme was unusual in discussing the play from a variety of perspectives, with extracts on 'Dreams and Meanings', including Freud on *Richard III*, an interview with the director, Steven Pimlott, and a gender history essay by Lisa Jardine, 'The Tongues of Women' (reprinted in the 1998 programme). Those for the smaller theatres – 1975, 1992 and 2001 – were simpler, with production details and quotations, if any, drawn from earlier main-house programmes.

All line references are to the Arden edition of *Richard III*, edited by Antony Hammond (London, Methuen, 1981), although words and punctuation follow the promptbook where the difference is significant. These verbal differences are printed in italics. Quotations from Barton (1963) and Noble (1988) are taken from the published versions of the adapted texts. In my discussion of the remaining ten productions, all non-Shakespearean additions to Shakespeare's text are printed in italics. Unless otherwise stated, all the productions were staged at the Royal Shakespeare Theatre (known in 1953 as the Shakespeare Memorial Theatre).

1

POLITICAL
RICHARDS

This chapter discusses three responses to *Richard III* as political history, in which the general interpretative focus was on the historical power struggle behind Richard's rise to the throne, and on its contemporary political parallels. These responses were embodied in productions directed by William Gaskill in 1961, Peter Hall and John Barton in 1963, and Adrian Noble in 1988. In the Cold War climate of the 1950s and 1960s, William Gaskill saw the play as presenting opposing ideologies, with Richard as a master of realpolitik who played others like chess pieces on his board. The two later productions expanded the political-historical canvas by performing *Richard III* in sequence with the *Henry VI* plays, in a cycle form initially inspired by Douglas Seale's post-war revival of the three parts of *Henry VI* at Birmingham's Repertory Theatre (1951, and at London's Old Vic in 1952–3). In 1963 Peter Hall and John Barton's adaptation extended Gaskill's reading of *Richard III* to these same histories, creating an epic saga, *The Wars of the Roses*, in which Richard's Machiavellian dissembling grew out of the corruption of earlier political processes at the hands of innate self-interest. Twenty-five years later, the production style of Adrian Noble's adaptation *Richard III – His Death*, as part of the 1988 *Plantagenets* trilogy, mirrored what many considered to be the superficiality of political engagement in the 1980s by portraying 'a society obsessively preoccupied with politics at the level of signification' (Shaughnessy, 56), and one dangerously susceptible, therefore, to Richard's performative skills.

When Peter Hall founded the RSC in 1961 he made one rule, 'that whenever the Company did a play by Shakespeare, they should do it because the play was relevant, because the play made some demand upon our current attention' (Trevor Nunn, in Berry, 1989, 56). To keep the work 'relevant', Hall wanted to play modern drama alongside Shakespeare, and turn the company into a 'highly-trained group of actors ... with antennae stretched towards our world of contradictions ... expert enough in the past and alive enough to the present to perform the plays' (Hall, 1964, 43). With this in mind he established a second permanent base for the RSC at London's Aldwych Theatre, to house non-Shakespearean work and host an annual festival of modern European theatre. He also invited directors and designers from avant-garde theatre companies to work on the classical repertoire. The most prominent of these were Joan Littlewood's Theatre Workshop in Stratford East and the English Stage Company at London's Royal Court Theatre, both of which developed their ensemble work using, among others, the techniques of Bertolt Brecht and the ideas of the French Theatres of Cruelty and of the Absurd. Therefore, when Hall asked the director William Gaskill, the designer Jocelyn Herbert (both from the Royal Court) and the designer John Bury (from Theatre Workshop) to work at the RSC, he knew that he was bringing the margins to the centre, and must have expected unconventional results.

William Gaskill and Jocelyn Herbert came to Stratford in 1960 for Hall's first season as Artistic Director. Gaskill was experienced in modern French theatre, ballet and mime, and in 1956 had worked (then unofficially) with George Devine to launch the English Stage Company with John Osborne's *Look Back in Anger* – the same year that the visiting Berliner Ensemble also knocked British theatre sideways. As Gaskill put it, once kitchen sinks and alienation devices had begun to repoliticize English theatre, especially the relationship between stage action and audience, 'design could never quite be the same again, and I knew I had to rethink everything' (Gaskill, 14). Jocelyn Herbert, then the company's scene-painter, felt the same. She was impressed by the visual modesty of the permanent set, inspired by the Berliner Ensemble, that had been a feature of Devine's first season at the Royal Court. Later, when she saw this simplicity being spoiled by decoration, she resigned and took her new 'minimalist, object-centred approach' (Trussler, 325) to the RSC.

The cross-fertilization that drew Gaskill and Herbert back to Stratford for the 1961 production of *Richard III* also inspired the RSC's experimental season, directed by Peter Brook at the London Academy of Music and Dramatic Art the following year. Entitled 'Theatre of Cruelty', this was a medley of new and established modern plays, and one Renaissance text (Thomas Middleton's *Women Beware Women*), which tapped into current theatrical trends with its examination of 'man's deep instinctive lusts' (Hall, 1964, 46). It was this specific application of the French theatre director Antonin Artaud's theories to Renaissance texts that led Peter Hall to see the place of ritual and violence in the politics of Shakespeare's plays. And so, when he staged the early histories as *The Wars of the Roses* the following season, he drew attention to the same 'connection between catastrophe and unacknowledged instinct' that the 'Theatre of Cruelty' had identified:

> We live among war, race riots, revolutions, assassinations ... and the imminent threat of extinction. The theatre is, therefore, examining fundamentals. Man has developed some fine disciplines to curb his animal instincts, yet they are all imperilled by the nature of man himself. ... The Drama – through Beckett, Genet, Arden, Pinter, and many of our younger writers – is exploring this problem. Inevitably Shakespeare has been there already.
>
> (Goodwin, 46)

To some extent Hall's reading of Jan Kott's book *Shakespeare Our Contemporary* supported his view of history as a fatalistic force. Like Leopold Jessner before him, Kott saw history as a Grand

Mechanism binding the past to the present in an inexorable process: 'The implacable roller of history crushes everybody and everything' (Kott, 39). Hall invokes the same idea of continuity when he describes the relevance of the early histories to the present day: 'I realised that the mechanism of power had not changed in centuries. We also were in the middle of a blood-soaked century. I was convinced that a presentation of one of the bloodiest and most hypocritical periods in history would teach many lessons about the present' (Hall, 1970, xi).

This similarity has led critics to elide Kott's and Hall's interpretations of the plays. But there is an important distinction. Kott presents the human condition as 'an unalterable given which political action cannot affect' (Sinfield, 185), and he offers a profoundly pessimistic view of man's influence over history; whereas Hall suggests that man's instinct to dominate can be held in check 'by parliament, democracy, tradition, religion', and believes that Shakespeare thought so too: 'Shakespeare's conclusion is ... that history is a tragic pressure on all human beings, and unless they govern themselves and their institutions pragmatically, there is a perpetual natural tendency to return to chaos' (Hall, 1970, xiii). This emphasis on the positive power of democracy and democratic institutions to save man from himself becomes quite clear in John Barton's version of the early histories, and informs the largest piece of adaptation in *Richard III*.

Hall's belief in democratic structures was evident in the RSC itself. His new acting ensemble was founded on egalitarian principles, and *The Wars of the Roses* saga was designed to develop a joint spirit of artistic endeavour. The doubling of roles and the unfolding of character and relationships over the plays reinforced this process, as did Barton's text. His rationalization and clarifica-tion of a sometimes 'shapeless and ill-defined' dramatic structure (Barton, 1970, xvii) enabled actors to see their roles as psycholo-gically consistent and the plot as a coherent exposition 'of retribution, of paying for sins, misjudgements, misgovernments' (Hall, 1970, xiii–xiv).

This process of homogenization was relatively straightforward in the less well-known and, until this adaptation, less regarded *Henry VI* plays. Cuts, transpositions and Barton's pastiche additions were accepted because on the whole in 1963 they were not recognized. The better-known and initially more popular play, *Richard III*, however, drew a mixed response. Playing it as the conclusion of both *The Wars of the Roses* and *The Plantagenets* was praised for the resultant clarity of narrative, and for the manner in which historical events were made 'meaningful' to modern audiences. But it was also felt that adaptation weakened *Richard III* as a play. By the time the cycle had reached its finale, some in the audience were sickened and cynical: 'the effect ... [was] cumulatively deadening to the senses' (*Guardian*, 1964). This was partly because the pattern that adaptation draws out of the *Henry VI* plays is already present in the formal structure and language of *Richard III*. Richard's theatricality in the later play places him outside that patterning – 'I am determined to prove a villain' (1.1.30) – and so turns the epic narrative that adaptation seeks to clarify into the subject of the play. If, in trying to compensate for this inconsistency, the actor moves away from his earlier characterization to engage more fully with the audience, the integrity of the interpretation suffers and the disjunction with the *Henry VI* plays becomes clear, as some of the reviews reveal:

> *Richard III* presents the difficulty that ... it is largely a self-contained work. (*Times*, 1963)

> The dynamism of [Anton Lesser's] performance, and of the production as a whole, have spent themselves by the end of the middle play, making *Richard III* a curious anti-climax. (*Times*, 1989)

> The whole concluding part ... is not on the same level as the two earlier ones.... The problem is that *Richard III* is a different kind of play. (*S. Telegraph*, 1989)

> *Richard III* is a much more sophisticated play than Henry VI [*sic*]: Shakespeare made a quantum leap forward in using language and

verse to create character. Richard, too, is more complex than
anybody in the trilogy.   (*S. Times*, 2001)

Richard III seem[ed] longer-winded than the rush of often
unsophisticated but always arresting incidents that precedes
it.   (*Times*, 2001)

WILLIAM GASKILL, 1961

I

Gaskill's production was the first major staging of *Richard III* since
the release of the highly successful film version of the play
directed, in 1955, by Laurence Olivier, and it inevitably drew
critical comparison. Casting the Canadian actor Christopher
Plummer in the title role encouraged this, since in voice and, as
Figure 1 shows, in appearance his Richard bore a resemblance to
Olivier's crookback King. Gaskill's directive innovation, set beside
these visual echoes of the Olivier–Irving tradition, drew attack
and praise in equal measure. Some critics judged the production
a disappointment because Gaskill's choices were deliberately
different from Olivier's, while others acknowledged a new frame
of reference in the ensemble style. Bamber Gascoigne, for
example, saw a broadening of emphasis away from the central
figure to a court chronicle, focusing 'the spotlight ... on the web
no less than the spider' (*Spectator*), while the *Times*, in a review
entitled 'A bold break with tradition', applauded Gaskill's trust in
the post-war audience's capacity 'to believe that there are such
beings as monsters of cruelty'. This was a topical reference to the
trial of Adolph Eichmann, under way in Jerusalem as the
production opened, and reported daily in the British press.

  Although Gaskill played a relatively full text by comparison
with earlier Stratford productions, in terms of staging he believed
that 'less was more' (Gaskill, 18). His autobiography, *A Sense of
Direction*, praises the aesthetic and didactic qualities of Brecht's
'epic' theatre, because here the director maintains 'the objective

FIGURE 1 Motley's 1961 design left the stage bare but for this massive pillar, behind which Christopher Plummer's Richard often hid. Emblems, such as Edward IV's golden sun, were flown in front of the metal-mesh rear curtain.

control of the stage picture and its meaning' by focusing his audience on what will be instructive – 'moving his pointer round the stage like a school-teacher on a blackboard' (19). In Brecht's dialectical approach, the stage is blocked into left and right frames, and the audience invited to read the movement between these areas as part of the play's meaning. But for this to work 'there must be no unnecessary clobber. ... The human figure must exist in space with only such elements of architecture and physical properties as [are] absolutely necessary' (20).

He was helped here by the simplicity of Jocelyn Herbert's setting, 'light in colour, straightforward in conception, swift in movement, and spacious in *décor*' (*Tablet*), through which the language flashed 'like the trajectory of a shell' (*Observer*). The action was played on a single-level, scrubbed board stage dominated by a massive pillar stage right (shown in Figure 1). This 'Norman column', which served for both court and Tower dungeon, instantly established 'that we, too, were to be held within the precincts of a murderous bid for absolute power' (*New States.*). Called 'The Tower' in the set plans, it was chiefly associated with Richard, who would circle it in order to pause the action, or surprise everyone by suddenly appearing from behind it.

Across the rear of the stage hung a high metal-mesh curtain, fronted by a narrower and more finely meshed gauze screen in gold, both identifiable in Figure 1. At different points in the action, heraldic emblems on mesh sheets were flown in front of this screen to hang just above the Tower. These signposted the action rather like Brecht's placards, changing as the play advanced from Edward's tarnished copper sunburst (set in Figure 1), to Richard's silver and black boar (shown in the background to Figure 2), and finally to a black shield beneath a crown. The Tower and emblems were framed by a false proscenium arch, to the front of which the stage extended, past the real proscenium, on to an apron over part of the orchestra pit. Two staircases then allowed access from either side of this apron into the pit itself.

The silver, gold and jet colours of the metallic backdrop were picked up in the costumes – disappointing several reviewers who longed for Olivier's coloured heraldry. But what they considered mundanely drab others saw as richly dark, the steel grey and tarnished gold of corrupted grandeur. Many of the costumes had been 'distressed' (as the RSC would later term their deliberate ageing of materials) precisely to avoid the idealized medieval world that sumptuous costumes might suggest. It was an idea that John Bury adopted in his designs for the 1963 histories.

Richard Pilbrow's complex lighting enhanced the flexibility of this design, making it 'alternately, a landscape of skyscrapers and a well-protected West End jeweller's window at night' (*SA Herald*). And Marc Wilkinson's score matched the setting's steely coldness with a series of sharply discordant notes, dismissed by Edmund Gardiner as 'squeak-and-bump ... boar-hunt music' (*SA Herald*), but in which V.S. Pritchett heard 'a screech of horror, cruelty and unease' (*New States.*).

Setting, lighting and sound together brought a new, integrated production style to the Stratford stage. The Brechtian clarity of Gaskill's scene patterns, minimal stage furniture and the 'stark simplicity of action and groupings' cut 'a way through the maze' (*Guardian*) of the play. Byam Shaw's unfussy 1953 production had earned similar praise. Bamber Gascoigne, in the *Spectator*, voiced a hope that Gaskill's 'latest achievement ... will turn out to be a distinctive style of classical production' for the English Stage Company. In the event, however, it heralded what would become a recognizable RSC style.

II

The front curtain was perhaps the most traditional element of this production. For it rose on a totally dark stage, with only sounds – the 'sinister drumbeats and harsh flourishes from trumpets' (*Morn. Adv.*) – to indicate what was to come. Gradually a spotlight picked out Richard, his back to the audience, staring at the sun of York suspended above the stage. Beginning in a quiet, pleasant voice, he spoke the opening thirteen lines from this position. Then, turning on the line, 'But I, that am not shap'd for sportive tricks' (1.1.14), he dropped the mask of geniality and delivered the remainder of the speech 'in menacing tones' and with a 'hard and pitiless' look, directly to the audience (*Morn. Adv.*). A similar switch of tone followed his mock-grief at the imprisonment of his brother Clarence, where again the shift from compassion to coldness took the audience by surprise. Plummer gave no reason for either volte-face. Like Olivier, Gaskill added lines from *3 Henry VI* to Richard's opening soliloquies, but, whereas Olivier used them to ground Richard's hatred in familial rejection, Gaskill showed Richard icily disowning all emotional ties:

> *I had no father, I am like no father,* [Gaskill addition]
> I have no brother, I am like no brother;
> And this word 'love', which greybeards call divine,
> Be resident in men like one another,
> And not in me: I am myself alone
>
> (*3 Henry VI*, 5.6.80–3)

Later, as Richard contemplated wooing Anne, Plummer paused on the word 'love' in the lines –

> not all so much for love
> As for another secret close intent
>
> (1.1.157–8)

– and, turning upstage, took a few steps towards the 'Tower'. The thought of love appeared to trouble him, and so he moved towards a place of safety. But, unlike Olivier's Richard, he kept its cause a secret, even from his audience, and remained throughout an isolated, enigmatic figure.

Plummer's Richard was 'terribly misshapen' in appearance (*SA Herald*), 'a flailing ache of limbs like a battered swastika' (*S. Telegraph*), with a severely twisted spine, a withered arm tucked Prussian-style behind him and a 'spastic, crabbed-limp' (*SA Herald*). His face was also slightly twisted, his mouth 'slipping across' it in a half-grin (*SA Herald*). He shared with Olivier's Richard the same long, lank hair, parted to one side, and their make-up was almost identical, but his performance was his own. Where Olivier emphasized the devil Richard, Plummer stressed the quiet player, becoming 'a cynical puppet-master whose virtuoso manipulation of human beings is his only diversion in a world which scorns him' (*Spectator*). Reviews admired the calculating intelligence and the feline charm, 'throw-away wit and mobility of mind', of a suave confidence trickster (*New States.*), his mastery of the pause as counterpoint making him 'a model for Machiavelli: a conspirator who is always a jump ahead of his rivals, knows it, and delights in it' (*Tribune*). He kept his distance therefore from victim and audience alike.

The deception of Anne (1.2) reflected this shift from theatrical bravado to something more subtly underhand. Textual cuts took out all reference to the past, making his professed stoicism at his father's death (1.2.159–64) less to do with revenge than with his apparent inability to cope with emotion. He became the loveless boy unused to weeping who was suddenly disabled by a lovely face. As Plummer played it, Anne had not turned Richard back from thoughts of violence, but had melted a frozen heart.

The audience was never in doubt that this was acting, but the performance was naturalistic and potentially convincing: 'the royal mummer has been trained by Stanislavsky', Alan Brien noted in the *Sunday Telegraph*. His skill was signalled in small details. At one point the promptbook shows him perching on the edge of Henry VI's open coffin, watching as Anne moves angrily around him, the seemingly thoughtless irreverence declaring his mastery of the scene. It was a visual counterpart to his nimble, disingenuous deflation of her fury.

In the public scenes, too, Richard controlled the action. He prowled the stage as he spoke of 'sly, insinuating jacks' at 1.3.53, stopping to ask the same question of each member of the Queen's family in a mocking reversal of the excessive politeness he had shown as he arrived:

> When have I injur'd thee? When done thee wrong?
> Or thee? Or thee? Or any of your faction?
>
> (1.3.56–7)

And he ended with Elizabeth:

> Meantime, God grants that we have need of you.
>
> (1.3.77)

The Woodvilles, however, could not answer him face to face because he was never still. Circling the stage, he made others follow him or address his back. The distinctive blocking reinforced

Richard's directorial control, the 'lone chess player manipulating men and women like figures on his board' (*D. Mail*).

Only Queen Margaret (Edith Evans) disturbed Richard's cool mastery. The promptbook shows Elizabeth following Richard, trying to get his attention as he moved about the stage, deliberately challenging her status. But when Margaret interrupted the argument, Richard stood still, and turned away as she approached him. When he made to leave, she held him back with 'But repetition of what thou hast marr'd: / That will I make, before I let thee go' (1.3.165–6), and again with 'And leave out thee? Stay, dog, for thou shalt hear me' (1.3.216), her words daring to make him face her. It resulted in a rare loss of control for Richard, who made to strike her on the line, 'Thou elvish-mark'd, abortive, rooting hog' (1.3.228), before stopping himself and choosing instead the strategically placed word, 'Margaret'. The spell was broken, and Elizabeth's family closed in. No one seemed to notice how Margaret had momentarily shaken Richard's suave control.

III

Richard's isolation made him dangerously unpredictable. He arrived in the second court scene (2.1) alone and unannounced (lines 45–6 were cut), appearing from behind the Tower pillar to take the assembly by surprise precisely at the moment that King Edward marked his absence:

> There wanteth now our brother Gloucester here
> To make the blessed period of this peace.
>
> (2.1.43–4)

It was as if he had been listening all along.

Eric Porter's Duke of Buckingham was similarly skilful when it came to timing. He spent the scene observing Richard, noting at its close how he invited the others to precede him, and thereby set himself apart from Edward's court (2.1.140–1). As if signalling this observation, Buckingham pointedly invited Richard himself to depart with the line 'We wait upon your Grace' (2.1.142). Although the moment was obviously significant, it was not fully explained until the end of the following scene when, in an almost parallel situation, Buckingham proposed that they speak further on their journey to the prince (2.2.146–50). It was clear that in the interim they had joined forces, as Irving Wardle pointed out: 'There is a moment of appalling silence as the two guilty creatures see into each others' hearts, and the pact is made' (*Observer*). And Gaskill underlined the moment by taking the first interval at this point.

Wardle felt that Gaskill's focus on Richard's political partnership with Buckingham was a distinct improvement on the usual courtlier reading of Buckingham. It also fitted with Richard's delineation as a logical and realistic, though cunning, politician, rather than something inhumanly evil. Even so, the men's association remained uneasy, chiefly because they were too alike. Richard was an isolate and Eric Porter's Buckingham was equally strategic, 'a gaunt vulpine schemer' whose 'dry-witted stabs' (*Observer*) at humour, played here as failed attempts to fall in with his master's jokiness, underscored the tension between them.

Their joint assault on the court was a skilful blend of comedy and intimidation. This was first seen in 3.1, as both instructed Catesby how to sound out Hastings's loyalty, and the same teamwork controlled the council scene, 3.4. Richard arrived early and moved upstage with Lovell and Ratcliffe to conceal himself behind the Tower pillar. Once Buckingham had shown Derby, Ely and Hastings to their seats, Richard surprised everyone by suddenly appearing from the Tower, cued by Hastings's proposal to speak for him. Lovell and Ratcliffe, meanwhile, remained concealed.

The two dukes' sudden departure from the meeting was part of this performance. It left the remaining counsellors in a long and uncomfortable silence, which Richard shattered on his return not only with angry accusations but with the instant arrival of Catesby's soldiers at every door. Lovell and Ratcliffe then reappeared to take Hastings prisoner. In his allusion to George

Orwell's *Animal Farm*, Alan Brien identified these as the tactics of realpolitik: '[Hastings's] jolly, bustling, party wheel horse ... is led off to the knacker's yard just when he thinks the animal farm is his reward' (*S. Telegraph*). Hastings was led down into the pit, and the soldiers dismantled the council table, signalling clearly that there would be no consultation from now on.

More proof of the new order followed. As Hastings disappeared into the pit, so, with perfect timing, Richard and Buckingham brought out of it the props – body armour, a drum and swords – for their next scene (3.5). This visual irony set the staged 'attack' beside the secret violence of Richard's assault on the throne, and the scene played out the counterpoint. First the two men panicked the Lord Mayor by running round the pillar and beating the drum. Then, quite suddenly, they fell silent, as Lovell and Ratcliffe brought on Hastings's head. The head was not covered – an unusual decision, noted in reviews – and the sight of it unnerved the Mayor. It also invited a multilayered response from the audience. As the 'real' head became a stage prop, so the realism of Hastings's death destroyed the illusion of the mock attack. In turn, the visual horror jarred with Buckingham and Richard's calm defence of Hastings's death. (The apparent balance of their case was strengthened by the distribution of Buckingham's lines, 3.5.49–60, between them.) Thus the carnivalesque interplay of realism and performance in Gaskill's dialectical staging challenged the audience to recognize the gap between the action and the word that comedians and cunning politicians such as Richard consciously exploit.

The challenge continued in the Baynard's Castle scene (3.7). Soldiers now openly policed the stage, two of them sitting at the edge of the pit, as Clarence's murderers had done, gazing out into the audience. At the scene's close Richard drew both audiences – on the stage and in the auditorium – into his thanks for 'gently' colluding in his election: 'Farewell my cousin, farewell gentle friends' (3.7.246). But, with the soldiers looking on, the interval applause must have seemed rather like enforced support.

IV

Such was the efficiency of the coronation scene (4.2) in this production that Richard seemed to be establishing himself as the head of a Mafia-style business empire rather than a nation. This was brought out in the smoothness of certain details, such as Tyrrel's silent understanding that he should remove a ring from Richard's finger as security of passage to the boys. Richard's request for Buckingham's hand became a business-like handshake, similar to that with which they had sealed the promised earldom of Hereford (3.1.194–6). Perhaps Richard intended it to bring that offer to mind as he intimated murdering the boys.

The new King seemed to fear no treachery. He spoke to Buckingham with the court present, and was undisturbed by his friend's circumspect response to the idea of murder. All the same, when Buckingham asked leave to consider the plans, he was forced to negotiate an exit through the surrounding nobles and then through ranks of Richard's guards; a difficulty which revealed just how isolated Richard was, both from the cruelty that underpinned his court and from the world outside it. And this made him vulnerable. By the end of the following scene, news of Ely's and Buckingham's defections and the approach of Richmond's army had taken Richard by surprise. Nothing in the production had shown him as a warrior – in fact his references to recent battles were deliberately omitted from the wooing scene with Anne (1.2). He was a strategist, but it was political manoeuvring that utilized his wit. Military invasion was not something he had countenanced.

In this respect Richard differed from the other courtiers. Warriors all, they possessed a physical strength that Richard's extreme disabilities prevented him from matching. He shared this outsider status with the women at Edward's court, particularly Elizabeth Sellars's 'vain, hard and beautiful' Elizabeth (*S. Telegraph*) who was intimidated by its masculinity. She tried hard to play court politics, but threw out 'just a sufficient hint of the uncertain and self-made' (*SQ*) to explain the veneer of toughness which Richard could so easily attack. As an outsider himself he recognized her weakness. And it was through her, in 1.3, that he initially attacked the men.

As a whole, the performances of the women either disappointed the critics or were ignored by them, their response in part dictated by a critical tradition which still held that some of the *Richard III* women were 'Shakespeare's biggest bores' (*SA Herald*). Jill Dixon was thought to be weakly undercast as Lady Anne, and Bamber Gascoigne (*Spectator*) considered Edith Evans's imperious performance as Queen Margaret to be too grand and overplayed for such a modernist interpretation.

Gaskill's stated belief in ensemble theatre and his record of directorial control, however, suggest that his choice of actors was important to him. If the women seemed noticeably weaker than the men, or if those who did not, such as Margaret, appeared to be acting in a different play, then Gaskill probably had these effects in mind when he chose his company. Edith Evans had played Queen Margaret to Olivier's Richard on the London stage in 1945, and she brought with her the associations, values and acting style of 'classical Shakespeare' established in Sir Henry Irving's Lyceum productions at the end of the nineteenth century, and developed by later actors such as Olivier and John Gielgud. To cast her again as Margaret in a production that so openly departed from the traditional would be to emphasize anachronism both in character and in acting style. Gaskill seems to have used this to illustrate the fact that Margaret is from another age, presenting through her a historically deterministic world-view that was entirely different from Richard's rational materialism.

The second scene of female lamentation (4.4) was presented very formally, as Figure 2 suggests, with the three women finally seated on the ground in classical tragic mode. Reviewers noted the unusualness of this staging – with one critic regretting that Dame Edith should be made to adopt so undignified a pose – but none saw it as part of Gaskill's overall interpretation. Sidelined or rebuked by a male-dominated world, however, the women could do little else but weep and catalogue each death. By turning them

FIGURE 2 Edith Evans's Queen Margaret stands above the Duchess of York (Esmé Church) and Queen Elizabeth (Elizabeth Sellars) in Gaskill's staging of 4.4 (1961), as all three lament the cruelty of Richard, whose boar emblem looms overhead.

into choric voices, Gaskill employed a classical theatrical convention to illustrate the conventionally passive role that the world of 'masculine politics' (*S. Telegraph*) had left them little else to play.

When Margaret rose to leave, Elizabeth tried to detain her, following the old woman round the stage just as she had been forced to follow Richard in the first court scene (1.3). But by the time that Richard arrived she was using the same behaviour to the opposite effect, hounding him around the stage just as Margaret had done in 1.3. She too had learned the active power of grief.

The same was true of the Duchess of York (Esmé Church). By removing Richard's second 'wooing' scene (4.4.199–431), Gaskill increased the importance of her curse, which (as in the 1953 production) she directed at her son's greatest weakness, his inability to fight:

> Therefore take with thee my most grievous curse,
> Which in the day of battle tire thee more
> Than all the complete armour that thou wear'st!
>
> (4.4.188–190)

For those who sought to fathom Richard's reason for rejecting family bonds in his opening soliloquy (the words added from *3 Henry VI*), here was evidence that his mother knew how to attack his insecurities.

V

Gaskill's textual cutting of the play's final movement defined the confrontation between Richard and Richmond in terms of opposite world-views – Richmond embracing the bonds of shared humanity, and Richard manipulating others as if they were his goods. The final act established this contrast through the different degrees of preparation in the respective camps. In the King's tent there was a good deal of busy-ness, as Richard ordered wine and writing implements and issued orders for his armour, whereas Richmond and his men were calm and mutually supportive, welcoming defectors from the opposing side. The fact that Richard's encampment was arrived at via the pit formed a visual contrast between the open 'above-board' access to Richmond and the underground route to Richard's 'lair'.

Sadly the promptbook says nothing, and the reviews give few details, of how Plummer delivered Richard's nightmare soliloquy (5.3.178ff.). V.S. Pritchett noted that when Plummer 'awoke from his dream on the eve of Boswell [*sic*] and spoke the acid introspective passage beginning: "Richard loves Richard; that is, I am I", he reduced it to the level of a conundrum' (*New States.*). So it would seem that the conscience soliloquy was delivered in the same 'matter-of-fact, forceful, almost reasonable' manner (*Times*), and with the same unemotional logic, that characterized the other soliloquies. The staging of the visitation, however, was considered original and effective. As both commanders slept, Richard downstage of Richmond and leaning over his field-table, their surrounding guards rose from sleep to become the ghosts. Dressed in battle cloaks but now with chalk-white masks, they circled downstage and addressed Richard and Richmond one by one before exiting at different points of the stage. This doubling permitted a psychological reading of the moment, as if the soldier-ghosts were acting Richard's sleeping thoughts. If so, then the dream played out Richard's fear that future disloyalty might fulfil his mother's curse.

The confrontation between Richard and Richmond was equally innovative. Gaskill represented the opposing factions with a token handful of men – a metaphor that Bamber Gascoigne preferred to the convention which 'pretends that only a small corner of a vast army has been able to crowd through the wings and on to the stage' (*Spectator*). The end was also simple, as Richard and Richmond faced each other in silence on what was, for some time, an empty stage. This was the idea of John Barton, the fight director, who would use it again in the 1963 history cycle; and it would become a feature of the RSC production style. The stylization deliberately avoided the suggestion of excitement or heroism, an effect also intended by not using clanking armour. What few soldiers there were simply wore knitted chain-mail over their usual costumes. Although Robert Speaight (in *SQ*) regretted this absence of realistic sights and sounds, the staging maintained its dialectical focus on the confrontation of ideologies represented in Richard and Richmond. They fought with swords, but Richard also wore a mace and chain strapped to his withered arm which 'he flailed about him' to 'genuinely horrific' effect (*John O'L.*) as his fighting skills failed.

The underplayed and unspectacular ending, with Richard as the '"bloody dog" – a dead face attached to an anguished body', stopped the conclusion from 'collapsing into inflated heroics', according to Irving Wardle (*Observer*). In fact the final focus was divided. When Richard fell for the last time, soldiers arrived 'surrounding back of stage' (promptbook), and, flanking them, the ghosts of Richard's victims looked out from behind the rear-stage grilles. The image here of soldiers merging into ghosts was reminiscent of the earlier nightmare when soldiers had played out Richard's fears. As soon as he was dead, stabbed on the ground by Richmond (each blow accompanied by a music cue), the ghosts disappeared, leaving at least three possible readings in their wake: that the horrors of the past were now exorcized; that Richard was defeated as much by his new fear of deadly curses as by Richmond; or that the invading forces brought with them a form of justice that exists beyond Richard's cold logic, a moral judgement represented by ghost-soldiers in his Bosworth dream.

The closing action confirmed Richmond as a force for communal good. Signalling his victory, he threw his sword and gauntlets aside and knelt to be crowned by Stanley, while the soldiers, who had now replaced their swords with banners, declared their support by kneeling and echoing the final 'Amen'.

PETER HALL AND JOHN BARTON, 1963

Whether it was one of the most important theatrical events of the last century or 'the ultimate literary heresy: Shakespeare cut, rewritten, and rearranged' (Hall, 1970, vii), *The Wars of the Roses* adaptation has generated more scholarly debate than any other RSC production to date. What Peter Hall termed this 'impertinence' (vii), a trilogy adaptation of the three parts of Shakespeare's *Henry VI* and *Richard III* by John Barton and Hall himself, was an important part of the RSC's 1963 season, with a revival the following year contributing to a seven-play cycle from *Richard II* to *Richard III* produced to mark Shakespeare's quatercentenary. A BBC television version of the 1963 trilogy, broadcast in three instalments during April and May of 1965, took the productions to audiences across Britain, Australia, Canada and the United States. And finally a 'cleaned-up' text of the broadcast adaptation was published by the BBC in 1970.

In his introduction to these scripts, Barton justifies the adaptation on practical theatrical grounds. The less known and, in his view, only partly finished *Henry VI* plays would be uneconomical to stage in full, and the ever-popular *Richard III* might gain clarity and depth from the preceding histories. Peter Hall, however, defends the adaptation in ideological terms, admitting that his interest in the plays developed only when he saw their modernity as a consequence of the 1962 'Theatre of Cruelty' season. The early histories recorded the 'time-honoured practices of politicians', whose manipulation of the 'mechanisms of power' made the plays directly relevant to the present 'blood-soaked century' (Hall, 1970, xi). Theatrical pragmatism and political ideology therefore forged this collaboration.

Barton prepared the adaptation, reducing 12,300 lines of the original four plays by half, and adding 1,400 lines of blank verse to make approximately a fifth of the adaptation pastiche Shakespeare. *Richard III*, the least rehandled of the four source plays, lost two entire scenes (3.5 and 3.6) and fourteen characters, but gained a figure in the form of Princess Elizabeth, whose political importance was emphasized at the play's close. In the following discussion, all quotations are taken from the published version of the adapted texts, line references to Shakespeare's text are to the Arden edition of *Richard III*.

The final revision of the text, and the direction of the production, was Hall's responsibility, and his interpretation of the source plays steered both adaptation and staging. When Barton feared that the early drafts lacked a clearly defined shape, for example, Hall replied that this structural fluidity underlined 'the concept of order as a living, changing thing, both in the individual and the state' (Hall, 1970, xix). He read the plays as warnings against inflexible political mechanisms that corrupt the moral principles on which society is based, and the shifting quality of Barton's action would show how human instincts require to be '*constantly* checked' (xiv; my emphasis) by governmental structures that adapt to change. Adaptability would become a 'regenerative principle' (xiv) running counter to the vicious cycle of events. The constant threat of chaos was reinforced at the close of *Richard III* when Richmond, the figure of regeneration, rasped his sword across the steel floor as he walked away. He left the scene not 'the one miraculous exception to the otherwise universal human bestiality', as Alan Sinfield has stated (Sinfield, 186), but on a note of unease. The previous year Peter Brook's *King Lear* (1962) had sounded the same warning, with a final thunder roll threatening storms to come.

I

John Bury's design for the production was intended to reinforce the timeless significance of the events it catalogued. Bury had been recruited by the fledgling RSC in 1962 after several successful years with Joan Littlewood's Theatre Workshop in Stratford East, where, like Jocelyn Herbert at the Royal Court, he had started to integrate stage, lighting and sound design. He was resolutely against the 'fairytale unreality of canvas and scene paint' (Pearson, 37), and believed that the texture of the set, props and costumes added an important layer of meaning to the play. His central image for the trilogy was of steel, both in fact and metaphor 'the great steel cage of war' (Bury, 237). As the photograph of the set model shows (Figure 3), the floor was flagged in expanded sheet steel with a mesh surface and the walls clad in metal shields to protect and intimidate (an image taken from the treasury door in Tewkesbury Abbey which is reinforced with shields from the Battle of Tewkesbury): 'Nothing yields: stone walls have lost their seduction and now loom dangerously – steel-clad – to enclose and imprison' (Bury, 237).

For all their apparent solidity, these walls were actually three-sided towers, or *periaktoi*, capable of being moved into a variety of positions or swung off to clear the stage for battle scenes. Their flexibility added to the 'sense of rapid, vertiginous historical movement' (Shaughnessy, 46), with a sense of insecurity about the authority of history, created by direction and design, as Robert Speaight's comparison with Tania Moiseiwitsch's fixed set for the 1951 histories implied: 'walls of unbelievable solidity go round and round, and presumably up and up. In comparison, Miss Moisewich's [*sic*] timbers were stoically static' (*SQ*, 1964). The towers moved inwards as the plays advanced, until the high metallic walls of Richard III's slaughterhouse, 'something out of a nightmare concentration camp' (*Guardian*, 1963), closed the actors into a playing space that Richard himself controlled (this flexibility is suggested in the set model, Figure 3). This sense of violence was reinforced in the 'sound-picture', designed by Guy Woolfenden, that underscored the action, the noise of steel-tipped boots and weapons on the stage floor echoing back in steel shrieks made by a dagger drawn across piano strings. Sounds also covered scene changes, which were carried out in full view and, in Richard's play, by soldiers who unbolted doors or swept aside furniture as the action accelerated. Taken together, the speed of playing, the accompanying sound-picture and the schematic nature of the design reinforced repeated images across the trilogy. It was a patterning of text and action, along with the reappearance of symbolic props, such as the metal-studded council table, which charted fluctuations in power and, in particular, marked the increasing misuse of governmental structures.

The costumes matched the anti-illusionist realism of the set design. Recognizably historical in outline, they were made from modern synthetic fabrics which were coated with glue crystals, marble chippings and stone gravel – a process known as 'gunking' – to achieve a heavily textured effect. Under stage lights the texturing could appear rich or rotten as necessary, as in the contrasting appearances of Margaret and the court in Figure 4. Since, according to Bury, 'real materials need real light' (Pearson, 40), the majority of scenes were played in white light carefully angled to reflect off or be absorbed by the flat metal surfaces like natural daylight. The initially bright colours seeped out of the design as the trilogy unfolded, the men's costumes for example becoming 'rusty' and 'tarnished' with the corrosive years; an effect similar to that sought by Herbert's unromantic designs for the 1961 production, but with more playing time, and funds, to show the deterioration. Medieval pastels, veils and even velvets returned briefly to Edward's court in *Richard III*,

FIGURE 3 The set model of John Bury's design for the 1963 *Wars of the Roses* trilogy shows the metal-clad walls, or *periaktoi*, which closed in the stage for *Richard III*, and the small door which Richard preferred to use.

before the black leather and steel uniforms of Richard's 'thugs' darkened the stage.

II

The choice of the slight, boyish-looking actor Ian Holm as Richard, and the decision not to exaggerate either the deformity or the ugliness of the character, fitted in with the director's realistic approach – a physical scaling down of Richard into the 'naughty schoolboy' (*E. News*) and 'high-spirited minor' (*Times*) that made him into one of the pack, the culmination of a tribe of hungerers after power which the adaptation sought to portray. As Figure 4 shows, when Richard was seated his small stature and, by implication, his immaturity were emphasized. The coexistence of boyishness and ambition is captured in Figure 5, in which the slight, leather-clad figure glances backwards, but the raised boot is on the staircase and, at last, he wears the (over-large) crown.

FIGURE 4 Peggy Ashcroft's Queen Margaret harangues the seated Richard (Ian Holm) in 1.3 (1963), as Rivers (Roy Marsden), Queen Elizabeth (Susan Engel), Hastings (Hugh Sullivan), Stanley (Jeffery Dench) and Buckingham (Tom Fleming) look on. The metal walls are here set back to suggest the openness of Edward's court, a contrast with the confines of Richard's regime.

This sense of tribal greed began when Barton refocused events in the *Henry VI* plays to show the proto-democratic machinery of government, established by the former Lord Protector, Humphrey Duke of Gloucester, gradually passing into the hands of self-interested men. The use of physical force to establish and maintain power became increasingly sophisticated, evolving from the feudal defence of family honour in *Henry VI* to the individual's desire for power in itself in *Richard III*. This mounting chaos moved, in the final play, into a mechanically smooth process of legislation behind whose impersonal façade lay the subtle power of the political manipulators with their twentieth-century parallels. The young Richard was introduced in the second adaptation, *Edward IV*, as an acute observer of the political scene. Maintaining this quiet, almost self-effacing quality in the final play, Holm made

FIGURE 5 Ian Holm's leather-clad Richard (1963) mounts the steps to the throne, the dark costume outlining the hump and raised boot, which until now had been half-hidden beneath the cape (seen in Figure 4), and emphasizing his new signs of office – the chain, the hip-belt and the over-large crown (4.2).

Richard a product of his times, a cool, efficient and subtle politician, like Plummer's Richard, who worked within a system that he understood very well. In taking the throne this Duke of Gloucester skilfully misappropriated the democratic process established by his namesake, his initial success (and ultimate overthrow) endorsing Hall's concern, expressed in his 1963 programme note, that individual responsibility and governmental structures ought to regulate each other 'to check the selfish interests of men'.

Holm's Richard did not lack charisma, but the magnetism of his characterization lay in the detail, where the minimum of gesture, a facial expression or an exchange of looks said (almost) all. The text supported this minimalism. Richard lost many asides and rhetorical flourishes, diminishing both his delight in language and his familiarity with the audience, so that he became a self-contained, circumspect figure who treated his audience as enigmatically as he treated those on stage. References to him as an outcast of nature were eliminated, as were all comments on his abnormal childhood. Robert Speaight complained that the scale of this performance was 'too small and its pitch too low. . . . Nothing can make Shakespeare's Richard a quite credible character' (*SQ*). Holm's Richard, like Plummer's before him, was no demonic corruption of nature driven by his deformity against the world, but rather an extreme example of the power-logic to which, as Peter Hall saw it, 'any man in any age' could succumb (*TES*).

As a skilled political tactician who made systems work for him, Richard's early appearances did not disrupt the formal patterns of the play as ostentatiously as in some productions. He was more insidious. Typically the promptbook shows him entering unobserved through a small door in the rear wall of the set (in Figure 3 the door is shown stage right) and sizing up the situation before committing himself to the scene – a development of Shakespeare's characterization in *3 Henry VI* where Richard often observes discussion, and shows a marked preference for action over debate. This intolerance of words was aimed, in the final play, at the nascent democracy of his brother's court. Edward had continued Henry VI's attempts to secure peace by devolving power to his nobles, and he met them around a hexagonal council table (set across the proscenium in Figure 6), the symbol of government by consensus that had been an important innovation of the former reign. The ceremony which was played out behind Richard's opening speech – Edward's formal reinstatement of the recently imprisoned Hastings as his Lord Chamberlain – illustrated this desire for concord. Richard's disdain for what he saw as more weak leadership was evident in his reference to such reconciliation as 'idle pleasures' (1.1.31), and in lines added to his dialogue with Clarence blaming the 'base house of Woodville' for fostering Edward's interest in détente.

Richard's wooing of Anne (Janet Suzman) gave subtle signs of how he would oppose his brother. It was low-key and realistic, the text relieved of some of its conscious artifice, and Richard's metaphorical association with the super- or subnatural reduced. Richard's false modesty was also missing, his flamboyant command of rhetoric and skilful playing of the situation to impress the audience replaced by what appeared to be remorse.

All of this allowed him to win Anne's sympathy. Replying to her blunt question, 'Did thou not kill this King?' (1.2.103), the promptbook shows him dropping to his knees, evidently upset at the memory. The unexpected action prompted a much gentler delivery than usual of Anne's line, 'O, he was gentle, mild and virtuous' (1.2.106), as she too knelt to take advantage of his vulnerability by showing him his sin. On film Richard's reply, 'The fitter for the King of Heaven that hath him' (1.2.107), is thoughtful and serious, not inviting laughter, and most of the following exchange is unselfconscious on Richard's part. As he and Anne kneel close together, his declaration that her beauty has provoked his tears becomes a private, painful revelation. And this affects her, mollifying her anger as she is increasingly disposed to believe that love indeed lies at the root of his misdeeds, and will be the means of his redemption.

When Richard asked her for the second time either to kill him or to declare herself his, the promptbook shows Anne lifting the sword but then unexpectedly restoring it to him, speaking the words, 'Arise, dissembler' (1.2.188), as if she were creating him her knight. The action neatly reinforces the text's chivalric imagery at this point – as Richard kneels before his lady – by confirming that Anne saw herself as inspiring his change of heart. Her susceptibility to his address was made more plausible by the 'almost ...

reasonable' nature of Richard's quiet logic: 'We listen literally spellbound ... seriously considering, as Anne is doing, whether this assertion which strikes most of our minds as monstrous might not also contain some truth' (*Queen*). On film Anne appears to be convinced of Richard's spiritual repentance, and their interchange concluded, on stage and in the film recording, on this serious note, her lines denying Richard a farewell (1.2.226–8) cut to remove any sign of independent playfulness as she left him deep in thought. The scene was not played as the victory of persuasion over insuperable odds, therefore, but as something much more clinical: the masterly fulfilment of a pre-set plan.

Richard's delight at winning Anne was similarly muted. References to her curses and her conscience and to his devilish dissembling looks were cut from the text, placing greater emphasis on his disgust at her pity, and his pleasure in exploiting weakness for political ends. On film, Holm delivered the final section of the soliloquy – in which Richard contemplates his new attractiveness – with irony, identifying gullibility such as Anne's with the naïve benevolence of Edward's peacetime court.

III

Richard shared his censure of Edward's political changes with an astute Queen Margaret, played here by Peggy Ashcroft. Her first appearance came between 1.2 and 1.3, when the promptbook shows her moving, on film furtively, from the rear of the stage towards the throne. On film, she is just reaching out to touch it when the sound of approaching voices sends her scurrying away. She appeared in a dishevelled version of the battledress that she had worn in *Edward IV* (the second play of the adaptation), a grey-and-black-flecked pinafore, with the original chain-mail undershirt and hood replaced by a thin black polo-necked top, her long hair unkempt and now the same grey as her clothes. As Figure 4 shows, her body had lost the shape and stature of the younger Margaret and the gown hung loose, out of place and out of fashion. Her monochrome image reintroduced the world of war, and the unbending principles that had caused so many deaths in the preceding plays. None the less, these were the principles by which she and Richard judged Edward's new 'democratic' regime.

This shared desire to resurrect as well as to revenge the past offered a fresh reading of the 'bond' between Margaret and Richard. And it was this strange affinity that led Margaret to see him, in 1.3, as a danger to the court. Her intervention here came at the first suggestion in the play that Richard might be king:

RIVERS

    We follow'd then our lord, our lawful King;

    So should we you, if you should be our King.

RICHARD   If I should be? I had rather be a pedlar:

    Far be it from my heart, the thought of it!

                                    (1.3.147–50)

MARGARET

    Hear me, you wrangling pirates, that fall out

    In sharing that which you have pill'd from me!

                     (1.3.158–9)

Initially the court saw her as mad, ridiculing what seemed to be exaggerated anger. And certainly Margaret's ritualized rhetoric, particularly her use of reptilian imagery (cut elsewhere from the text), seemed at odds with the prevailing naturalism. (Gaskill had achieved the same anachronistic effect by casting Edith Evans in the role two years before.) As then, Richard was troubled by her presence. He tried twice to leave the scene but each time Margaret stopped him, first with words and then by standing in his path. Unable to look at her, he took himself to the edge of the stage and stared into the audience, listening intently, knowing that she saw through him, as her point of intervention had suggested and her curse later confirmed.

Richard's instinct was to leave, but, when he was prevented a second time by Margaret, the promptbook shows him sitting down on one of the benches, his face, on film, impassive as she stands above him, cursing. However, when she spoke the words

> The worm of conscience still begnaw thy soul!
> Thy friends suspect for traitors while thou liv'st,
> And take deep traitors for thy dearest friends!
>
> (1.3.222–4)

he sprang up to grasp at her. Recoiling at the attack, Margaret was horrified: 'Thou elvish-mark'd, abortive, rooting hog' (1.3.228ff.). With the intervening lines (225–7) cut, this extreme description of Richard followed directly after her logical prediction of his political demise, with the unfortunate effect of reversing the serious impact of her words. Richard's interruption of the description (1.3.234) then further deflated the moment (on film reducing the court to laughter), and her vital warning was ignored. Visibly relieved, everyone gathered in groups to comment on the interruption.

The unease between Margaret and Richard remained, however, as Tom Fleming's astute Buckingham observed. On the surface his calming intervention, 'Have done, have done!' (1.3.279) – a response prompted, as a result of textual cuts, by her view of Richard as a 'poisonous bunch-back'd toad' (1.3.246) – was an attempt to take the heat off Richard. But this 'wily old fixer cashing in on the prevailing hooliganism' (*Theatre W.*) also intended it as an overture to Richard, who immediately tested Buckingham's loyalty with the question, 'What doth she say, my Lord of Buckingham?' (1.3.295). He received the confirmation, 'Nothing that I respect, my gracious lord' (1.3.296). Their public formality – 'my Lord of Buckingham', 'my gracious lord' – jokingly sealed the private bond as, speaking through his laughter, Buckingham walked deliberately past Margaret to sit at Richard's side.

IV

The court that gathered in 2.1 was very different from that which had been seen briefly at the opening of the play. The King had become seriously ill and was attended by physicians who, photographs show, bled him with leeches, while, at his side, nuns prayed. The religious mood continued in the subsequent peace-making, with Edward insisting that each oath of friendship be taken on the Bible, and his concluding speech (using Elizabeth's words) suggesting that this was personal penance for the inter-necine conflict that had brought him to the throne: 'A holy day shall this be kept hereafter' (2.1.74). The King's private hopes, however, sat uneasily with the contrived ritual, exposing a gap between the intention and the act which Richard quickly took advantage of. Arriving, as the promptbook shows, the moment he was mentioned (as if, like Plummer's Richard, he was waiting in the wings), he shook hands eagerly with his former enemies and humbly asked their forgiveness, his enthusiasm contrasting markedly with those who had just awkwardly pledged their peace. When Elizabeth (Susan Engel) then knelt to ask for Clarence's pardon (2.1.76–7), the promptbook has Richard falling to his knees to announce that 'the noble Duke is dead' (2.1.80). Both of these gestures – peacemaking and kneeling – repeated the preceding action, as Richard mimicked the democratic piety of Edward's court while at the same time calculatedly exploiting its prevailing mood.

It was here that the new partnership between Richard and Buckingham came into play. Buckingham's question, 'Look I so pale, Lord Rivers, as the rest?' (2.1.84), which is, in fact, addressed to Dorset, usually as an aside, was now directed very publicly to Rivers, with the hint that he might have some cause to monitor the responses to Richard's news. Rivers rebutted the insinuation but his anger only implicated him further, as Buckingham had planned. This exchange of words (2.1.84–6) now followed Richard's reference to the late delivery of Clarence's reprieve (2.1.90–1), with Richard looking pointedly at Rivers as he described the 'cripple' messenger who had arrived too late – the subtext being that Rivers knew of the delay. The subject surfaced a third time at the scene's close when Richard privately criticized the Queen's family to Bishop Morton of Ely:

> Mark'd you not
> How that the guilty brother of the Queen
> Look'd pale when he did hear of Clarence' death?
>
> (2.1.136–8)

This co-ordinated attack showed how Richard and Buckingham worked events to their advantage, aiming their 'performance' not at their Woodville victims but at the watching clerics, particularly Morton, who held some sway at Edward's court. It was the influential audience that mattered.

Further textual revision eased the way in which Richard and Buckingham moved into positions of authority following Edward's death. By conflating 2.1 and 2.2, telescoping individual responses to the unexpected turn of events, and by intercutting Rivers's advice to his sister (2.2.96–8) with that of Richard and Buckingham (2.2.101–3, 115–16), Barton concentrated power-seekers around the weakened throne. Queen Elizabeth's extended grieving for her husband (2.2.34–7, 39–46, 66–71) was replaced by a new speech stressing her concern for her place in the realm, and hinting at voluntary withdrawal from the political scene. Buckingham realized that this would clear the way for Richard to control the throne. So, seizing the initiative, he mentioned the new king (in words of advice originally given by Rivers):

> Drown desperate sorrows in dead Edward's grave
> And plant your joys in living Edward's throne.
>
> (2.2.99–100)

And Hastings quickly seconded the proposal (using more of Rivers's words):

> Ay, it is meet so few should fetch the Prince.
>
> (2.2.139)

Thus, before the Woodville camp had realized it, Richard and Buckingham were in control.

V

The central section of the production, 2.3 to 3.7, outlined the way in which Richard and Buckingham harnessed the political machinery of government to achieve the crown. Richard already had military support. His quiet intervention in the funeral procession (1.2) had met no resistance from the accompanying soldiers; indeed, they closed and bolted the doors on Richard's prearranged nod. The adaptation went on to show how Richard consolidated power by targeting his persuasion at such institutions as the army, the church, the Civil Service and eventually the popular vote. He worked within the system, carefully exploiting the mismatch between the tentatively new structures of democracy and the inflexible, but often hollow, value-systems represented by feudal rites. As Peter Hall wrote in the 1963 programme for *Richard III*: 'The political interest is that Richard III and Buckingham take the greatest care when they're seizing the throne to act constitutionally. It's the classic coup d'état, with legal sanctions.' Hall also foregrounded the role of the populace in rubber-stamping the 'legitimacy' of Richard's rise. Public opinion was important in Richard's plans, as the sight of his henchmen, Ratcliffe and Catesby, eavesdropping on the citizens' conversation in 2.3, revealed. The scene itself opened semi-chorically, with the third citizen's new lines drawing a comparison between the child-king Edward's accession and the causes of the recent civil war – 'Woe to that land that's govern'd by a child!' (2.3.11), continuing:

> Witness the late accurs'd intestine jars
> Which rent our realm and which we still do bleed for ...
>
> (Barton, scene 59)

This fatalism was challenged, however, by the second citizen, who identified political abuse of the law behind the general woe (in a version of the Scrivener's words from 3.6.10–11):

> Here's a good world the while! Why, who's so gross
> That seeth not this palpable device.
>
> (3.6.10–11)

Yet, as the third citizen observed (again after the Scrivener at 3.6.12), it is far safer to blame fate and do nothing than actively to speak out and risk similar punishment: 'Yet who's so blind, but says he sees it not?' This reworked dialogue makes Richard into one more overreaching politician, his actions little different from those of Henry VI's protectors. Even the second citizen felt himself powerless against repeated and seemingly universal corruption at the top. Thus Barton's alterations shifted the focus away from Richard's plotting on to the citizens' sense of impotence in the face of such events, and the collusion that this collective silence signifies.

It was the young princes who had the potential to break such fearful silence, as Prince Edward's return to London (3.1) showed. Buckingham and Richard had organized the event as a public relations exercise and the moves were meticulously planned. But the self-possessed young king stopped the show by stating, 'Where is my uncle Rivers? Where is Clarence?' (Barton, Scene 61) – an interruption which clearly irritated Richard, as his patronizing response, shortened to four lines, suggests:

> Sweet Prince, the untainted virtue of your years
> Hath not yet div'd into the world's deceit;
> Those uncles which you want were dangerous:
> God keep you from them, and from such false friends!
>
> (3.1.7–8, 12, 15)

This ought to have been the last word on the subject. But the Prince's retort, 'God keep me from false friends! but they were none' (3.1.16), revealed that he was nothing like the political innocent that his uncle had expected.

Barton's adaptation made the princes into a team, their subtle yet polite interrogation reflecting Richard and Buckingham's own technique. When young York questioned the necessity for a Lord Protector, his intelligent curiosity replaced the famous request for Richard's dagger and a pick-a-back (3.1.110, 129–31):

> What needs a Lord Protector? I have heard
> That in King Henry's time there was one such,
> Who was so troublesome that men remov'd him.
> May they not do the same with you, good uncle?
>
> (Barton, scene 61)

And, when Prince Edward turned from the discussion of Caesar's Tower to enquire about the long imprisonment of his great uncle Mortimer, the neatness of his tactics troubled Richard. The aside – 'So wise so young, they say, do ne'er live long' (3.1.79) – was more than ironic in its private acknowledgement that such acumen would prove a threat were it allowed to reign.

Buckingham organized the Prince's public return to London, but Richard stage-managed the coronation council (3.4) himself. The threat that the princes posed, it seemed, required stronger measures than a simple PR exercise. The scene opened with each council member – Ely, Norfolk, and Derby, Buckingham, and finally Hastings – arriving separately, according to the prompt-book, via the narrow doorway to take their places at the hexagonal council table centre stage (see Figure 6). Newly studded with 'EV', this symbol of cabinet democracy already announced the King's intention to continue his father's plans for government by consensus and debate. Richard's opposition to that idea was evident in the timing of his arrival, just as each member had voted on the coronation date by placing his hand palm down on the board. He then went into private conference with Buckingham, during which it was agreed that the Duke would go immediately to Guildhall. Buckingham's departure thus left Richard in control. But then, according to the promptbook, he too left the stage. After what is, on film, a lengthy and uneasy silence, he returned and further disconcerted the nobles by laughing as he accused 'Edward's wife, that monstrous witch' (3.4.70) of witchcraft, encouraging everyone (but Derby) to take this as a joke against himself. Not until 'Off with his head!' (3.4.76), therefore, did Hastings realize that Richard was deadly serious – by which time Catesby had thrown wide the double doors to let the soldiers in.

As Hastings was marched away, the promptbook has a second group of soldiers, stormtroopers, moving forward to 'smash' the table flat with their hands, their action, a parody of the earlier voting procedure, making it as clear as in Gaskill's 1961 production that any nascent democratic process was now dead. Figure 6 shows

FIGURE 6 Hastings (Hugh Sullivan) is taken prisoner by Richard's soldiers in 3.4 (1963), watched by one of the stormtroopers who then destroy the table, and the democratic style of government that it represents.

Hastings's arrest, and, in the background, the figure of a stormtrooper. The sounds of their violence, and those of marching feet, echoed through the auditorium as the lights dimmed.

Richard's silencing of democratic opposition culminated in his Baynard's Castle nomination as King. It also heralded a change in the Richard–Buckingham partnership. The Duke had failed with the citizens at Guildhall, whereas Richard had succeeded in the council chamber, so Richard no longer needed his MC. Busily unaware of his altered role, Tom Fleming's Buckingham still commanded the event, the promptbook showing him ordering the removal of the torture wheels, on which hung two of Richard's victims, and distributing clerical costumes to the actors as the crowd arrived. On film he faces the crowd even when he is addressing Richard, and later watches them intently as Richard speaks. And the text shows him editing his words in the light of their response, refocusing the argument away from the princes' illegitimacy, for example, when several citizens object. The citizens did not therefore appear foolish or irrelevant, as in some productions, but as open to rational persuasion – albeit staged, as Buckingham believed, by Buckingham.

Richard therefore let the people win him over with a public repetition of his wooing tactics with Anne. As they departed, Richard called out, 'Farewell, gentle friends', adding the apparent afterthought, 'Farewell, good cousin', as he tossed his prayer-book down to Buckingham (a reversal of Shakespeare's text at 3.7.246). Both promptbook and film show Buckingham catching the book, as, on film, he laughs off this dismissal as part of the performance. But Richard had spoken the aside unsmilingly. As the scene darkened, the film shows him seated on the walls, swinging his legs back and forth and drumming rhythmically against the metal – a signal, as the sound drowned out the laughter, of Buckingham's dismissal from Richard's political stage.

VI

A sense that Richard was unassailable, and change impossible, hung darkly over the closure of 3.7. But the opening of the production's second half revealed the gathering of a determined opposition. This was initiated by Bishop Morton of Ely, played by Jolyon Booth, whom Barton introduced into the Tower scene (4.1) with news of Anne's imminent coronation. Fearing what this meant, Elizabeth was shown advising Derby (not, as in Shakespeare's text, her eldest son Dorset) to join Richmond overseas, her warning supported by Anne's added words:

> Ay, often have I heard my husband swear
> He means not only to uproot his foes,
> But any man that ventures to befriend them.
> Since, then, he hath no greater foe than Richmond,
> Who is the only heir to Lancaster,
> Fly hence, my lord, ere you be pluck'd away,
> Even as Lord Rivers and Lord Hastings were.
>
> (Barton, scene 66)

But Derby, played by Jeffrey Dench as the loyal public servant, was not convinced:

> Ah, would I knew where true allegiance lay,
> And which of them should be my rightful master!
>
> (Barton, scene 66)

His unease highlighted the dilemma faced by conscientious men who see the games that politicians play yet fear that interference might corrupt themselves rather than improve matters. And it repeated the citizens' concern outlined in 3.2. However, Derby's hesitation at potential treason was balanced by Ely's willingness to play along with Richard for the greater good. Barton's (and Shakespeare's) sources, Thomas More's *The History of Richard III* and Edward Hall's *Chronicle*, present Bishop Morton of Ely as a key figure in Richard's downfall precisely because he was capable of playing politics to moral ends. His cunning, together with Derby's vigilance against personal corruption, would now drive the counterplot.

The promptbook shows Catesby's sudden arrival with four stormtroopers interrupting the discussion, as he informs Anne officially (as Derby does in Shakespeare's text) that she 'must . . . be crowned Richard's royal queen' (4.1.31–2). Nonetheless he took with him the Tower guards who had overheard the earlier discussion. The move added to the growing sense that Richard's spies were everywhere, and Ely and Derby began to move fast. As the stage emptied they sealed their opposition to the new regime by outlining what Shakespeare reveals much later in the play, an alliance between Queen Elizabeth and Richmond (Derek Waring), to be confirmed by his marriage to her daughter:

> ELY   . . . go sound Elizabeth:
>   Tell her, the fearful cause of all our sorrows
>   Is the unnatural and bloody strife
>   'Twixt York and Lancaster and haughty Woodville:
>   Which foul division may not be resolv'd
>   But by regrafture of these houses' blood
>   Through marriage betwixt Richmond and her daughter.
>
> (Barton, scene 66)

Derby would remain in England and persuade his mother to agree, while Ely joined Richmond in France, a plan that should confound whatever the guards had overheard.

Thus the adaptation established Ely and Derby as focalizers of a redemptive political stratagem that set itself firmly against Richard's increasingly totalitarian structures in the drama's second half. Barton also redefined Elizabeth's role in Richard's defeat, again following the chronicles, by making her part of a larger political plan to restore some element of democracy to the state through Richmond.

Richard's coronation (4.2) heralded the sinister brutality of his new regime. It took place at night, the scene lit by burning torches that, reviewers commented, illuminated the heads of his victims hanging either side of the huge entrance doors. When Richard arrived, the promptbook records the sound of the door bolt echoing round the auditorium, and, on film, the surrounding soldiers face outwards as if warding him from the citizens whom he had so recently called friends.

Asking Buckingham to help him reach the throne (4.2.1), on film Richard leans on the Duke's sword rather than the proffered hand. Later, when introducing the subject of the princes, he repeats the gesture as he points up the double meaning of 'indeed':

> O, Buckingham, now do I play the touch,
> To try if thou be current gold indeed.
>
> (4.2.8–9)

The gesture was important in emphasizing that the unspoken subject was not really the death of the princes but Buckingham's loyalty – in deed – in what would be a permanently subordinate role. When Buckingham later withdrew, therefore, it was to reflect on his political position, not to wrestle with his conscience. And, when he resolved to flee, it was not in fear of his former partner, but because, in the light of what seemed Richard's new-found self-sufficiency, Richmond offered better means of reviving his political career.

VII

Plot and counterplot – one to secure the throne by murder and the other to shorten Richard's reign – ran side by side, establishing a pattern for Act 4 in which each of Richard's horrors was moderated by some hope. When, for example, Buckingham's departure was followed by news of Ely's defection to Richmond, the promptbook shows that the messenger was Derby (the original messenger is Ratcliffe). Richard's response (in a lengthy addition by Barton), to rid himself of Anne and replace her with young Princess Elizabeth, would have threatened Derby's counterplot had he not been there to overhear:

> Though it was my hope
> In marrying her to knit my house with Lancaster,
> Since she is barren, she can serve no purpose ...
> What issue from this maze? It boots me much
> The world should take me true heir of York:
> Therefore I must contract another marriage,   [Barton, scene 67]
> To stop all hopes whose growth may damage me. [*Richard III*, 4.2.59]
> ... Whom should I wed, then, but Elizabeth,
> My brother Edward's daughter? There's my way: [Barton, scene 67]

By developing the historical counterplot in more detail than in the original text, Barton strengthened the dramatic emphasis on Richard's defeat by political forces at home as much as by outside invasion. Lines added to 5.3 (and adopted in several later productions of the play) show Derby informing Richmond of the Queen's conditional approval of the marriage:

> All comfort that the dark night can afford
> Be unto thee, my kinsman and my King.
> I bring you greetings from dead Edward's Queen,
> Who prays continually for Richmond's good:
> If thou dost thrive, her daughter shall be thine.
>
> (Barton, scene 74)

The proposed marriage pact with Richmond was crucial to Richard's fall in this production. By introducing it much earlier than in Shakespeare's text, Barton identified quite separate political interests for Elizabeth and Richmond in Richard's demise. The pact also introduced an element of ambiguity into Richmond's motives, as, with a single alteration from 'proudly on' to 'to usurp' in Richard's reference to the ambitious Richmond, 'And by that knot looks *to usurp* the crown' (4.3.42; my emphasis), Barton drew a comparison between the two men, each keen to secure political power by the same alliance.

Derek Waring's first appearance as Richmond (5.2) underlined this complex reading. The promptbook shows him arriving with the Bishop of Ely, whose added presence emphasized the organized opposition that had initiated Richmond's return. But he then walked downstage alone, and addressed his first words to the audience just as Richard had at the opening of the play, 'Fellows in arms, and my most loving friends . . .' (5.2.1ff.). On the final couplet –

> True hope is swift, and flies with swallow's wings;
> Kings it makes gods, and meaner creatures kings
>
> (5.2.23–4)

– Richard entered for the next scene and paused for a moment upstage, according to the promptbook, directly opposite Ely. The villain and the man of God therefore stood for a moment behind Richmond, like the good and evil angels in a morality play. The image was complicated, however, by the overlapping scenes (a technique used in Byam Shaw's 1953 production) which linked Richmond and Richard as 'meaner creatures' ambitious for power. Richmond's private interests were, therefore, neatly distinguished from those of the nobles, such as Ely, who had assisted his invasion and whose instrument he was.

The secret pact with Richmond added a dimension to the women's encounter with Queen Margaret, and Elizabeth's reception of Richard's wooing in 4.4. Margaret knew nothing of the agreement, but the audience could evaluate her counsel to the other women in its light. In practical terms, the unpredictable effect of the curses with which she proposed to rid the earth of Richard compared poorly with the material advantages of a pact with his potential successor.

Barton's cutting diminished the choric element in the women's repetition, making the prevailing tone of the scene a naturalistic one, against which the incantatory voice, retained solely in Margaret's speeches, seemed little more than repetitious private grief. Delivered from a side bench, her catalogue of revenge (4.4.38–43, 46–8, 55–8) became a partial, off-centre history of death. She was not exultant or bitter; and when she was asked to teach the other women how to curse (4.4.116–17), her voice hid nothing of the personal cost that hatred exacts from those who feed it:

> Think that thy babes were sweeter than they were
> And he that slew them fouler than he is.
> Bettering thy loss makes the bad causer worse:
>
> (4.4.120–2)

The complexity of Peggy Ashcroft's reading here sustained the production's focus on the shared responsibility for Richard's rise. Margaret sensed that to unpack her heart with words was self-indulgence. And by now the audience knew that a strategic alternative to cursing lay in challenging politicians at their own game. Hers was, therefore, an incongruous ritualizing of history when set against the pragmatism of the plot already in hand.

Cuts in the subsequent dialogue between Richard and his mother modified her disappointment in him. She no longer saw him as a hell-hound but voiced personal hurt at his refusal to listen. It was a naturalistic exchange, much like the same moment in the 1961 production, and as a consequence her words predicting his defeat hit Richard hard. On film his eyes widen with shock at this rejection.

Richard's response was to dismiss his mother and the assembled troops and attempt a matter-of-fact approach to 'wooing' Susan Engel's Elizabeth: 'Now madam, list to me'

(Barton, scene 70). His monosyllables and half-line replies, advanced from later in the scene where they imply diminishing authority, suggest that he saw the situation as cut and dried:

ELIZABETH
Say then, who dost thou mean shall be her King?
RICHARD
Even he that makes her Queen: who should be else?
ELIZABETH   What, thou?   (4.4.265–7)
RICHARD   Ay, even I. [Barton, scene 70]
ELIZABETH
How canst thou woo her?
RICHARD   That would I learn of you.
ELIZABETH
And wilt thou learn of me?
RICHARD   Madam, with all my heart.
                                        (4.4.268, 270)

But this approach simply added force to Elizabeth's longer speeches, with their bitterly ironic emotion, particularly when she refused to match Richard's efficient pace. When he began to substantiate his case with some show of remorse for the past, it was clear that her resistance had unnerved him. Textual cuts took him swiftly from remorse to blunt clarification:

> If I have kill'd the issue of your womb,
> To quicken your increase, I will beget
> Mine issue of your blood upon your daughter.
>   (4.4.296–8)

But cuts also held back Elizabeth's response. Moreover, Elizabeth's superiority was suggested by their relative positions. She stood as Richard knelt, trying desperately to think of something to swear by. He had used the same move in wooing Anne (1.2), but here the chivalric pose was ineffectual because Elizabeth challenged every vow.

The promptbook shows her taking the initiative in kissing him on 'Bear her my true love's kiss' (4.4.430). He then spat this away in disgust before dismissing her with 'Relenting fool, and shallow, changing woman!' (4.4.431). On film, he grasps her in a greedy, almost violent embrace, which she receives impassively. And again he spits. Both versions grant Elizabeth the upper hand and make it quite clear that she has not changed her mind.

VIII

The dramatic import given to this political counterplot made the appearance of the ghosts at Bosworth less influential in Richard's fall than in previous productions. The metallic 'sound-picture' by which John Bury indicated the undercurrent of violence in Richard's rise was supplemented in this scene by dragging chains, although none of the ghosts actually wore them. In fact, the promptbook shows them happily liberated from the constraints of this life, their naturalistic movements and familiarity towards Richard representing a clear break with performance tradition. Clarence perched on a table edge and hugged him. The two princes played a game of tag around him and Anne cradled his head. Henry VI put his hand over Richard's mouth to stop him speaking (as if recalling how Richard had stifled the King's speech before stabbing him at the close of the previous play), kissed him and, placing a hand on his head, appeared to bless him. In general the ghosts commiserated with Richard on the inevitability of his defeat.

The promptbook gives little evidence of how Ian Holm spoke Richard's conscience speech (5.3.178–207), but on film he picks out the patterned metre to construct a calmly objective debate with himself, retaining the lengthier sense units rather than infusing the questions with jerky panic as some Richards have done. Only with the realization, 'I shall despair' (5.3.201), does he nervously bite his finger ends. Even so, the words themselves are spoken calmly, as if despair is the only logical response. Once voiced, they trigger Richard's recollection of the recent curses, and he hesitates. But it is a momentary panic, after which his tone is one of resignation to the blunt fact of despair. Overall it is an emotionless and highly rational reading of his situation, very like

Plummer's in 1961, acknowledging a lack of emotion and of conscience in himself that is now past remedy. But fear has shaken Richard, and when he tells Ratcliffe, 'I fear, I fear' (5.3.215), it is the fear of fear of which he is afraid. And this experience lets him know, perhaps for the first time, the shrinking fear of others:

> Come, go with me;
> Under our tents I'll play the eaves-dropper,
> To see if any mean to shrink from me.
>
> (5.3.221–3)

In contrast to the fearful suspicion in the King's camp, as the promptbook shows, Richmond's men woke him (symbolically, perhaps) with wine, and fresh water to wash before battle. Here was a man preparing for victory who had no doubt of his support. His oration to the troops drew ordinary citizens to the stage edge to hear and cheer him, and then to join his army, exactly as Richard had feared. Richard, however, delivered his oration to a stage empty of all but a single soldier on guard beneath the black boar banner, and a sense of this isolation, reinforced by Holm's slight figure, was voiced in his opening uncertainty, 'What shall I say more than I have inferr'd?' (5.3.315).

When the rhetoric eventually came, judicious cutting kept Richard's focus on Richmond's political ineptitude. Even so, on film he has to search for words before coming up with 'a milk-sop' and 'a paltry fellow' (5.3.326, 324), their weakness inadequate to the thumping gesture that accompanies their delivery. As if realizing this, Richard puts his fist inside his crowned helmet (which he wears in Figure 7) and addresses it as if it were another figure, a hand puppet or captive audience, and this gives him confidence. His voice strengthens and grows sterner as the rhetoric gains force. Now, however, there are two faces: the fearful Richard, weak and isolated, and the iron mask that Richard has projected as king, the unyielding self-image that he has always aspired to, represented by a hollow shell.

FIGURE 7 Derek Waring's Richmond meets and defeats the metal-caged Richard (Ian Holm) in 1963 (5.5), chiefly because Richard's unwieldy armour and fighting implements – a sword, a ball and chain and a battle mace – prove more hindrance than help.

On stage the rousing exclamations addressed an empty space:

> Fight, gentlemen of England! fight, bold yeomen!
> Draw, archers, draw your arrows to the head! ...
> Inspire us with the spleen of fiery dragons!
> Upon them! Victory sits on our helms.
>
> (5.3.339–40, 351–2)

As Richard ended, the stage filled with noise and smoke, his dragon-fire supplied by four huge canons gaping on the audience. He was encased in a heavy half suit of black armour for the battle, seen in Figure 7, with his face now invisible inside the helmet-crown, the weaker arm protected by a shield while the other wielded a spiked ball and chain, just as Plummer's Richard had in 1961. The ugly implements of warfare, including a ball mace, are seen hanging from his waist in the photograph. As brutality encased in metal, he resembled the production's central image, 'the great steel cage of war' (Bury, 237). The human scale of Holm's interpretation disappeared inside this monstrous image, as if, in despair, the man had become a war machine.

In a final irony, Richard's ball and chain became his fetter. Having lost his shield in the fight, his sole defences were the mace and this unwieldy implement, which he swung madly round his head to keep Richmond at bay. The fight, however, proved long and too exhausting. Production photographs show that the ghosts stood in a line across the rear of the stage to watch the action, as they had in 1961. The photographs also suggest that the stage battle was very like that on film where, eventually, Richmond catches hold of Richard's chain and winds him in, severing it to disarm Richard before, as noted in reviews, stabbing his dagger through the visor in a vicious victory. He then stood, unarmed and amazed, above the hump of metal as Richard's dying whimpers echoed around the auditorium. On film it is not clear how far Richard finally gives himself up to death. The ambiguous image, both on film and in the stage production photographs, is of the chain binding the two men together, like an umbilical cord.

Once the Bishop of Ely had confirmed death, he removed the coronet from Richard's helmet and knelt as Richmond crowned himself. Then, speaking of unity, the new King drew together the banners, the white rose and the red, which hung above the stage. The whole army knelt to echo his final 'Amen' (5.5.41), and the space emptied, leaving Richmond walking slowly down the forestage to retrieve Richard's sword. Before turning upstage to leave, however, he looked out, calm but unsmiling, into the audience. Then, as he walked away, he let the sword drag across the steel-flagged floor behind him, releasing sparks and a screech that ricocheted around the space. Since both his own and Richard's swords were three-quarter-sized, sliver-shaped implements (seen clearly in Figure 7) rather than the unwieldy broadswords of the earlier two plays, this trailing action must have been deliberate. The metallic screech lingered as the stage lights dimmed, a thinner version of the sound that had tracked Richard's rise, and an eerie recollection of his death shriek. It was a threatening note that, while it did not drown out Richmond's rhetoric, denied the play the comfortable closure that he had prayed for: 'one leaves the theatre with an uneasy feeling that the wheel of history has gone full circle and will turn again … and again' (*SA Herald*, 1963).

ADRIAN NOBLE, 1988

The RSC's second major adaptation of Shakespeare's first tetralogy came twenty-five years after *The Wars of the Roses* with Adrian Noble's production of *The Plantagenets*, staged at Stratford in the autumn of 1988. In his introduction to the published texts of the plays, Noble describes them as dramatizations of the medieval past for a Tudor audience, and outlines Shakespeare's role as that of editing the chronicles for the stage: 'Shakespeare is telling the story of his race. Perhaps it would be more accurate to say that Shakespeare was *creating* the story of his race' (Noble, viii).

So by shaping what was already an epic narrative to meet the same theatrical requirements that Shakespeare himself recognized – of clarity ('clear narrative convenience'), shape ('the dramatic advantages of shape and focus'), simplicity ('the need to simplify the actuality of politics') and effect ('to marshal the events in order to achieve a particular dramatic effect') (Noble, viii) – Noble saw his adaptation as simply taking Shakespeare's editing a little further. He did not want, like Hall and Barton, to mine the plays for modern political parallels: 'We all had to learn to value narrative over "character moments" and to value story-telling over psychology' (xiv).

The twentieth century's role in this production lay in the medium, therefore, not the message. Noble saw Shakespeare's compilation of his source material as similar to that of drama-documentary, a genre of television that was relatively new to Britain in the 1980s (Noble, viii), and so he initially invited Charles Woods to prepare the text. (Woods's BBC television drama-documentary *Tumbledown*, about the Falklands conflict, had hit the headlines earlier the same year.) The series' title, *The Plantagenets*, however, recalled another popular television genre, the soap-opera serial (particularly those of the 1980s such as *Dallas* and *Dynasty*), with its indication that the action would be seen in terms of a family saga rather than as the political history that *The Wars of the Roses* had implied.

I

The production's design had a cinematic quality befitting Noble's parallel with drama-documentary. Narrative clarification came through visual symbols, whether in the emblematic use of heraldic devices to characterize each reign – the triple sunburst hanging over Edward's court and the similar but more jagged circular saw spinning across Richard III's wasteland (seen in the background to Figure 10) – or in the staging, where the full depth of the playing space was used to create images of pageantry, warfare and flight. And, as in television documentaries, the narrative devices editorialized the text. Scene changes, for example, told a story, highlighting the juxtaposition of events by overlapping action in a theatrical version of the cinematic fade, or indicating narrative parallels by reworking the same stage image. This reiteration came in *Richard III*'s execution scenes; Rivers and Grey at Pomfret (3.3), Hastings at the Tower (3.4) and finally Buckingham (5.1). On each occasion the prisoners crossed the stage in single file, from left to right, along a shaft of bright light coming through a doorway from the offstage execution chamber. Once they had disappeared from sight, Ratcliffe stared after them for a moment until an ominous boom signalled that execution had taken place. He then gave a single sharp bow of the head, and strode away.

The director and Bob Crowley, the designer, worked within the RSC 'style' of staging that had been inspired by John Bury's approach to the earlier *Wars of the Roses* cycle. Some aspects of the adaptations were, in fact, identical, such as the gradual fading of colour in set and costumes as the plays progressed. Both productions had a stage floor made of metal, although Crowley's filigree mesh sheeting, seen clearly in Figure 8, allowed more delicate effects, such as when light and smoke rose through it 'like the sidewalks of Manhattan' (*Observer*). Bury's anti-illusionistic approach in *The Wars of the Roses* had used 'Brechtian' white light to militate against what he saw as this form of picture-stage falsehood. He was concerned to convey meaning through individual props, or 'image objects', as he termed them (Pearson, 39), such as the council table, and, in a single stage set, 'the great steel cage of war' (Bury, 237), using images from the text, albeit one with pastiche additions. Noble and Crowley's cinematographic scenic images, however, created a separate but parallel set of meanings to those in the text. To accommodate these, a good deal of Shakespeare's verbal imagery was cut. In its place, each picture offered an imaginative correlative of that which Noble felt lay at the heart of individual scenes, as the promptbook titles – 'Hunt', 'March', 'Refugees' – indicate. Together they formed 'a constantly changing picture-scape of light, movement and colour' (Smallwood, 1993, introduction, 14). Where Bury's realistic imagery had tried to be anti-heroic, Crowley's sophisticated neo-medievalism, conveyed in the fabrics and subtle colour mixes of the interior designer's palette, was spectacularly epic. Audiences were invited, as sophisticated consumers of cinematic image and design, to read – rather than, as Bury had proposed, to feel – the 'texture' (Pearson, 37) of the plays. Some reviewers felt that Noble had sacrificed 'a totally cohesive production for some spectacular isolated moments' (*Int. Her. Trib.*). And at points in *Richard III* the histrionic nature of the Noble/Crowley staging became unintentionally confused with the self-conscious artifice of the play.

The eighteen-week rehearsal period provided an opportunity, rare for main-house productions at the RSC, for set and costume designs to evolve alongside the company's exploration of the text, and for the final production to emerge organically from the artistic process. The prepared text was also revised during

FIGURE 8 Adrian Noble's blocking for 1.3 (1988) isolates those members of the court whom Queen Margaret (Penny Downie) curses. Richard (Anton Lesser) stares angrily into the auditorium, stage right, while, stage left, Queen Elizabeth (Joanne Pearce) stands horrified at what she hears. Temporarily without the crown (it lies behind on her chair), Elizabeth and the court watch her predecessor hold the stage.

rehearsals, as a result of actors' unease with some of Woods's 'conceptualized stage directions' (Fiennes, 100), which they felt sacrificed too much of the language to visual effects. Even so, in hammering out their own text (Noble, xiv) the company removed 1,285 lines from *Richard III*, now titled *Richard III – His Death*, including one full scene (3.6), and reduced the play by a third.

II

The opening lines were delivered in part as a victory speech, with Anton Lesser as Richard standing on a table beside the new King and circled by the celebrating court, voicing everyone's relief that war had ended and peaceful unity was theirs. Richard's gesture to their brother Clarence to come closer with the lines –

> And all the clouds that lour'd upon our house
> In the deep bosom of the ocean buried.
>
> (1.1.3–4)

– welcomed his return to the dynastic fold; although it was also an ironic premonition of his later dream and death by drowning. And, as the performance video shows, the first thirteen lines concluded happily with trumpet fanfares and applause. Then, as Elizabeth ran up to join her husband on the table, Richard leapt down and out of the celebration into spotlight. The rest of the speech was spoken from the *platea*, or side-stage edge, to the theatre audience, with, on video, the party frozen in tableau behind. This *platea* image of Richard, plotting to destroy the pretty picture, would recur throughout the play. He had done the same at the end of *Edward IV* by capping Edward's closing couplet with the first word of his own play, 'Now!' That closing tableau was reconstituted in this opening scene, and Richard's threat to destroy it repeated on the line, 'And hate the idle pleasures of these days' (1.1.31). Then, looking back briefly at the image of what might have been, he lobbed a champagne bottle at the golden sun. As the glass hit home, the court dispersed in panic, and an ominous crash initiated Richard's journey to the throne.

This sudden shift from public scene to private conversation at first suggested Richard's intimacy with the audience, particularly when his words seemed to respond to their imagined 'comments'. But, on video, Lesser's emphasis in the rhyming couplets (lines 39–40) and later in

> What though I kill'd her husband and her father?
> The readiest way to make the wench amends
> Is to become her husband, and her father;
> The which will I ...
>
> (1.1.154–7)

was edged with irritation at what he saw as the audience's wilful obtuseness. Here, and in his soliloquy at the close of 1.2, he showed frustration at their failure to 'keep up' with, and admire, his cunning intellect. As Lesser put it: 'whether Richard is happy about needing them is another question, which gives the relationship another dimension' (Lesser, 149). His dismissal of 'Simple, plain Clarence' (1.1.118), isolated here by cuts, voiced his general disdain of gullible inferiors. The relationship between Richard and the audience was, therefore, not as frank as his opening familiarity implied, and Noble reinforced this distance by omitting many of his asides, as Gaskill and Barton had done in 1961 and 1963.

Richard's early appearances in the play are physical interruptions of processions or court meetings, and Noble's staging reinforced this. But, when Richard played against the formal patterning in wooing Anne (Geraldine Alexander), the emphasis was placed on his transgression of the linguistic code, turning their keen encounter into one of register, not rhetoric. Cuts in the text gave him single-line responses to her lengthier attacks, allowing Lesser's naturalistic performance to run rings, literally and figuratively, around Anne's formal speech. His capping of her half-line, 'I hope so!', with 'I know so' (1.2.117) identified who would control the scene. He was close enough at this point to have kissed her, and the video shows him pausing long enough to suggest that he might, before moving away, his unpredictability teasing Anne. When at first sight she made to strike him, he stayed her arm and calmly said, 'Sweet saint, for charity, be not so curst' (1.2.49), so that his words and action nimbly redirected all her force against herself. He did the same when she picked up the sword and lunged at him (1.2.183). His advice, 'Nay, do not pause', drew audience laughter since she clearly showed no inclination to delay. Thus Richard blocked her actions with words that surprised her with the unexpected, not with a valid counter-argument.

The videotape shows how Lesser underplayed some lines, almost throwing them away. Others he delivered as if amazed at his own thought. This last came when he spoke of weeping (1.2.157). Wiping her spittle from his cheek, he found it wet with tears and paused a moment to contemplate the 'miracle'. Since he was seated at the time on the edge of Henry's open coffin (as Christopher Plummer had been in 1961), he looked down into it, letting his amazement at her powers remind Anne of her own shock at his ability to make the dead king's body bleed again. The recollection made her weep with guilt at the apparent power of her own sexuality.

As Anne was confused almost into capitulation, therefore, her last act of independence was to deny him a farewell kiss, but this seemed only to diminish her in Richard's eyes. Once she had gone, he urged the audience to respond to his success by pointing in amazement at the stage space where he had been so daring, as if directing them as he had directed Anne. But they withheld applause. He had 'won' Anne with unpredictability, not wit, and, like her, the audience seemed uncertain how to take him and uncomfortable with the collusion that he required.

III

The court scenes (1.3 – shown in Figure 8 – 2.1 and 2.2) suggested sumptuousness, in the heavy red velvet curtains draped across the central rear-stage entrance, and in the lighting: a golden haze above the stage and, at floor level, royal blue, which, along with the textured gold edge of the stage, suggested carpeting. This textured border, seen clearly in Figure 8, was a permanent fixture, although in the court scenes it continued as an edging to the rear-stage curtains, seen to right and left in the background of Figure 8, thus placing a two-dimensional frame around the action very like the illuminated border of medieval manuscripts.

Movement was operatic, as groups of figures arrived from side entrances at the proscenium arch or advanced downstage from the central curtained entrance. Their placing on the stage, marked out clearly in the promptbook and seen in Figure 9, denoted loyalties. Elizabeth (Joanne Pearce) swept across the space in a gold gown hidden beneath a huge gold-and-white fur cape (shown in Figure 8 as she stands downstage left), a costume that underlined the operatic nature of both her performance and the staging. At first she gravitated towards family groups, as if she needed to give and receive support, and was quick to look to her brother Rivers and to Stanley for advice when Richard's attacks began. Initially her role was domestic rather than political.

For the same reasons that applied to Ian Holm's 1963 performance, most reviewers felt that Lesser's boyish Richard blended easily into the society that he came from, although this was more evident in the *Henry VI* adaptations – where the motivation for his ambition stemmed from admiration of his father, not from physical deformity – than in *Richard III*, where he suddenly seemed 'to have had an entirely different upbringing to that of his brothers' (*D. Telegraph*, 1988). Richard's deformity was defined by a small hump on the left shoulder, a raised boot, and one arm strapped across his chest (seen as he stands front stage right in Figure 8), all of which became less prominent after the London transfer. Aggression formed a significant element in the interpretation, compensating as it did for maternal deprivation, which manifested itself in the final play as an instinctive physical response whenever he was threatened. Now, however, Richard became more of a physical isolate on stage, and his actions were both faster and noticeably less predictable than everyone else's. Dressed not in the rich bright colours of the court but in close-fitting black velvet, he marched angrily from his liminal position at the 'carpet' edge (seen in Figure 8), veering awkwardly around the other courtiers either to head off Elizabeth mid-stage or to stand centrally before the crimson curtain while Margaret whispered to Buckingham on the forestage. Such moves disrupted the formal picture that the curtain/carpet frame enclosed.

Penny Downie's Margaret also stood out against the court's elegance. At first she sat unobserved at the back of the scene (1.3), next to one of Elizabeth's two nun-like attendants (seen in the background of Figure 8), but the promptbook shows her rising when Richard entered and slowly moving down the left side of the 'carpet' to the front as she listened to, and commented on, their dispute. Returning, she intervened from the centre back, but was not recognized by the court until she threw back her veil to reveal a crown. The photograph shows how well her costume – a long dust-grey gown with sleeves almost hiding her hands, and a veil worn as a stole – marked her out, like Richard's costume, from the rest. So did her demeanour, with Downie feeling an air of 'detachment and wry humour' about Margaret in this scene, 'a sense that she is really enjoying being there' (Downie, 134). In Figure 8 she holds the centre stage.

By the time of the second court scene, a conflation of 2.1. and 2.2, the golden lighting had partly given way to a hazy blue across the rear stage, into which chill light moved King Edward, clearly very ill. The sombre tones tinting the golden peace reflected the unease with which he now tried to unite everyone in handshakes. He then stood to one side, looking on with pleasure at his apparent success. Opposite him, and also separated from the rest, stood Buckingham, his isolation marking the threat that he posed to this picture of harmony. And then Richard arrived. His news of Clarence's death drove Edward to the wheelchair that he had staunchly rejected at the opening of the scene, signalling that any hope of an improvement in his health was gone.

The mourning women held the centre stage immediately after Edward's death, while, on the margins, Richard and Buckingham canvassed support. The promptbook shows that both men quietly 'worked the room' as the women wailed, so that, by the time that Rivers mentioned the new king at 2.2.96–8, Buckingham was able to present his plans for the Prince's return as something of a fait accompli. Here again Richard had used the focal action to his advantage, with Noble's staging achieving the same effect as Barton's reorganization of the text at this point. At the close, Richard sealed his pact with Buckingham in a handclasp not unlike a 'hi-five', the two men standing on the forestage where a jagged crimson shadow had begun to creep across the blue-and-gold border – the first image of the circular saw emblem with which King Richard would replace Edward's golden sun.

IV

The citizens' scene (2.3) opened up the action to the outside world, a detail underlined on video by autumn rain and figures scurrying across the stage somewhat anachronistically under umbrellas. The speaking citizens were all lawyers, their lines, reduced by almost half, divided among four figures dressed alike in black robes and skull caps and bearing legal documents. This visual and textual uniformity made them choric, not individual as in the 1963 adaptation, and their voices those of the professional rather than the common point of view. Although their dialogue was interrupted by the arrival of Lovell, masquerading as a messenger, the scene was less politically significant than in the Hall/Barton text. Played at speed, with running figures adding to the sense of urgency, its function was to show the law as buffeted by the winds of Richard's change.

This uneasy world was temporarily shut out by a cream curtain, the material divided into squares like blind windows, which was drawn across the full width of the stage to form a backcloth to the following scene (2.4). On video, this sound reinforces the happy domesticity of the action as Elizabeth, her younger son and the Duchess of York (Marjorie Yates) put Prince Edward's clothes and toys into a large wooden trunk. They seemed to be packing away the young man's childhood – although certain of the playthings, such as a paper crown, had a wider resonance – with the implication that the new reign would bring a new maturity to the realm. But the previous scene, the blind windows and, soon, news of the Woodville brothers' imprisonment, indicated otherwise. (Noble's introduction of the paper crown here thinly echoed young York's disturbing reference to the past in Barton's adaptation.)

The arrival of Prince Edward drew a contrast between the young man's seriousness and Richard's immaturity (3.1). The uncle obviously resented having to defer to his nephew, and, as the video shows, he took some time to force his weak knee down before the King. Later, as Edward passed the time by questioning the Tower's history, Richard was forced to look to Buckingham for answers, an embarrassment which so irritated him that he addressed the comment, 'So wise so young, they say, do never live long' (3.1.79) directly to the Prince, although he rephrased it when Edward asked for clarification. (All of Richard's other ironic asides were cut from the scene.) He seemed equally out of his depth when Hastings spoke of sanctuary, turning again to Buckingham for a response. However, when the Cardinal went on to reject Buckingham's argument, Richard silently placed himself between the two men and stared at the cleric, the hand on the dagger quite enough to make him change his mind.

Richard's method of acting against the spoken word reached its zenith in Hastings's arraignment, the recruitment of the Mayor and, at Baynard's Castle (3.4, 3.5 and 3.7), the removal of the Scrivener's soliloquy (3.6), allowing Noble to merge these three scenes. A long refectory table was placed across the proscenium, towards one end of which sat Ely and Stanley, with Ratcliffe and Buckingham at the other. Hastings sat midway, facing the audience. This made him the last to notice Richard's arrival down the stage behind him, and he was still struggling to his feet when Richard brushed aside all deference and invited everyone to sit. He did not join them immediately, however, but moved across to place his hand gently but firmly on Stanley's shoulder, making him jump with fright. The moment passed, as everyone turned to business, but the video shows how Richard built on the unease; he drummed his fingers on the table for some while before beginning, 'My Lord of ...', and then broke off to look around the table before adding, 'Ely', much to Stanley's clear relief. These intimidating silences increased after Richard returned with Buckingham at 3.4.59, letting him initiate speech and action, and suddenly accuse Hastings of treachery with a speed that was intended to mask the lie.

Once Richard and the others had departed, Hastings was left seated at the table, unable to take everything in, while Ratcliffe calmly completed the execution warrant. He then closed his folder, stood up, pushed in his chair, and politely ushered the Duke upstage into the shaft of light, and along it to an offstage death.

Richard's request for Hastings's head before dinner justified staging the next scene (3.5) in the same chamber and at the same table as the coronation council. An added word at the close also ensured that Buckingham brought the citizens '*here* to Baynard's Castle' (3.5.97). By locating all three scenes in the same room, Noble made it Richard's theatre, a space where he played for political power by varying the same script. The single venue reinforced the slick efficiency of Richard and Buckingham's double-act. It also imprisoned the narrative momentum inside the artifice of Richard's stage.

The action in these scenes shared similarities. When Richard and Buckingham emerged from the shadows (where the video suggests both men had waited while Hastings was dispatched) they cleared the council papers to allow the table to be set for supper. Richard then slipped into his seat just as Buckingham hailed the arrival of the Lord Mayor behind him – the moves exactly matching Richard's arrival behind the unsuspecting Hastings in the previous scene. When Richard turned in his chair to add his welcome, he pretended to mistake Ratcliffe and Lovell (then entering upstage) for enemies, and his sudden shout disconcerted the Mayor enough for Buckingham to press him to sit down and calm himself. Grateful for this, the old man swivelled into the seat beside Richard and faced the audience, just in time to hear Lovell announce, 'the head of that ignoble traitor . . . Hastings' (adapted from 3.5.22–3) as, with a flourish, he removed the cover from the silver salver on the table to reveal the same. Wineglass in hand, Richard sat back and perused the dish as he might the menu, but the Mayor sat transfixed with shock. Not surprisingly the elderly gentleman's speedy acquiescence in the execution took little prompting, and with palpable relief he scurried off to report it to the citizens.

With the Mayor gone, dinner was served to Richard and Buckingham, although Richard's plan that the citizens should be spoken to without delay meant that Buckingham left hungry.

Richard then dined alone, eating cheese off his dagger while waiting for Buckingham's return (the rest of the scene, along with 3.6. having been cut), and breaking the lengthy silence only when he touched a wineglass with the knife to order a refill. The audience watched him eat. Finally, pointing the dagger at Hastings's head, he looked out at them and asked the Scrivener's question:

> Who is so gross
> That cannot see this palpable devise? [sic]
> Yet who's so bold but says he sees it not?
>
> (3.6.10–12)

Since here the phrase 'palpable devise' [sic] referred to Hastings's death and not, as originally, to the legal document indicting him, the inquiry showed Richard acknowledging the transparency of his deception. He was admitting, therefore, that his source of power was the threat of death, not the manipulation of the law that Shakespeare's text reveals, and Hall had emphasized in 1963.

To some extent Richard's question rendered the Baynard's Castle scene superfluous, since it implied that there was little need to gull the citizens of their support, particularly for a Richard so little given to self-dramatization as this one. The threat of death alone would be enough. The performances before the Mayor (3.5) and the Mayor and citizens (3.7) in this production simply underlined the people's complicity in their own deception, rather as a theatre audience is complicit in the deception of the stage – the very link that Richard made when he addressed his question to the audience as if they too were his dupes. The scenes themselves lost much of their complexity because Richard's verbal dexterity, particularly his manipulation of the law, was replaced by comic business, and the oral record of the outsider – the Scrivener, the citizens and to some extent the Mayor – virtually disappeared.

The parallels between Richard's Baynard's Castle performance and that in a theatre were self-evident, both on stage and in the video recording: 'the appearance of a theatrical curtain was perhaps intended to remind the audience of their complicity' (SS).

Buckingham met the citizens, many of them lawyers, before a shimmering gold proscenium curtain, while 'backstage' the table became a makeshift altar placed below a bedsheet backcloth crudely daubed with a black crucifix. When Catesby drew the curtain back (reversing the opening of 2.4), Richard was upstage kneeling at the altar, a monk's robe thrown around his shoulders and a prayer-book in his hand. On either side of him Lovell and Ratcliffe, dressed as monks, swung censers and intoned prayers. White light, set at floor level, threw melodramatic shadows on to the backcloth, with Richard and later Buckingham in follow-spots, all of which drew attention to the artifice of this 'kind of black mass' (SS).

The crowd appeared to be as conscious as the theatre audience that this was all a show. When Richard replied to Buckingham's invitation by mentioning his inadequacies as a future king (3.7.158–60), many of them, particularly those identified as lawyers, applauded his refusal. They also voiced dissent at Buckingham's criticism of young Edward's claim to the throne. When Buckingham departed in disgust, the crowd was sharply divided, the Mayor desperate that Richard should agree, others attempting to leave but held back by their more fearful colleagues. Kneeling at the stage edge to be 'blessed' with holy water in exaggerated style by the 'monk' Catesby, Richard snapped the order to recall Buckingham, showing his frustration at the crowd's refusal to play the scene as he had planned. When he then accepted the nomination there were still murmurs of dissent from the kneeling crowd. So, stressing each syllable as if he were administering an oath (as illustrated), he reminded them that:

> God doth know, and you may part | ly see,
> How | far | I | am | from | the | de | sire | of | this.
>
> (3.7.234–5)

He then threw off the clerical gown to reveal his hump, and, stepping up and on to the altar, placed his good foot on the outsized Bible in a blasphemy that illustrated the hypocrisy of every word. For Martin Hoyle, in the *Financial Times* (1989), this terrifying ability to 'snap into psychopathic viciousness with a scream of almost animal rage' was a strength of Lesser's performance; although Charles Osborne, in the *Daily Telegraph* (1989), found it absurdly melodramatic, 'a compendium of comic effects rather than ... real malevolence'.

The citizens gasped in horror at this, and several tried to silence the frightened Mayor as he shouted a solo, 'God bless your Grace: we see it, and will say it' and 'Amen' (3.7.236, 240). But Ratcliffe simply took the lid off the silver salver. At the sight of Hastings's head Baptist-like on the platter, everyone joined in with 'Amen'.

Anton Lesser admitted that it had been difficult to find 'the right note on which to play this scene' because of the comic business with Hastings's head, but he felt that in the end the staging showed how 'Richard and Buckingham are merely seeking to fulfil a formula: it must be *recorded* in the annals, that on such-and-such a date, under duress of the people, Richard accepted the crown' (Lesser, 152). The immediate dispatch of messengers was intended to convey this; although that is one of the points that the Scrivener's scene, cut from this production, makes. Noble also cut Buckingham's account of the Recorder speaking to the people, removing further textual evidence that those responsible for the 'annals' mistrusted Richard.

This elision of Richard's narrative with that of the adaptation was matched in the staging, aspects of which – the theatre curtain, the backcloth and the lighting of Richard's mise-en-scène – had appeared elsewhere in the production. The Baynard's Castle performance came very close, therefore, to parodying the style of image-making which had dominated the play. At Richard's invitation the audience came to see the violence as humorous, the scene with the Lord Mayor and aldermen as farce. And the citizens' failure to be deceived by such theatrical fiction had the potential to undermine the theatre audience's response to the more sophisticated spectacle – the 'high-octane theatricality' (Noble, xi) – of Noble's documentary tale.

V

In a slightly more sophisticated way, the coronation scene was also a mockery of spectacle, with Richard processing down the stage in full regalia before spinning round and, emitting a childlike whoop of joy, galloping up the 'stacked-up steps' (*Independent*, 1988) of the throne and curling into it as in a womb. It had echoes of the 1984 interpolated coronation ritual, discussed in chapter 3. He then lounged sideways across it, one good leg lolling over the arm, as he spoke conspiratorially to Buckingham, then Tyrrel and finally his Queen, occasionally raising himself to peer nosily round the rear of the chair as a child might, for fear that anyone else was there:

> The pathos of that image is important at this pivotal point in the play, the wild excitement of leaping into that seat followed in a second or two by the loneliness and stillness of the little figure dwarfed by it. . . . This is his zenith, from which he can only descend.
>
> (Lesser, 153)

Richard looked directly at Anne, who was standing alone at the front of the stage, when he informed Catesby that she was 'sick and like to die' (4.2.57). This drew her towards the throne, but on video Richard overlooks her silent protestations as he continues with his plans (4.2.60–4), until she turns, half falling down the steps, and drags herself on all fours out of his sight. The action confirmed the coldness of Richard's comment as he watched her go: 'Tear-falling pity dwells not in this eye' (4.2.65).

Two scenes marked the icy climate of King Richard's realm – the arrival of the women at the Tower (4.1), and their meeting with Richard en route to Bosworth (4.4). Both scenes were set in winter, the first a snowscape and the second a barren plain shrouded in smoke rising from the gridiron earth. And in both pictures women were bearing burdens across a vast expanse of stage. In 4.1 they approached the Tower merrily, bells underscoring the Yuletide image of Elizabeth dragging a sledge of gifts – including a rocking horse and a sack of toys – through falling snow. In the later scene blanketed figures carried carpet-bags across a smoking waste, 'shawled refugees of the dynastic fall-out' (*FT*, 1988). These bags can be seen scattered on the ground around the women in Figure 9. The contrast of scenic images marked the speedy decline in England's fortune under Richard, from potential peace to hell.

Scene 4 opened with Margaret's former enemies trailing past her as she stood centrally on stage, her fixity underlining her certainty in Richard's 'bitter, black, and tragical' demise (4.4.7). As in the 1963 production, her pleasure was tempered with some pity, particularly when the Duchess rebuked her for triumphing in woes that she once shared (4.4.59–60). Sitting with them on the ground (Figure 9), Margaret took the old woman's hand and began to tally up the deaths (4.4.63–70) in a gentler voice, as if acknowledging their shared experience; 'it's as near as she ever gets to an apology', Penny Downie admitted (Downie, 137). And in their turn the other women, who bowed their heads at the harsh truth, accepted that each had fallen prey to greed and hatred. The moment implied something of the same unity as that in the 1963 production. Cuts before and after her conclusion –

> Thus hath the course of justice whirl'd about,
> And left thee but a very prey to time.
>
> (4.4.105–6)

– made it apply to all three of them; 'in a strange way they become one', as Downie put it (138), and as their positions in the photograph suggest. At the end of the speech, the video shows Margaret taking off her crown, picking up one of the bags and leaving for France. The force of 'her whole spirit' (138), however, brought the other women to their feet and, hearing the sound of Richard's warlike drums and trumpets, they determined to voice their angry grief:

> Then in the breath of bitter words let's smother
> My damned son, that thy two sweet sons smother'd.
>
> (4.4.133–4)

FIGURE 9 In *The Plantagenets* (1988), all three women – the Duchess of York (Marjorie Yates), Queen Margaret (Penny Downie) and Queen Elizabeth (Joanne Pearce) – eventually sat upon the ground in 4.4. Around them lies the luggage with which Elizabeth and the Duchess were fleeing, like refugees, from Richard's land.

The arrival of Richard's army marching singly across the rear stage was a mirror image of the patterned death scenes, and this suggestion of execution was reflected in the jagged metal 'sun', a black circular saw disc which travelled above the stage behind them in time with the advance, shown in Figure 10. Although it symbolized an unstoppable force, the image was ambiguous. Up to this point, any advancing action in the play had crossed the stage from left to right. The retrograde movement of the troops from right to left, therefore, stood out as different, and implied retreat. Meanwhile, behind it all, the anticlockwise movement of the giant cog-wheel wound time slowly back to Richard's end.

The Duchess of York, played by Marjorie Yates, brought the movement to a halt by standing in the soldiers' way and forcing them to listen, as shown in Figure 10. Richard stared at the ground as she spoke her curse, but when she left he made a sudden move

FIGURE 10 As Richard's black, serrated-edged sun emblem (1988) rolls behind his advancing army (4.4), the Duchess of York (Marjorie Yates) halts the action. Cradling his helmet-crown, Richard (Anton Lesser) stops to listen, as later he will listen to the ghosts in 5.3. Queen Elizabeth (Joanne Pearce), exhausted and numbed with grief, looks on, stage left.

towards the retreating figure, a dagger in his hand. Then, almost immediately, he turned the blade into himself, stabbing his deformed hand several times in obvious frustration. It was a momentary lapse in self-control, the action betraying something of the self-hatred that his mother's lifelong rejection of him had engendered:

> She has prevented the progress of his war, has literally stood in the way of the war machine ... and then she hits him with all those emotionally painful memories ... and it rattles him more than he had expected ... he feels he must hurt, must mutilate himself because if he doesn't he will kill his mother in his rage at what, in his eyes, she has been responsible for. (Lesser, 154)

Words had always troubled this Richard, even from his early scenes in *The Rise of Edward IV*; his desire to kill Margaret at the end of that play had been to end her words, 'Why should she live to fill the world with words?' (*3 Henry VI*, 5.5.43), and he had killed her husband Henry for the same reason, 'die, prophet, in thy speech' (*3 Henry VI*, 5.6.56). Once more his impulse was to silence the speaker, but, in a prophetic act, he turned the anger back onto himself.

When Richard saw that Elizabeth had noticed this, however, he pulled himself together and ordered the army on while he spoke to her in private. Ignoring or not hearing his words, Elizabeth began to leave as well, so, as the video shows, Richard scurried forward to prevent her, grabbing a rag doll from the top of her carpet-bag as he mentioned young Elizabeth. This stopped her in her tracks. When he went on to affirm love for the Princess, however, he repeatedly tossed the doll in his hand, even chastising it at one point as 'petty Richmond', setting up a conflict between word and deed which reinforced the Queen's fear that he intended to harm her child.

For the first part of their dialogue Elizabeth sat on a carpet-bag, and Richard addressed her from across the proscenium. But the promptbook shows him moving closer as he spoke of making amends with grandchildren. Then he knelt beside her, teasing her with the doll, and finally thrusting it into her lap in anger when she still refused to accept his vow that Elizabeth's life would be, 'As long as heaven and nature lengthens it' (4.4.353). At these words Elizabeth seized her chance, and, showing what she had learned from Margaret, she pushed him further – 'As long as hell and Richard likes of it' (4.4.354) – daring him to vow his love (textual cuts removed the intervening confrontation at 4.4.355–65) and then revealing just how little he had left to swear by:

> That thou hast wronged in the time o'er-past.
> (adapted from 4.4.395–6)

Increasingly enraged by her refusal to let him complete his word, and agitated by the truth of her arguments, Richard circled the stage like a caged animal. Finally he stepped in and delivered the speech, 'As I intend to prosper and repent' (4.4.397ff.) while dragging her brutally downstage by the hair. The omission of the concluding lines (4.4.412–17), where Richard almost begs her to think of the future, not the past, to 'plead not my deserts but what I will deserve', meant that he ended with the more brutal assertion:

> It | cannot | be | a | voi | ded | but | by | this;
> It | will | not | be | a | voi | ded | but | by | this.
>
> (4.4.410–11)

As at Baynard's Castle his staccato delivery emphasized each syllable, as if he knew that she was unlikely to believe him. And he was right. She hung from his hands as the doll now hung from hers, his violence negating every word.

Despite her physical discomfort, Elizabeth's reply sounds surprisingly calm on video, a fact which gave her words an ambiguity similar to Richard's:

> Write to me very shortly,
> And you shall understand from me her mind.
>
> (4.4.428–9)

He then kissed her violently on the mouth before tossing her aside, pausing on his way out to deliver his dismissal: 'Relenting fool, and shallow, changing woman!' (4.4.431). But he found himself detained by Ratcliffe's arrival with news of Richmond's invasion, and this sent him into a flurry of indecision. Throughout their dialogue, the video shows Elizabeth crawling around the floor gathering the toys and clothes that have tipped out of her bag. Her later promise of a marriage between Princess Elizabeth and a victorious Richmond (delivered using Barton's 1963 addition) therefore came as no surprise.

VI

The golden blur of light and a trumpet flourish that heralded Richmond's arrival in England immediately transformed the prevailing gloom into a scene of hope, reinforcing as it did Simon

Dormandy's heroic reading of the role. Here was 'a genuinely courageous and politically blameless young man, who seriously believ[ed] God to be on his side' (Smallwood, 1993, introduction, 15). The video shows Richard, on the other hand, reaching Bosworth in semi-darkness, his followers like himself clad all in black, and their voices echoing slightly in the gloom. The tents, represented by huge backcloth flags – black with a silver boar for Richard, green and red with a Welsh dragon for Richmond – were raised side by side across the mid-stage, and tables set for each protagonist before them. Richmond prayed before settling to sleep on the ground, while Richard sat up drinking, clearly unsure of what the day might bring.

His greatest threat, however, came from the past, the ghosts of which awaited him on the other side of the tent wall. As it slowly descended they were revealed as a group of Lazarus-like statues in a white icescape, 'an appalling consortium, slowly dissolving as each comes shrouded down for his individual prophecy' (SQ) before drifting uneasily back to limbo, from where they swelled the chorus of 'Despair and die!' Something of this 'consortium' can be gathered from the ghosts' appearance on Bosworth Field, shown in Figure 12. At first Richard sat back and listened bemusedly, like a dreamer 'fascinated by the extraordinary juxtaposition of weird things' (Lesser, 155). But when the ghost of Rivers arrived he stood up and attempted conversation, as if trying 'to come to a wheedling arrangement' with him, according to one review (Independent, 1988). He also tried to silence Anne and Buckingham, each of whom had once sought to interrupt him; although, when he failed to gain the Duke's attention, he searched vainly on his belt and in the table drawer for a dagger to do the job.

Once the other world had disappeared again behind the banner curtain, Richard sat down and poured himself a drink. He was shaking so much, however, that he knocked the goblet to the floor and then fell himself as he went to retrieve it, screaming, 'Have mercy, Jesu!' (5.3.179) at the sight of the red wine, with its associations of 'retribution, deliverance, sin, forgiveness, ceremony, final judgement' (Lesser, 155) (the business mentioned here by Lesser was cut after the London transfer). Recovering slightly when he realized that it had only been a dream, he eased his panic with the joking question, 'Is there a murderer here?' (5.3.185). But the reply was spoken seriously, 'No. Yes, I am' (5.3.185). With much of Richard's subsequent equivocation omitted (5.3.186–91), this blunt admission led swiftly to the quiet conclusion:

> I shall despair. There is no creature loves me,
> And if I die, no soul will pity me –
> And wherefore should they, since that I myself
> Find in myself no pity to myself?
>
> (5.3.201–4)

Try as he might to dismiss thoughts of despair, however, the cool honesty of these last two lines was not wholly convincing. And when he tried to laugh it off by repeating the word 'fear' to Ratcliffe, 'Ratcliffe, I fear, | I | fear!' (5.3.215, my emphasis), the joke half acknowledged the emotion, with its unspoken need for the love and pity that he could not give himself. When, shortly after, Norfolk privately delivered the taunting message found on his tent (5.3.305–6), Richard read the note aloud to prove his fearlessness. But as he read and then lobbed the screwed-up paper into the wings (the action a weak echo of the opening champagne bottle) his bravado barely covered his unease: 'There is a terribly simple but profound understanding here; this is it, this is how it's going to be' (Lesser, 156).

Richmond delivered his battle oration from a table bathed in golden light, the staging recalling Richard's victory prologue. On this occasion the quickly improvised stage enhanced Richmond's plain speaking integrity, and its *platea* position allowed him to include the audience as his troops; in both, Richmond's simplicity outdid Richard's Baynard's Castle show. His was a ringing endorsement of the morality of rebellion against tyranny, the message made rather more choric than individual by cutting his refusal to be ransomed and all references to material gain

(5.3.258–61, 266–9). In the light of the Hall/Barton adaptation and 'given current orthodoxies', this was 'probably the most radical aspect of the production', according to Robert Smallwood (1993, introduction, 15).

As Figure 11 reveals, Richard's oration was delivered from the top of the metal cage in which he had murdered Henry VI. Rising from below centre stage, it took Richard's diminutive form into a powerful but precarious mid-air position. The photograph shows that, as it ascended, a handful of his supporters clung to the metal sides like children on a climbing frame, their shadows cast in half-light on the stage floor. The rest of the space, however, was quite empty. Clad now in black body armour, with a huge spiked shield buckled protectively over his hump and weaker arm, and another, seen in the photograph, held in his stronger hand, Richard the fighter, like Holm's Richard before him, addressed a void: 'There is the Henry V style in the oration ... "What shall I say" – but now it is all visibly a waste of time' (Lesser, 158).

The battle scenes had deliberately degenerated into chaos as the trilogy advanced, and Bosworth reflected the hollowness of Richard's words, conveyed as it was in cries, screams and drumbeats rather than the physical encounters of the earlier plays. In fact, the deflation of battlefield heroics was common to all three political interpretations. As Richard's call for a horse echoed around the stage, his preoccupation with finding Richmond caused him to wound Catesby without realizing it. When the protagonists finally met, it was a long and difficult encounter, with Richard knocking Richmond's sword away before losing his own. This he replaced immediately with the tattered standard dropped by the dying Catesby, and defended himself well enough to knock his more obviously powerful opponent to the ground. Just as he was about to finish Richmond with his dagger, however, he looked up to see a phalanx of the ghosts advancing slowly down the stage. Transfixed for a moment by the sight, and by their words, 'Despair and die', he failed to notice Richmond grasp the fallen banner and force it upwards through the humped shoulder,

FIGURE 11 Richard (Anton Lesser) addressed the 1988 auditorium audience (5.3) across a stage empty but for his few supporters, who clung on to the metal cage like children on a climbing frame. Richard's diminutive stature was emphasized by his precarious position on the cage, while the protective spiked shoulder armour and shield underlined his vulnerability.

lancing it like a boil. The moment is captured in Figure 12, silhouetted by the ghosts. The 'contorted beetle that was Richard' (*TLS*) then slid down the wooden stave, blood and sinew spewing from the wound, and was finally pinned at Richmond's feet. Spread-eagled on the ground, he stared in horror at it.

The promptbook shows that the ghosts stayed on stage to watch Richmond receive the crown from Stanley. Keeping it in his hands,

FIGURE 12 At the close of Adrian Noble's 1988 production (5.5), Richmond (Simon Dormandy) pinioned Richard (Anton Lesser) like an insect through the armoured hump, the opportunity created and witnessed by the shrouded ghosts of Richard's victims.

however, the new king enquired after Stanley's son George, and it was the news of the boy's safety that prompted him to pardon those of Richard's men who would accept defeat. He then spoke of uniting the dynasties that had almost destroyed each other across the three *Plantagenet* plays, his concluding prayer, 'a heartening major chord' (*Independent*, 1988), shorn of any sermonizing about the punishment of future treachery (5.5.35–9). Finally he held the crown aloft while the closing music underlined the image of a nation harmoniously reunited. Hall and Barton had signalled the dawn of an uneasy future at this point, but Noble's final tableau looked back 'with majestic symmetry' (*Independent*, 1989) across dramatic and historical time. Behind the foreground future of Richmond's smiling band, the sunrise colours drained away through Richard's black and blood-soaked present to the wintry spectres of the past. The lighting imitated the effect of a camera pulling back to show the closing panorama, with the golden glow of Crowley's picture frame intensifying as the music soared.

For some this was a fitting conclusion to a dynastic saga told through spectacle and image, a plush affair ostensibly far removed from the didacticism of its RSC predecessor:

> the extirpation of this nodule of unnatural malignancy looks especially cathartic when you see it ... as the ceremonial, almost sacramental resolution of a nation's long ordeal.... The cycle closes with majestic symmetry, triumphantly vindicating this cavalcade of carnage, genealogical vendetta, and grand dynastic designs.
>
> (*Independent*, 1989)

As the *International Herald Tribune* observed of the entire saga, 'there is something immensely reassuring about a company of 40 advancing towards the footlights to play out some vast dramatic national anthem of blood and death and restoration.'

Others, such as Michael Ratcliffe, were disappointed that Noble's picture-pageant endorsement of consumer capitalism questioned 'neither the message nor the triumph' of Tudor history (*Observer*) – despite a programme quotation from the Spanish ambassador to the Tudor court noting how Henry VII himself 'purged and cleansed' England of all 'doubtful' royal blood. One review suggested that the production's lack of 'shaping spirit, no use of history and therefore no meaning' exactly captured 'the prevailing liberal bewilderment' (*Morn. Star*) of the late 1980s. And indeed its emphasis on self-projection, particularly the references to interior design in the 'illuminated' stage pictures, might have been read as a soft-focus reflection of Peter Hall's concern about the devaluation of community, especially at a time when the Prime Minister herself had announced society's demise. But when the production began to elide the artifice of Richard's power with that of theatrical spectacle, it was more difficult to differentiate between stage image and political deception, as the drama's ironic dimension, including its outside commentatory voices, disappeared inside the picture frame.

Since 1945, political readings of the play have eagerly reflected current events or the contemporary political climate, drawing not least on the example of Hitler's rise and systematic pursuit of power, and on the subsequent Cold War in world politics. And the seriousness of this realist reading has taken the play well away from the one-man melodrama it had become on stage in the early years of the last century. Commentatory voices, such as those of the citizens and the women, have been given greater prominence, and not only is Elizabeth allowed her powerful scene with Richard (4.4), too often dismissed as a repetition of 1.2, but she is shown to be politically engaged in the final action. Both of these – the citizen voices and Elizabeth's political influence – are elements which Shakespeare developed from chronicle accounts.

However, the consistency of structure and style that this realist political approach required – underpinned, certainly in 1961 and 1963, by the directors' stated ideological stance – has been at the cost of the play's comic elements, and, in particular, of its ironic self-consciousness as drama. Directors tended to subsume the play's theatricality within their own staging, and minimize the eccentricity of Richard's shape and audience asides, thereby diminishing that dimension of the play, and of Vice-figure Richard, which stands disruptively outside political ideology and historical account.

2

PSYCHO·SOCIAL RICHARDS

ll the productions discussed in the last chapter and in this were interested in the material context of Richard's rise, and each presented him, in large part, as the product of his political or social circumstances. In the productions examined in chapter 1, Richard was shown to capitalize, skilfully and single-mindedly, on the political conflict which surrounded him. The interpretations discussed in this chapter generally saw Richard as a victim, psychologically and emotionally damaged by the flawed belief structures, expectations and codes of the society that the court represented; flaws which his rise to power both exploited and exposed. Stratford has seen three of these strongly psycho-social interpretations of the play – directed by Glen Byam Shaw in 1953 and Terry Hands in 1970 and 1980 – and a fourth, directed by Elijah Moshinsky in 1998, in which the response was less fully developed.

Glen Byam Shaw carefully established Richard's social background in his 1953 production by giving place to the surrounding figures and events, and by casting an unusually gentle, apparently vulnerable protagonist – a reading similar to that suggested in pre-war productions at the Old Vic by Henry Cass (1936), and Tyrone Guthrie (1937). Played by Marius Goring, Shaw's Richard was an emotional cripple, broken and then rejected by an uncaring, irresponsible society; a man not a monster, who was the subject of history rather than its construct.

To date, Stratford's most daring advocate of the psycho-social approach has been Terry Hands, whose two productions peopled a social landscape very like Byam Shaw's, though far more sinister. Hands's protagonists shared the innate vulnerability of Marius Goring's childlike characterization, but their values were more obviously distilled from the world which spawned them. In the 1970 production, this was a primitive society just emerging into civilization. A decade later, it was one in which established social and religious structures offered no more than superstitious scaffolding for instinctual fears.

Although Elijah Moshinsky's was the most recent of the four interpretations, it was the most old-fashioned in that it revived aspects of the Irving–Olivier tradition that the other two were reacting against. This was a commercial venture for the RSC, closer in both principle and intention to pre-war unsubsidized productions, with Richard as the sort of virtuoso soloist that Olivier's stage and film performances defined. The limited length of the run, with a brief provincial tour taking in Stratford before a short London transfer to the West End's Savoy Theatre, enabled Robert Lindsay, highly acclaimed and sought after for television and film performances, to take the star role. Yet these same commercial requirements denied Moshinsky the range and strength of casting in the lesser parts that the RSC's usual permanent company and repertoire allow, particularly in *Richard III*. A West End transfer also reduced the playing time to no more than two and a half hours. Had the production remained a barnstorming star vehicle, however, it might have been more of a critical success. But Moshinsky's and Lindsay's decision to present Richard's victimhood as a reason for his single-minded villainy, and so turn the production towards a psycho-social interpretation, presented problems. For, as Byam Shaw's and Terry Hands's productions showed, if Richard is to be seen as a product of his environment, he needs to be set within, and against, a clearly defined social context. The broad lines of Moshinsky's textual adaptation, design concept and casting, which were largely driven by practical requirements, worked against such detailed definition.

The following discussion pairs the productions according to similarity rather than chronology, not only because the development of ideas between Hands's two productions invites their comparison, but also because Moshinsky's is the closest post-war Stratford production to the tradition out of, and against, which Byam Shaw built his response.

GLEN BYAM SHAW, 1953, AND ELIJAH MOSHINSKY, 1998

I

The decision to replace pictorial elaboration with simple architectural suggestion in the single set for Glen Byam Shaw's 1953 season marked an important change in Stratford's approach to design. Motley's design, most of which can be seen in the coronation scene (Figure 13), consisted of 'a series of sharply pointed arches, making the effect of two triangles pointing down-stage, with their right and left center' (SQ) linked by a canopy, and set on a central platform from which wide steps at either side curved in to a forestage (the forestage can also be seen in Figure 14). Two doors on either side of the proscenium arch gave on to this forestage. In *Richard III* the right-hand door was used both as Hastings's house and balcony (3.2.) and for Richard's appearance on the leads at Baynard's Castle (3.7), while the left door, named the Tower entrance in the promptbook, 'became associated with the entrance to a place of execution or murder' (SQ). Through here the dying Clarence was dragged, the two Princes unwillingly took their last walk, and Rivers, Vaughan, Grey and Buckingham passed to execution, a hooded figure waiting for them on the stairs within.

In some ways the design recalled the permanent set, of two wooden staircases joined by a balcony, which Tania Moiseiwitsch had designed for Stratford's 1951 history plays. But Motley opened

FIGURE 13 Motley's setting for the 1953 coronation scene (4.2) shows the twin triangles pointing downstage, with heraldic banners closing in a series of arches which, at other times, framed views through to the rear. The edge of the right-hand proscenium door can just be seen. Richard (Marius Goring) takes the hand of Buckingham (Harry Andrews) before the throne dais, while the court looks on.

up the playing space to the rear wall to let the action move more freely, and so gave three-dimensionality to character and event. Banners and plain or figured backdrops, seen in Figure 13, closed in the arches for interior scenes (with a 'Death cloth' for the executions), but at other times the audience could look through to the space beyond, where citizens passed over the stage or soldiers awaited command.

Lighting effects were used to transfer scenes from court to battlefield, and reviewers praised the memorable stage pictures these created (*D. Telegraph*), focused as they were on solid figures, not on a painted scene. Figures 13 and 14 show that costumes were medieval in style, the men wearing tabards and sometimes cloaks, and the women in soft pastel-coloured robes with headdresses, or

FIGURE 14 In what is probably a posed picture of 1.3 (1953), Queen Margaret (Joan Sanderson) curses Marius Goring's Richard, seated on the steps. They are watched apprehensively by Buckingham (Harry Andrews), Derby (John Bushelle), Hastings (Tony Britton), Rivers (Donald Eccles), Queen Elizabeth (Rachel Kempson), Dorset (William Peacock), Vaughan (Peter Duguid) and Grey (Dennis Clinton).

black widows' weeds. In general the men sported long, dark hair, with heavy make-up and half-beards or moustaches defining their faces as strongly masculine. Motley's identification of opposing factions by costume colour helped to clarify the subtle regrouping of individuals as events advanced. Along with the design of set and lighting, this co-ordinated approach reinforced the drama's structured social background by defining gender roles, throwing subordinate characters into relief, and introducing a world beyond the court peopled by those whose lives hung on the main events.

Rob Howell's setting for Elijah Moshinsky's 1998 production owed more to the Victorian picture-stage than to Motley's 1953 design. Massive Gothic side and rear walls dominated a rectangular playing space, the proscenium edge of which opened out into a triangle with its apex jutting out into the stalls audience. This downstage promontory gave Richard in particular, but also Richmond and Margaret, a commanding position from which to address the audience or, turning, to stand and watch the main events. Two doors in the rear wall gave glimpses into distant chambers, framed figures as they entered, as shown in Figure 15, or simply threw light on to the darkened stage. From the first court scene (1.3) until Baynard's Castle, and then, with the exception of Bosworth eve, until the end, these rear and side walls were fronted by a heavy chain curtain (seen as background in Figure 15) which cast swaying shadows across the stage and clanked as figures passed, an echo of the court's unease. Corin Buckeridge's music score evoked the medieval cloister, with solo choristers and Gregorian plainsong building to a full choir in the closing battlefield communion.

The costumes matched the heavily medieval setting (shown in the court's appearance in Figure 15). Figures were weighted down by cloaks and lengthy, dark-coloured robes, which hindered movement but allowed for striking static poses. The royal women, whose dresses varied the colour scheme a little with dull purple, moss green and, in Anne's case, white, wore close-fitting medieval headdresses reminiscent of nuns' hoods, with an added coronet for Elizabeth, and later Anne. Their arms were covered and, for Elizabeth, restricted by the caped bodice of her gown, emphasizing the constraint imposed by medieval modesty. All the nobles at court carried long staffs topped with heraldic emblems, seen in Figure 15, in portable versions of those that dominated Hands's stage in 1980. These identified the rank and possibly the faction of each peer, although only Richard's boar was instantly recognizable. Nothing in the costuming itself marked age, status or family loyalty, as it did in 1953. The followers at court – soldiers, servants and lesser functionaries – were all dressed as monks and nuns, their colour-coded habits appearing to signal good or evil intent. Clarence's murderers wore black, those bearing Henry's body wore white, and a few others, presumably of uncertain moral status, wore robes of brown and cream.

FIGURE 15 Robert Lindsay's Richard (1998) stands centre stage to vent his anger on Siân Thomas's Queen Elizabeth in 1.3. Almost every member of the court bears a staff of office or of nobility, signalling the importance of status in this scene. To the rear the metal chain curtain hangs open at the door to Edward's chamber, where doctors minister to the sickly king.

This clerical background might have signalled Edward's retreat into the cloister as a penance for past wrongs, as Hands's 1970 production implied. But Moshinsky's text and stage direction offered little support for such a reading. Heavy textual cutting, including all references to the civil war, in fact prevented any detailed definition of the play's historical or social context and drained the play of 'political resonance' (*Guardian*, 1998), whether in fifteenth- or twentieth-century terms. This was because Moshinsky and Lindsay, who worked together on the staging, had decided to take the play back 'to an original format' precisely to avoid the sort of 'modern equivalent' (Lindsay in *E. Daily Press*) for its historical world that political responses to the play had found. In the event, this 'original format' owed more to theatrical tradition than Elizabethan authenticity, rooted as it was in the sort of nineteenth- and early twentieth-century stagings of *Richard III* exemplified by Henry Irving at the Lyceum, and revived here in the uncomplicated contrast of a vaguely medieval/ Gothic background and a villain-king.

Olivier had created the same binary opposition, with the same heavy cutting, in the first half of his 1955 film, but his cuts were replaced with visual references to court factionalism, gossiping discontent and royal adultery on which the villain preyed. Moshinsky's court was too indistinct to present a convincing catalyst for Richard's discontent: 'Lindsay has nothing to compete with. Richard's foes are petty and virtually interchangeable bureaucrats, all of them swaddled in billowing robes like so much washing on a line' (*E. Standard*). Even the citizens, who, as outsiders, comment on the power-struggle, were made part of Edward's cloister (a monk and a nun), their reassigned comments rendering them even more chorally insignificant than in Noble's 1988 production.

II

A strong contrast between Richard and the court in the 1953 production was fundamental to Byam Shaw's reading of the play. Marius Goring's appearance as Richard, shown in Figure 16, broke with the tradition of 'the tall, dark, twisted Crookback, to whom we have become used' (*S. Mercury*). More particularly, he presented a striking contrast to the overt masculinity of the other nobles, with his deep 'anthropoid' forehead (*S. Mercury*) and pale, almost white, complexion, framed by lanky, red, shoulder-length hair, suggesting an effeminate weakness and vulnerability. His appearance implied 'that a sense of his own deformity has shaped the twisted mind of Richard', which the *Times* saw as a distortion of 'the theatrical values of the character'. He wore black leather, in a style described by one critic as 'what we now call a "space suit"' (*Man. Guardian*), which accentuated his tall, slight frame and drew attention to the built-up left boot and thin leg encased in a half-calliper. It suggested physical immaturity, in shape half man, half child.

FIGURE 16 Marius Goring's Richard (1953) displayed obvious physical disabilities, with a raised left boot and leg iron and a deformed hand. His wide forehead, lanky red hair and pale face drew attention to the staring eyes, and deceptively suggested a childlike quality in the man.

But Richard's opening stance also revealed a man of action, his broadsword resting across his right shoulder, part soldier, part rebel. (Figure 17 offers a posed version of this.) On 'Grim-visaged war hath smooth'd his wrinkled front', he lowered the sword and leaned on it 'as a walking stick', according to the promptbook, placing his heavy-booted left foot on the forestage step to indicate how 'rudely stamped' he was, and then transferred the sword into his clawed left hand on the words, 'Deformed, unfinished'.

FIGURE 17 Standing before a sword-and-shield starburst and heraldic beasts, in a posed version of the opening moments (1.1) of Byam Shaw's 1953 production, Marius Goring's warrior Richard showed nothing of the innocent vulnerability on which he later played.

Together these movements made ironic play on the assumption that deformity rendered Richard harmless. His apparent immaturity concealed a fighting man.

Byam Shaw's choice of Marius Goring for this complex interpretation was significant, because the actor's reputation lay in naturalistic, Ibsenesque roles based on a shrewd observation of human nature. So much so, in fact, that the *Times* felt his 'inveterately realistic imagination' would be unsuited to portraying villainy twice as large as life. But Byam Shaw wanted a naturalistic

Richard whose behaviour, if not his appearance, showed his attempt to be one among a group of men. This too the *Times* disliked, since Goring could not therefore, 'succeed in making himself inescapable'. Ivor Brown in the *Observer* felt that it was interesting to see Richard 'now pinned on the psychiatrist's table and acted modernly', but the *Times* clearly longed for a more conventionally obvious villain: 'there really is no room for the suggestion that he might have died a good old man if he had not been born so ugly'. The *Scotsman* was equally unimpressed at the absence of traditional business, such as Richard tearing the prayer-book to tatters and flinging it into the street below at the close of 3.7. Significantly, Robert Lindsay played just such a piece of business – throwing Richard's prayer-book high into the air – at the same moment in 1998.

Lindsay's Richard was in many respects the villain that Goring's critics would have welcomed. With long, dark hair, a large hump on the left shoulder, a pronounced limp which caused him continual pain, and a deformed left hand protected by a pottery claw, his appearance underlined the Olivier inheritance. As Olivier's film Richard had stood a while in reverie before limping forward to acknowledge the camera's arrival, so Lindsay's Richard stood briefly at the opening of the play in the rear-stage doorway and watched the falling snow, his frame swathed in a 'black drop-sleeved cloak' (*E. Standard*), seen in Figure 15, which slid behind him as he limped towards the forestage promontory.

He seemed to have emerged into the night air from the indoor confines of his brother Edward's court, wrapping himself in his own 'winter of discontent' (a specific reversal of Richard's opening lines, where wartime winter is displaced with summer peace). The effect emphasized Richard's melancholic isolation, and linked it with the cold outdoors. In fact all of Richard's early scenes took place outside in what appeared to be the precincts of a monastery, where he wooed Anne, where Edward died (on a convenient tomb), and where the coronation council was held, amidst the sort of elegantly carved stone stalls found in abbey cloisters. Only after Richard's coronation, his cloak now blood-red, was the action set inside the walls, where the centre stage was dominated by a long refectory table, covered in the same red cloth and heavy with documents.

Lindsay's Richard was a mixture of the skilled comedian and the bemused lost boy. His underplayed facial expressions and mannerisms punctuated by single punchlines were familiar from the actor's role as Michael Murray, the northern council leader, in Alan Bleasdale's 1991 television drama series, *GBH*. Lindsay's Richard shared the shoulder-shrugging tic that had indicated Murray's psychological breakdown, and both roles used Lindsay's northern voice. Richard and his brother, Edward, spoke with a similar Yorkshire accent, despite the fact that everyone else in the family, including their mother, the Duchess of York, used a standard RP voice. (Reviews were incorrect in reporting that the entire family was identifiably northern.)

As with some other details of the production, such as the cloister setting, it was not made entirely clear to the audience what this selective use of the northern accent meant. Robert Smallwood suggested that, in a court where the majority spoke 'standard' English, a Yorkshire brogue was a 'virtually inescapable' signal of intellectual inferiority; a signal which therefore overlooked the fact that Richard's 'dazzling' intellectual virtuosity drives much of Shakespeare's play (*SS*). It was a view endorsed by Richard's comical inability to answer the young king's questions in 3.1. Michael Billington described Lindsay's Richard as 'a baffled joker, with a strong Yorkshire accent, who cannot quite believe how much luck plays into his hands' (*Guardian*). On the other hand, both voice and mannerisms could have been intended to reinforce links in audience members' minds with Michael Murray in *GBH*, who, part victim of sinister political and emotional forces, fought to maintain his control – to comic effect.

Lindsay tempered Richard's comedy with the same under-current of unease, both physical and psychological, that he had shown in *GBH*, signalling this in Richard's habit of swaying from foot to foot and of nodding his head sideways as he spoke. His severe treatment of the younger prince in 3.1 had about it an element of petty revenge for his humiliation by the elder brother, which also hinted at something of Richard's insecure childhood. The boy was evidently frightened of his uncle, and hesitant to greet his brother until Richard's shout of 'Boy!' commanded him to kneel before the King. Young York's later bravado became an extreme reaction to this fear, much, perhaps, like Richard's. A line interpolated into the opening soliloquy, 'Why love forswore me in my mother's womb' (*3 Henry VI*, 3.2.153), had grounded this insecurity in a loveless childhood. As Lindsay put it, 'from the bottom of his soul [Richard] loathes women.... He thinks women are promiscuous, manipulative and dangerous' (*E. Anglian*). And when he turned back at the end of the second soliloquy (1.2.162) to ask the audience, 'Can I do this and cannot get a crown? / Tut, were it further off, I'll pluck it down' (*3 Henry VI*, 3.2.194–5) – words, also imported by Olivier, from Richard's first soliloquy in *3 Henry VI* – it was clear that his was an ambition driven by revenge and a desire to be noticed, rather than a Machiavellian political plan.

Richard was particularly delighted, therefore, to have sexually aroused Anne in the wooing scene (1.2), a fact signalled by a lengthy final kiss that extended almost into orgasm as she whimpered in delight. This 'weird sex appeal' was another detail shared with Olivier's Richard (*D. Mail*). Instead of leaving, Anne clung on passionately to him, but Richard stayed unmoved. He simply glanced over her shoulder at the audience in order to announce the first success in his revenge against the sex: 'Was ever woman in this humour woo'd?' (1.2.232).

His second success was against Margaret. Anna Carteret played her as a fierce and bitter woman determined on revenge, although the specific details of her desire for vengeance seemed less important here than in a more politically orientated interpretation of the play. Textual cuts to reduce the running time had, after all, deleted much of the reference to the recent past on which the logic of Richard's criticism and Margaret's condemnation of the court in this scene rely. Nor did her appearance make reference to the past, since the production's minimizing of historical detail meant that, unlike Peggy Ashcroft (1963) and Penny Downie (1988), for example, she was neither battle-worn nor ancient. In fact her moss-green dress, full-skirted with a train, and Tudor headdress made her, if anything, fashionably ahead of the other royal women. She also carried, or trailed, a long green stole, which, when worn, looked like ivy wrapped around 'some mossed-over tree trunk' (*SS*). Her green uniformity gave the figure a symbolic quality, as though the cycle of revenge that she proposed derived not from political ambition but from a more primeval instinct.

On video, her vocal fury in 3.1 certainly belied her sophisticated appearance. As she cursed Richard, he began a deep-throated growl, half mocking her animal anger and half angry himself, which grew louder as he tried to drown her words. Finally he moved behind her and grasped her throat as he stopped her words with 'Margaret' (1.3.234), at the same time disarming her of the small dagger with which she was fending off attack. The moment formed a contrast with his disarming of Anne (1.2), but brought out the same bitterness in his reaction to women. Their emotional eloquence seemed to trouble him. Taken in the light of this production's focus on the private rather than the political Richard, Margaret's railing seemed to epitomize the maternal love by which he felt himself forsaken before birth, and the maternal hatred which he had subsequently felt.

III

Goring's Richard played on his apparent childlike vulnerability in the opening scenes of the 1953 production. The wooing of Anne reduced him to tears, and they, in turn, moved her to pity him. Promptbook details such as the hint of sensuality in Anne's gentle return of his sword to its scabbard, and the parting gift of a rose from her dress, endorsed the naturalism created by textual cuts. Her initial cursing was curtailed, and the stichomythic exchanges between the two of them reduced, to intercut the shorter speeches in a more realistic way. Cuts made Richard less consciously witty, and his control of the debate less overt, so that his dialogue with Anne became almost convincing. He certainly had fewer opportunities to signal an awareness that he was performing. Further cuts in Richard's concluding soliloquy also modified his actorly conceit, removing references to the 'devil and dissembling looks' and grounding his achievement in the convincing 'truth' of his feelings. His delight derived from amazement that, however briefly, Anne let him forget the 'intense inferiority complex' that he felt for 'his unbalanced body' (*Leam. Spa Cour.*)

The same naturalistic detail established the factional opposition at Edward's court. For instance Richard's henchmen, Hastings, Buckingham and Derby, waited uneasily for his arrival in 1.3, at which point Hastings diplomatically ensured that he acknowledged the Queen's presence with a bow. Elizabeth later used a similar gesture to stop Dorset from drawing his sword in response to Richard's taunts. Both actions showed hatred barely hidden beneath courtesy, and revealed a group of diplomats who eased the warrior Richard's path at court, even as their quiet smiles endorsed his outspoken disdain for the Queen. The formality exaggerated Richard's naïvety, a lack of courtly sophistication that he could neither hide nor turn to his advantage as he had in wooing Anne. Here was the gap between the public and the private man that gave rise to Richard's fear of betrayal by such apparent friends as Buckingham, and later triggered his defeat. As Ivor Brown in the *Observer* saw it, Richard was 'a human being ... soured into savagery by his jealousy of normal men'.

The arrival of Queen Margaret (Joan Sanderson, seen addressing Richard in Figure 14) brought the court's barely concealed antagonism into the open. And by the end of the scene the veneer of decorum which sustained Elizabeth's authority had disappeared. Fearing what Richard would do next, she turned from her departing family and crossed the stage, alone, to address Richard and his faction with the loaded question, 'Lords, will you go with us?' (1.3.322). But Richard simply froze her out. The promptbook notes, 'no one looks at QE – she turns to Rivers', and Rivers comes to her rescue with the promise of support as he hurries her away: 'We wait upon your grace' (1.3.323).

Edward's was a court struggling to cope with a new order organized along bureaucratic instead of feudal lines. This was revealed in the prominence of paperwork and documents in the public scenes, and through the figure of Lord Hastings. The promptbook shows that, at the opening of 2.1, he took charge of a document that King Edward had just signed (probably Clarence's belated reprieve). Then at the coronation council (3.4) he busied himself with another, this time for Richard's signature (perhaps his approval of the Prince's coronation). But, while Richard dipped his pen twice in the inkpot, he did not actually subscribe his name. When Buckingham later held up a document at Baynard's Castle (3.7) and asked Richard, 'Tomorrow may it please you to be crowned?' (3.7.241), this could well have been the unsigned paper from the council scene. Richard's dislike of such documents, however, had been established in the opening scene, when he met Hastings leaving the Tower (1.1.121ff.). The ex-prisoner was accompanied by Catesby, Richard's henchman, who handed his master a document to peruse as the two nobles spoke. Its contents were not revealed, but it could have been a royal pardon, which would establish Hastings as another obstacle in Richard's path to the throne.

Such realistic details in the depiction of the court, and Richard's usurpation of it, helped to create the impression of change from open conflict to bureaucratic government in ways possibly familiar to a post-war audience.

The narrative movement between scenes reinforced this naturalistic approach, particularly in Byam Shaw's portrayal of the passage of time. He merged events, either by retaining characters on stage as the scene changed, or by overlapping action. The young King Edward, for example, arrived in state through the bower of arches at the start of 3.1, just as his mother and brother left for sanctuary through the Tower doorway at the close of 2.4, with Cardinal Bourchier and the Bishop of Ely, included here in both scenes, remaining on stage to establish continuity. Sometimes the fluency of action was also symbolic, as when both boys left through the Tower door. Their departure formed part of a pattern highlighting Richard's destruction of society's legal and religious securities, each movement of which was associated with the doorway: young York sought sanctuary in the Tower; he was released from it despite clerical unease; and the two boys departed up the same stairs to their deaths. Thus Tyrrel's entrance from the Tower staircase after the princes' murder (4.3) completed the pattern, and Richard's plan.

Moshinsky's 1998 production eschewed this sort of realistic detail. Although Lindsay had stated that the court was full of 'dubious, power-seeking people' (*E. Anglian*), it was surprising how little the text and stage business allowed it to be seen. Instead of historical context, the production drew attention to Richard's control of events. When Edward died on stage (the text conflated 2.1 with 2.2), Moshinsky foregrounded Richard's reception of the news by placing him on the forestage promontory facing the audience, where he dropped to his knees, shaking with silent laughter, before turning to speak tearful words of comfort to the Queen. The intercutting of 2.4 with the citizens' dialogue (2.3) likewise placed Elizabeth's narrative inside the frame of Richard's plot.

This focus on Richard presented problems, however, in the central section of the play (from 2.2 to 4.3), where Richard and Buckingham (David Yelland) work their skilful way towards the throne. In most psycho-social interpretations, Buckingham's arrival provides the emotionally insecure Richard with a degree of, admittedly self-interested, friendship, shifting the dramatic focus from Richard's troubled response to women (who do not reappear until Act 4) to his political partnership with Buckingham.

In 1998, however, this relationship was a major casualty of the extensive textual cuts. By cutting 3.5, in which Hastings's death is presented to the Mayor, Moshinsky advanced the action from the council scene (3.4) (which now incorporated the Scrivener's comment, 3.6) to Baynard's Castle (3.7), thereby maintaining the impetus of Richard's success, but removing vital evidence of the partnership on which it rests. Unfortunately, David Yelland's portrayal of Buckingham as a smooth-tongued, medieval version of a Cabinet Secretary compounded the problem. His slightly weary, paternalistic tone of voice suggested just enough of the disinterested diplomat to explain his official role at Edward's court as that of a 'blandly faceless spin-doctor' (*E. Standard*) – so faceless indeed as to give no hint of self-interest. By cutting their performance for the Mayor, therefore, Moshinsky diminished the private basis of the partnership, removing evidence of Buckingham's arrogant ambition, and Richard's grounds for risking a similar deception at Baynard's Castle.

IV

Two intervals marked out Richard's progress in the 1953 *Richard III*. The first came between 2.2, when the Prince is sent for from the north, and 2.4, where the young Duke of York is taken into sanctuary (2.3, the citizens' scene, was cut). It signalled a transition from Richard's private manipulation of the court to his and Buckingham's political deception of the public. The second break came between 3.7, the Baynard's Castle scene, and 4.1, the women's arrival at the Tower, the point at which most single-interval productions place the break. Between the intervals, the figure of Buckingham became increasingly prominent, even to the point of threatening Richard, as his role in 3.5 revealed. Both men began the scene seated on the steps, arming themselves and discussing acting skills. But, when Buckingham and Catesby stood behind the Mayor with daggers to 'assist' his acceptance of Hastings's death, the game moved under Buckingham's control. Reassigned lines gave him the lion's share of the explanation, leaving Richard weeping silently over the basket containing Hastings's head. The *Times* reviewer noted that this strengthening of Buckingham meant that Harry Andrews's performance as the Duke was 'often in danger of sweeping Richard into a corner of the stage'. And the *Birmingham Post* regretted the 'insufficient buoyancy of spirit' in Goring's Richard, which, while it showed 'mental arrogance', had none of the 'tyrant's relish of power politics'. In this production, power politics were Buckingham's domain – a frequent danger in such psycho-social interpretations, where Buckingham takes on some of the intellectual wit and cunning more usually associated with Richard, and where, in a strong performance, he can so drive the action that he steals the audience's interest and attention.

Byam Shaw's textual cuts ensured that Buckingham concerned himself with usurpation by manipulation of the law, whereas Richard was happy to use any means, including violence, to achieve power. At the close of 3.1, Buckingham sent Catesby to test Hastings's loyalty, but now (with 3.1.174–7 cut) Buckingham made no reference to Catesby's tactics. It was Richard who did so, stopping Catesby halfway up the steps. After Catesby had left, further cuts (3.1.187–90) made Buckingham's question, 'what shall we do if we perceive / Lord Hastings will not yield to our complots?' (3.1.191–2) an immediate reaction to Richard's intervention. The promptbook then shows that he 'reacts' to Richard's answer, 'Chop off his head, man' (3.1.193). The offered earldom of Hereford seemed here to be Richard's attempt to placate the uneasy Duke.

When Buckingham left 3.5 to speak to the citizens at Guildhall he promised Richard:

> Doubt not, my lord, I'll play the orator
> As if the golden fee for which I plead
> Were for myself . . .
>
> (3.5.94–6)

But, with the rest of his dialogue cut, this parting joke sounded like a potential threat to Richard. Recognizing this, Richard took independent action by issuing new orders to Lovell and Catesby, and later 'hurries' (promptbook) in two bishops for the Baynard's Castle scene without Buckingham's knowledge (Buckingham's lines 3.7.46–47 were cut). Once he was crowned he increased the number of soldiers around him, and replaced political advisers, such as Buckingham, with those from his military past whom he could better trust. Final proof that Buckingham was out of favour came as their dialogue gradually edged the Duke off the central platform, then off the stage, and finally down the forestage steps towards the pit.

The cool, seemingly impersonal relationship between Richard and Buckingham in the 1998 production made Buckingham's desertion to Richmond (Jo Stone-Fewings) a less significant betrayal than in 1953. After the coronation (4.2), they met alone and in private across the long refectory table, now a symbol of the gulf between them. Once Buckingham had left to consider the proposed murders, Richard addressed the absent Stanley as part of what were now private musings about Richmond – all of which signalled a troubled isolation. He also returned to the uneasy swaying movements of 1.1, as he wandered, alone and at something of a loss, around the table and its weighty documents. His rejection of Buckingham, when it came, was less a threat to the Duke – who seemed finally to acknowledge the limited strategic intellect of the man he had made King – than a further sign that Richard was losing his hold on sanity. The focus of his decline was not the desertion of friends but the abiding sense of inadequacy and insignificance that resurfaced as soon as he had the crown.

V

The Duchess of York's curse (4.4.184–90, 195–6) was a key turning point in both productions, carrying particular weight in that of 1953, where Byam Shaw cut Richard's later dialogue with Elizabeth (4.4.199–431). Shortened by four lines in this production, the curse no longer mentioned Richard's enemies; his mother did not wish him dead, but that he might lose the energy to fight. And Richard's silent response showed that her attack on his fighting prowess – the one skill in which he equalled other men – had hit home: 'he sat and let the play move around him ... particularly when listening to the cruel words of his mother' (*D. Herald*).

The concluding scenes showed Richard's mental unpreparedness to fight stemming from this sense of betrayal rather than the outside workings of a retributive force. In the end Richard had only his own strength to rely on, a belief highlighted in the transposition of a couplet from the end of 4.3 to the close of 4.4:

> My counsel is my shield.
> We must be brief, when traitors brave the field.
>
> (4.3.56–7)

In 1998, it was the Duchess of York's description of Richard's wayward infancy (4.4.166ff.), delivered as she tweaked her son's ear, which hurt him. He grasped the hand and held it, causing her to wince with pain, as he whispered:

> If I be so disgracious in your eye,
> Let me march on and not offend you, madam.
>
> (4.4.178–9)

His tone was bitter, and as he released her hand brutally on the word 'offend' he intended it to hurt. She was clearly frightened. But so was he. His hand shook uncontrollably as the Duchess (Dilys Hamlett) braved the intimidation and cursed her son, caressing his hump and his deformed hand, and finally kissing him as if in blessing before hurrying away. It was an unequivocal condemnation and delivered with gentle cruelty.

The third kiss of the play came later in the scene when Richard embraced Elizabeth. It began as a last-minute gesture, but changed to something more emotional as, kissing her on the lips, he suddenly searched for the same sexual response that he had earned from Anne. But Elizabeth pushed him from her in horrified surprise, and hurried away. Richard stood in disturbed silence for some time, twitching, before dismissing her as a 'shallow, changing woman' (4.4.431), although the disgust also appeared to be directed at himself.

The production's focus on Richard as a victim of his psychological demons, rather than increasingly subject to moral guilt, culminated in a Bosworth nightmare confined entirely to Richard's mind. No ghosts appeared on stage, and the audience were given no more detail of Richard's visions than they were of Richmond's. As both men slept, in open tents pitched side by side on stage, nothing differentiated the good son from the bad but the way in which, on waking, each interpreted his unseen dream. Richard's reaction alternated between that of the comedian, who laughed off the experience, and that of the small boy, frightened enough to draw his dagger, like young York, in self-defence. In the absence of the ghosts, however, the voices that condemned him were his own.

VI

Both productions concluded with a detailed battle scene. At the last, Goring's Richard returned to the feudal values of the recent wars, a point emphasized in his formal declaration that warfare should replace conscience and the law:

> Let not our babbling dreams affright our souls;
> Conscience is but a word that cowards use.
>
> (5.3.309–10)

By cutting the preceding reference to the note on Norfolk's tent (5.3.305–8), Byam Shaw made Richard's fighting words not mere defiance, but a decision to put the clock back to an earlier, doubtless mythical, world of clear-cut issues where might was right. It was a world in which this Richard could succeed.

As a soldier, Goring's Richard was in his element. And the fellowship of soldiers was important to him, with Ratcliffe's reassuring hand and the words, 'a good direction, warlike sovereign' (5.3.303) inspiring Richard to swing his sword again over his right shoulder and recreate the defiant image with which he had opened the play. At the close of the oration, lines transposed from earlier in the scene made his final cry one of fraternal valour even in death:

> March on! Join bravely, let us to't pell-mell –
> If not to Heaven, then hand in hand to hell!
>
> (5.3.313–14)

And death came in an equal fight, Richard leaping on Richmond with daring athleticism and dying as the warrior he always believed himself to be.

At the close, Richmond signalled to his soldiers offstage. They entered, filling the scene with banners, and Derby proclaimed 'courageous' (5.5.3) Richmond king by first offering him the crown and then placing it on his head with the injunction, 'Wear it, enjoy it, and make much of it' (5.5.7). Richmond spoke a slightly abbreviated final speech, underscored by music, although the promptbook gives no indication of his movement or delivery, after which the music built to a crescendo, the banners were raised and the curtain slowly fell.

Lindsay's 1998 Richard also died a warrior, going into battle with the selfsame cry as Goring's Richard (5.3.313–14), but standing quite alone, looking downwards into a bright light beneath the centre stage as if looking into hell itself. The wall of chains then crashed to the ground, creating a heaped and cratered landscape over which the rival armies scrambled, and disclosing an audience of ghosts. Despite this, Richard fought for life. Several times, during a lengthy single-handed fight, he would have defeated Richmond had not the ghosts, weaving and cursing their way awkwardly (and for the actors somewhat dangerously) between the combatants, physically prevented it. Young York began the attack by leaping on Richard's back and shouting, 'A horse! A horse!', as he had done in 3.1. Finally Richmond found an opportunity to stab his opponent through the hump, after which Richard was dragged screaming from the stage, the echo of his cry lingering long after he had disappeared.

This departure was required by the staging of 5.5 as an act of battlefield communion, where Richard's body would have been an awkward presence. Richmond's closing words were spoken, in exhaustion and with obvious humility, by a devout and earnest leader of men. He gave the victory to God and, kneeling, took the sacrament alongside his soldiers to the sound of a Te Deum – a counterpart to the Kyrie with which the play had opened. The faith that once concealed itself behind the cloister walls was now held openly and defended by a valiant king.

There was, however, a counterpoint to this pious closure in the figure of Margaret, standing on the promontory, watching. Her reappearance was ambiguous; either she represented the hateful alternative to such Christian communion, or, standing in Richard's place, she qualified Richmond's self-possessed authority, as the victorious mother-figure watching the young man.

TERRY HANDS, 1970 AND 1980

Terry Hands has directed *Richard III* at least four times, in productions that share fundamental similarities. In 1965 he staged the play at Liverpool's Everyman Theatre, and, between his two RSC productions (1970 and 1980), he directed it in Paris for the Comédie Française (1973), where he refined many of the more extreme ideas seen earlier at Stratford and in Liverpool. Some of these modifications reappeared in the 1980 RSC production, along with pieces of textual adaptation and stage action derived from Byam Shaw's 1953 promptbook. Hands's own promptbooks are very informative, as will be evident from the following discussion, and, although I have summarized lengthier pieces of business, each specific detail is drawn from the stage manager's notes.

Hands has never shared his fellow directors' interest in the political dimension – or what he called the 'fat and watery exterior'

(*Rev. Special*, 1981) – of Shakespeare's histories. He seems concerned less with the chronological patterning of the past than with the place and condition of the individual at the centre of that history, or the 'real problem, which is a disease of the heart' (*Rev. Special*, 1981). His ambitious project, begun just after his 1970 production of *Richard III*, to stage both the *Henry IV* and *Henry VI* tetralogies at Stratford derived from this interest in protagonists, not politics. With Alan Howard playing the majority of title roles (in *Henry IV* he was Hal), and Abdul Farrah's famously minimalist designs, Hands's intention was to explore character and relationships rather than to re-create the historical or political moment. The fact that the productions were neither chronological nor confined to one or two seasons emphasized this non-historical approach. When, in 1977, the opportunity arose to conclude his productions of the *Henry VI* plays with *Richard III*, Hands chose *Coriolanus* instead, preferring to compare the psychological development of two men – Henry and Caius Marcius (both played by Alan Howard) – at odds with their respective societies, than to follow English politics.[1] In the event the sequence took a decade to complete. The first and final plays – *Richard II* and *Richard III* – were delayed until the 1980 season, when Hands directed them as companion pieces but with his emphasis firmly on character, not chronology.

The following discussion intercuts discussion of the two Stratford productions in order to offer a comparative analysis of Hands's interpretation and techniques.

I

The stage floor for the 1970 production, designed by Abdul Farrah, was textured paving, divided by a metal inlay, in the form of an inverted cross, running the full length of the playing area. This was bounded on three sides by grey walls with, to the rear, a stained-glass triptych screen, each section of which moved independently, and through which, at key moments, blood-red light filtered across the paving stones. Both the stone floor and, in the background, the glass screen are shown in Figure 18. The

FIGURE 18 Norman Rodway's Richard (1970) went into the final battle (5.5) weighed down by a huge boar's head helmet, his broken sword representing his weakness against Richmond at the end. The photograph, possibly posed, also shows the three stained-glass screens, here forming an illuminated background to the symbolic staging of the final battle, which culminated in the Dance of Death as the figure of Death himself led Richard from the scene.

acting space presented a world dominated by icons, from the tall standards topped by the heraldic beasts of patriarchal nobility, to the seven-foot female figure, called 'the Virgin' in the promptbook, which enshrined fertility and womanhood. When opened, as in the first court scene (Figure 19), it displayed a crown of thorns set centrally at the level of the womb. Figure 20 shows how Helen

FIGURE 19 As Queen Margaret (Sheila Burrell) speaks to Buckingham (Ian Richardson) in 1.3 (1970), her dishevelled, unwashed appearance contrasts strongly with his sophisticated version of the male courtiers' heavily textured uniform. Primitive badges of masculine power – a fur collar for Hastings (Barry Stanton), and starburst-toothed neckpieces for Dorset (Richard Jones Barry) and Vaughan (Michael McGovern) – tie in with the Virgin-shrine emblem of womanhood which towers over them, its circlet of thorns just visible at womb level.

Mirren's Anne took on something of this Madonna-figure's appearance at her coronation, her robes forcing her to stare straight ahead, her hands bearing the orb and sceptre propped up by puppet-rods, and her face at the centre of an oval collarpiece edged with a starburst of cruciform dagger hilts. There was a crown above her head and, seeming to emerge from her belly, a huge boar's head. It was grotesquely unnatural iconography which revealed a society insecure in its beliefs and structures, a world 'clangourous and pagan' (*New States.*), in transition from 'rabid barbarism' to 'unrelenting Christianity', as Gareth Lloyd Evans saw it (*Guardian*, 1970).

The costumes shared this blend of the primitive and the symbolic, making use of newly developed fur-fabric and material textured with RSC 'gunk', a glue-like substance that produced a three-dimensional design. The basis of most costumes was grey

FIGURE 20 The unmistakable symbolism of Terry Hands's 1970 production is shown clearly in 4.2, as Richard (Norman Rodway), dressed for his coronation and sporting a golden boar's head and matching leg-brace, discusses the murder of the princes with the more elegantly attired Buckingham (Ian Richardson). Anne (Helen Mirren) looks ahead, the silent, impassive female imprisoned in her sword-and-crucifix collarpiece, her head appearing as if on a platter and her arms supported by crutches.

fabric painted with a gridiron pattern, which gave the court a certain uniformity and retained the hint of recent conflict in its patterned armour-effect. Over this the nobles wore a range of tabards, coats and cloaks topped, as in Figure 19, by pointed metal collarpieces in a starburst design. Barry Stanton's Hastings and sometimes Norman Rodway's Richard wore shaggy fur collars, with Richard's dominated by a huge boar's head on the right shoulder, shown in Figure 20. Jerkins were held together with leather straps, belts and buckles, and everyone wore boots, mostly thigh-length. The emphasis was on masculinity, although in a rougher and more primitive sense than in 1953.

The sick and prematurely aged appearance of Patrick Stewart's Edward IV made him the least self-regarding, and the least obviously royal, figure at this court. Glimpses of jute bandages beneath his open nightshirt suggested decay and penance. Ian Richardson's Buckingham was the most sophisticated courtier. He wore a sleeveless cream coat over a part-silk jerkin, the coat, trailing elegantly on the ground, giving his smooth and calculated movements an authority that others, especially Richard, lacked (as Figure 20 suggests).

The ambiguity in set and costume design carried through into Michael Dress's music, which veered sharply between 'strident discords and ethereal ... effects' (*Morn. Star*), sometimes electronically produced, sometimes just the human voice. Used to signal scene changes, to underscore the play's darker moments and, in particular, to colour Richard's lines, its inconsistency of style and sound, according to reviews, contributed to the production's overall dissonance.

In a court obsessed with status, the women seemed to be viewed as a group rather than individuals, with their costumes and the requisite long blond hair defining their function, from a patriarchal perspective, as sexual and procreative. Anne and Elizabeth (Brenda Bruce) wore close-fitting, full-skirted gowns, with a jute-linen coat and cowl hood for Anne, and an elegant black cloak for the Queen. Elizabeth's court headdress was a snood topped by a coronet, hiding the blond hair worn loose in the final scenes. Anne wore her hair down in the wooing scene. Jane Shore, who was a prominent figure both at Hastings's lodgings and at Edward's court, was brazenly sexual in a white shift dress with a train of dark velvet, and, unlike the other women, she wore a considerable amount of jewellery, perhaps gifts from lovers. In sole contrast to these younger women, the elderly Duchess of York wore a black habit and her hair entirely hidden beneath a white-edged wimple. The prominence and the age-range of the women in this production was increased by the inclusion of two other female figures in the early court scenes: Clarence's young daughter Margaret (already in the text) and Elizabeth's teenage daughter, Elizabeth (an added figure).

The simple practicality of Queen Margaret's battle-worn appearance set her apart from everyone but Edward. As Sheila Burrell played her, in a quilted tabard held by a thick leather belt over a jute tunic, her feet roughly wrapped in strips of bandage, her hair unkempt and prematurely grey (all seen in Figure 19), she placed herself outside both the coded sexuality of the women and the symbolic masculinity of the men. Her primitive appearance both underlined and undermined the court's nascent civility.

Hands's 1980 production of the play refined his earlier concept. This time Abdul Farrah's stage set, consisting of a cyclorama and a floor of ridged rubber with corrugations running the full depth of the steeply raked stage, was less cluttered and almost entirely black. Metal chains hung across the rear wall and, for public scenes, heraldic standards, similar to those in 1970 but more elegantly stylized in design, slotted into the stage floor. Similar standards appeared in the season's companion production of *Richard II*, although those 'iconic and heraldic ornament(s)' had become 'totems' by the later play (*TLS*). The stage floor and, in part, the banners can be seen in Figure 21. Major effects were achieved by lighting, with more illumination than was then usual at Stratford directed from the wings to capture figures in pools or shafts of light. This nocturnal, spotlit effect, 'like searchlights pinpointing enemy planes in battle' (*Guardian*), deliberately denied the audience a clear picture, and, in direct contrast to John Bury's lighting in 1963, any notion of a universal view – a lack of clarity which comes across in the production photographs.

FIGURE 21 On the black neutrality of Farrah's corrugated stage floor (1980), Barbara Leigh-Hunt's wild and angry appearance as Queen Margaret (1.3) undermines the studied sophistication of the court, the tattered remnants of her battledress and bandaged feet a stark contrast with the satin and jewels of Queen Elizabeth (Domini Blythe) and understated elegance of Buckingham (Derek Godfrey). Alan Howard's leather-clad Richard crouches between them, listening.

One critic described events on this highly raked, side-lit stage as 'operatic in ... pageantry and methods of projection ... you notice how the interpretation of scenes is being subjected to design' (*Listener*). The steep incline forced actors to travel either straight down the stage or straight across it, since anything diagonal was physically awkward, resulting in movement that was more geometric than naturalistic. It limited the actors' spontaneous behaviour and made intimate conversation virtually impossible. The figures in this pattern were costumed primarily in black and white, adding to the chessboard effect and making the appearance of colour a bold statement, such as in Lady Anne's red dress or Jane Shore's bronze one.

There was conspicuous wealth and sophistication in this court's appearance, with costumes that worked twentieth-century details into basic medieval forms. Buckingham (Derek Godfrey) was now one of several courtiers who wore the uniform Prussian-style black suit with jackboots, although a gold circlet on his forehead denoted his superior rank. Domini Blythe's Queen Elizabeth wore an elegant silver silk draped dress, with a jewelled headdress (seen in Figure 21) very like the snood and crown worn by her 1970 predecessor. This time, however, she was heavily made-up and carried a small dolly bag on her arm – details which might have suggested a degree of sophistication had not her 'coarse-grained' accent (*Guardian*), and tendency to use the bag to emphasize her arguments, undermined the impression. Anne had long blond hair, as in 1970, but now a dark velvet cloak concealed a close-fitting velvet and satin dress, the materials refined, their texture sensuous. And the dress, exposed during the wooing scene, was blood red. The women's costumes implied an underlying individuality not suggested in 1970.

This was a wealthy and self-centred court. Dukes and nobles, the more senior identified by slim gold headbands, shared a simple elegance, which, though it contrasted with the earlier court, displayed the same anxiety about appearance and social place. This time, however, David Suchet's Edward IV set the standard. He showed nothing of his predecessor's penitent asceticism. Wearing a gold robe over his nightshirt, and his crown the entire time, and with a huge crucifix around his neck (see Figure 22) suggesting more display than faith, he epitomized the hypocrisy of his court.

FIGURE 22 Despite the presence of his bejewelled mistress, Jane Shore (Catherine Riding), Edward IV (David Suchet) warns his sophisticated courtiers (2.1) – Grey (Rob Edwards), Rivers (Brett Usher), Hastings (Bruce Purchase) – against perjury. The crucifix he wears is too large to be anything but show, the King's hypocrisy typical of the court in this 1980 production.

II

The action of the 1970 production opened with a play-within-the-play. The court and King Edward entered at the rear of the stage, the majority of them wearing animal masks 'to create the world of Richard III – a world of curses, bleeding corpses, bestial emotion, sudden and unpredictable death',[2] and running on wildly. They stopped suddenly when the King was centre stage and backed uneasily before kneeling. Richard now spoke the first thirteen lines of his prologue, but no one registered his presence until he mentioned his deformity, at which point they all fled. His appearance, with close-cropped, spiky hair and wide, frenzied eyes, explained what could have seemed their fear. The primitive emphasis in his costume, a blend of black leather, shaggy fur and metal, with various additions such as a large boar's head on his right shoulder, reinforced the notion that here was something little more than animal, crudely dangerous in its uncivilized immaturity, as Figure 20 shows. Norman Rodway had played Thersites in *Troilus and Cressida* the previous season, and some reviews noted the parallels with this 'scrofulous, infantile monster' (*New States.*). J.C. Trewin detected contemporary echoes: 'he has made him a skinhead of our own time, and there's something of the skinhead personality in the way he commits his unspeakable villainies with a cold humour' (*Birm. Post*).

But if Rodway's Richard seemed uncivilized, he was the product of an unsophisticated society, where social and religious structures offered little more than superstitious scaffolding for instinctual fears. The 1953 production had shown an England in transition from medieval feudalism to early modern values, but Hands's society was emerging from the wild, the struggle between imposed order and instinct implicit in the opening contrast between the semi-religious deference to monarchy and a superstitious terror of the beast. The continuation of the animal imagery in the heraldic emblems that dominated the court scenes appeared to emphasize this. D.A.N. Jones recalled Hands's production of Triana's *The Criminals*, 'the Cuban surrealist piece about bad children playing cruel games', as he noted how much this staging foregrounded the children – 'little peevish boys' – in the play (*Listener*). Rodway's misshapen Richard was an embodiment of his society's fears and, in his arrested socialization, the victim of them.

The early scenes showed Richard's immature game-playing as he 'ganged up' with Clarence to threaten Brakenbury, or twisted in and out between Hastings and Jane Shore in 1.1. His first encounter with Helen Mirren's Lady Anne (1.3) was physical.

She tried to beat him off with the processional crucifix she carried, but he wrested the weapon from her and turned it upside-down to lean on, in a striking blasphemy. When the body of Henry VI then began to bleed, the sight so fascinated him that he moved in and stared at it for some time, like a child.

Richard's debate with Anne was broken up in the same naturalistic manner as in the 1953 production, turning his responses into the monosyllabic truth-avoidance of a naughty boy:

RICHARD
Say that I slew them not?
ANNE
Then say they were not slain.
RICHARD
I did not kill your husband.
ANNE
Why then he is alive.
RICHARD
Nay he is dead.
ANNE
And, devilish slave, by thee.
RICHARD
And slain by Edward's hands.
(1.2.89–94 intercut)

The playfulness continued as the promptbook shows him stalking Anne around the coffin, leaping over it and trapping the edge of her cloak in an attempt to block her escape. He caught at it again when she tried to run away after spitting at him, missing her but taking the cloak with him as he fell. His next line, 'Thine eyes, sweet lady, have infected mine' (1.2.153), therefore, was prompted by an embarrassed Anne, exposed now in her close-fitting robe. With the following three lines cut, Richard pressed his advantage by continuing with 'Those eyes of thine from mine have drawn salt tears' (1.2.157), the text dropping all of Richard's references to soldierly stoicism, and his disingenuous claim to being tongue-tied, in order to reinforce the spontaneity of this emotion.

As in Byam Shaw's interpretation, therefore, Anne was won over by Richard's vulnerability. He reached out for her hand and, failing, fell again. As he looked up at Anne, his rebuke, 'Teach not thy lip such scorn' (1.2.175), implied that her disdain was for his physical weakness, not, as in the full text, for the idea that he could ever be tongue-tied. It was a criticism that made her re-examine the nature of her hatred, and she paused to listen, so lost in thought that she even let him kiss her. By the time that Richard offered her his sword at 1.2.178, they were standing face to face on an apparently equal footing, so that, holding her gaze as he knelt, he dared rather than invited her to kill him.

The early physicality of their opposition gradually moved into smaller and more sympathetic gestures. Having given her his ring, Richard took it back, according to the promptbook, and slipped it gently on her finger as she hugged him. To reciprocate, she put her cloak around his shoulders, as a mother might around a child – although reviews also note a 'vigorous, sentient' quality in Helen Mirren's performance that seemed to suggest 'a kind of kinkiness' in Anne's attraction to this mad boy (*New States.*). At the close of their exchange, both left the stage separately, but the promptbook has Richard returning through the exiting procession, having removed the cloak. This theatrical separation of the wooing from Richard's comment on it, as if he left as lover and returned as actor, pointed up the lack of conscious performance in the wooing itself, which in its naturalistic elements disclosed much of Richard's psychological vulnerability. As Ronald Bryden noted, 'For once the royal hunchback is not just a great role, but a man playing it to disguise a self he loathes ... the man behind the mask' (*Observer*).

The opening speech in 1980 differed significantly from the 1970 production in that Richard was alone on stage. He first appeared behind a translucent curtain, an upright figure who delivered the first thirteen lines without a move. Then on 'But I, that am not shaped for sportive tricks' (1.1.14) he slowly twisted into painful deformity and began to walk downstage, a stumble at one point showing how far the disability impeded him. It was an opening which mirrored that of *Richard II* (directed by Hands in the same season with Howard in the title role), where Richard was also introduced with choral music and behind a gauze. The parallel implied that the protagonists – 'little boys, inspiring different sorts of maternal instincts, with golden hair and sensitive faces, very decorative [and] demanding' (*Listener*) – shared an inherent potential for good and evil. Their respective plays then showed how differently society played its part in nurturing one and denying the other. Richard III's assumption of deformity in full view implied a character confined not liberated by his abnormality; where Richard II saw himself in a mirror, Richard III looked at his distorted image in his dagger's blade. His demise, therefore, seemed the outcome less of his choice to prove a villain than of his victimization, his passive 'determination', by those who acted as his mirror, and from whom he had originally acquired his perverse view of life.

This was underlined in Alan Howard's appearance as Richard, which drew far more attention to the devices enabling him to cope with his deformity than to the deformity itself. 'His left leg is encased in a silver chain on to which he hangs as if it were a horse's halter' (*Guardian*); a pulley device that made him move with 'jerks and drags' and with obvious pain – 'You can't help making excuses for this monstrous man' (*S. Wales Argus*). Unfortunately no photographs can be found of this device, which might have been cut after the London transfer.

The introspection hinted at in Rodway's Richard was strongly emphasized in Howard's performance, although Howard shared few of his predecessor's infantile ways. When Hastings and the added figure of Jane Shore met each other in 1.1, Howard's Richard seemed excluded by their constant kissing, not fascinated as Rodway's had been. Outlining his plan to marry Sinead Cusack's Anne, Richard paused wistfully after 'Not all so much for love', as if he longed to know such feeling. Significantly the rest of Richard's sinister thought – 'As for another secret close intent' – was cut (1.1.158).

A tall actor, Howard wore a close-fitting leather jump-suit, with silver buckles and studs – a Hell's Angel version of Goring's 1953 space-suit. A small dagger was concealed inside the right sleeve, and he would release this automatically, with a flick of his withered hand, to point 'his vicious verbal barbs' (*Glasgow Cit.*). Here his right arm was the weaker. His left leg was encased in a surgical boot and attached by pulley to his left arm, which exaggerated his incapacity to move; although, the *Sunday Times* observed, he was so often 'obliged by the director to perform feats of extraordinary agility that the idea of his being crippled made no sense at all'. His hair was dark and curled (see Figure 23), giving at times an angelic appearance that Richard would instantly destroy with a side-face smirk.

He played both angel and devil in winning Anne, blending the child-like vulnerability of Goring and Rodway with a darker sensuality and a violence that his appearance already hinted at. The scene repeated the physicality of the 1970 confrontation – she still viewed him as a fiend and defended herself with a crucifix – but when her cloak fell to the floor, caught on Richard's foot as she knocked him over, it disclosed a provocative red dress. His reply, 'Your bed-chamber' (1.2.114), which accompanied the revelation, reinforced the suggestion that Richard had aroused a hidden sensuality in Anne.

Textual cuts accelerated the pace of the action towards an overtly sensual, almost orgasmic climax very different from that in 1970. Richard's actions brought them physically closer – when she spat at him he grasped her hand and later stroked her hair – and his presence seemed to sway her more than his words. Once they were close he also seemed to melt, turning the tearful recollection of his father's death into a personal confidence. Richard recollected himself, however, when he saw capitulation in her eyes. On the line, 'Teach not thy lip such scorn' (1.2.175), he went to kiss her, but instead, pretending anger at her response, produced the dagger from his sleeve and forced her to hold it to his bared chest. When she released the blade, as he knew she would, it neatly fell into his waiting hand. Figure 23 captures the sensuality of the moment, just before Anne's right hand drops the knife.

Richard's closing soliloquy suggested honest amazement at this achievement, a revelation, according to the promptbook, underscored in light and sound. He was both impressed and repulsed by this ability to provoke female desire (*TLS*). As he spoke, he crossed to the proscenium arch and looked back at the scene of their encounter as if at a performance, dividing the event from his comment on it in a way similar to Rodway's departure and re-entrance at this point in 1970.

III

Both Byam Shaw and Hands showed courtiers jockeying for positions in a new social order, but in Hands's 1970 production the aggression was less diplomatically controlled. Richard struck Lord Grey on the line, 'To thee, that hast nor honesty nor grace' (1.3.55), and Elizabeth, played by Brenda Bruce, responded with a barbed comment as he turned to leave, 'You envy my advancement, and my friends'' (1.3.75). This was active provocation on Elizabeth's part, not self-defence as it sometimes suggests, and the interchange that followed, contained now within a shorter and logically simpler structure, became a confrontation about the relative authority of a woman and a deformed man in the new post-war world. It ended in Elizabeth's defeat, with Hands repeating Byam Shaw's business as Richard silently rejected her weighty invitation, 'will you go with me?' (1.3.321).

The verbal brawling in this scene amply justified Margaret's scathing comment:

> What? Were you snarling all before I came,
> Ready to catch each other by the throat,
> And turn you all your hatred now on me?
>
> (1.3.188–90)

But the pack replied with taunts, as they refocused the gender/ power argument on her, moving to encircle her, as Figure 19

FIGURE 23 The sexually charged moment, in 1980, when Anne (Sinead Cusack) accepted that Richard (Alan Howard) had killed for her love (1.2). She signalled her capitulation by dropping the dagger. He proved he was lying when it landed neatly in his waiting hand.

shows. Margaret responded in kind, matching her formal imprecations to the pattern of their abuse. The stage action appeared to reinforce the parallel as, in the promptbook, she stabbed a dagger into her hand on every curse and the court crossed itself with each injury. Margaret's brutality did not come from a past world; she was a mirror-figure who reflected the primitive base of this society to itself. And this linked her with Richard.

The instability of the court's religious scaffolding was exposed, in 1970, in the reconciliation scene (2.1), which Edward staged as a ritual sacrament. He appeared at court a sick man and a penitent, his emaciated body wrapped in rough jute bandages and his wispy hair unkempt. First he removed the crown and laid it on a reliquary. Then, crawling forward to join his family in a circle around an incense burner, he drew others such as Buckingham into the kneeling congregation and invited each to make his peace. However, the ceremony was uneasy because only the King appeared to have faith in the ritual. And, when this was broken into by Richard's news of Clarence's death, the instant regrouping of the factions revealed the fragility of the social bonds that Edward held so dear.

The credit for this theatrical coup was Buckingham's, as the promptbook note of his and Richard's surreptitious handshake shows. The two men then left the 'church' together, although Richard returned almost immediately to beg his mother's blessing (in lines transposed from 2.2.104–11). The unexpectedness of this prompted a rebuke from Ian Richardson's Buckingham, who had re-entered and was standing at the side of the stage: '*Tut, tut, tut. I* wait upon your grace' (adapted from 2.1.142). He seemed to be asking Richard to choose between family and friendship by re-creating the embarrassing confrontation with Elizabeth in 1.3 (another situation perhaps devised by him). After a lengthy silence, Richard dutifully returned to Buckingham, who then 'removed his own left glove, transferred it to his right hand, lifted it slowly over his right shoulder – was he about to strike Richard with it? – and then held out his bare left hand towards Richard's good arm' (*SS*). It was, as Peter Thomson notes, 'a sealing of Buckingham's (and Richardson's) authority' (*SS*). Both the private reprimand and the public coup identified the Duke as the Machiavellian manipulator at Edward's court; one who recognized flaws in the new society, and saw in them and in Richard's dangerous immaturity the means of his own rise. As Richardson himself observed, 'Buckingham is everything Richard wanted to be – the Renaissance prince, the aristocrat, with manner and breeding to go with it' (Cook, 41).

Noting how, in this 1970 production, Richardson's authority 'shines and reigns' as Buckingham, Gareth Lloyd Evans pinpointed the flaw in making Richard so entirely dependent on the ambitious Duke, for Richardson's Buckingham would not need to stoop so low; 'this Buckingham would never be a fall guy to this Richard' (*Guardian*). Exactly the same had been said of Byam Shaw's interpretation. Richardson had suggested something of the same deviousness as Catesby in 1961, and would later play Richard himself in 1975 (discussed in chapter 3), but his performance as a fiercely intelligent and wily schemer found its widest audience in the role of Francis Urquhart, the modern Machiavel, in the 1990 television adaptation of Michael Dobbs's political novel *House of Cards*.

Buckingham's growing influence over Richard's wildness, and so over the state, was charted in the public scenes of Act 3, which now opened with the citizens' dialogue, transposed from 2.3. The speakers were members of a crowd gathering to welcome the new King, their lines reorganized to represent the different viewpoints of a soldier, a woman and a priest. Of the three, the priest was most vociferous against Richard. As he warned, 'Oh full of danger is the Duke of Gloucester' (2.3.27), the promptbook shows a spotlight falling on the figure of Prince Edward, and then on Buckingham as he moved forward to guide the young man down the stage.

Buckingham controlled the coronation council (3.4) with equal subtlety. He suggested that Richard withdraw after an over-loud threat to 'chop off' Hastings's head, (although his diplomacy could not prevent Richard leaving a prop arm in Hastings's hand as he pronounced execution). However, the darker consequences of that judgement bore his hallmark, as Lovell and Ratcliffe stabbed Hastings in the back while marching him away. Buckingham may have regretted Richard's outburst, but its sentiments were exactly his own.

Hands closed the first half of the 1970 production on this horrific image of what was to come – an unusually early break. The increasingly open violence of the second half made it clear that physical force, Buckingham's chief form of intimidation, was Richard's only source of power. The Mayor's deception (3.5), on which the second half opened, was an ideal chance for Buckingham to harness Richard's prankish predilection – as he implied in added lines taken from *3 Henry VI*:

RICHARD

    Why, I can smile, and murder while[s] I smile,
    And cry 'Content!' to that that grieves my heart,
    And wet my cheeks with artificial tears,
    And frame my face to all occasions.   [*3 Henry VI*, 3.2.182–5]

BUCKINGHAM

    Tut, I can counterfeit the deep tragedian,
    Speak, and look back, and pry on every side,
    Tremble and start at wagging of a straw,
    Intending deep suspicion. Ghastly looks
    Are at my service like enforced smiles,
    And both are ready in their offices
    At any time to grace my stratagems.   [*Richard III*, 3.5.5–11]

RICHARD

    I can add colours to the chameleon,
    Change shapes with Proteus for advantages,
    And set the murderous Machiavel to school.   [*3 Henry VI*, 3.2.191–3]

BUCKINGHAM

    Can *we* do this, and cannot get a crown?
    Tut! were it further off *we'd* pluck it down.   [*3 Henry VI*, 3.2.194–5]

The final couplet is Richard's in the original text, but here it makes Buckingham the more ambitious man. What followed was both farcical and frightening, as Hastings's head was tossed from Richard to Buckingham and finally to the Mayor, who fainted with the shock. It was a repetition of the game of catch played at the close of Edward's reconciliation scene (2.1), when Richard and all the children had tossed a skull taken from a spilled reliquary. On that occasion Buckingham had confiscated the 'ball' and reprimanded Richard. Now he joined in the game.

    Physical threats were less blatant at Baynard's Castle (3.7) – when the Mayor shouted 'No' at the mention of Richard's 'empery'

(3.7.135), the promptbook shows Ratcliffe surreptitiously twisting his hand to change this to a 'Yes' – but the sense of silent terror was widespread. Buckingham's frequent pauses (marked in the prompt-book) suggested how reluctant the citizens were to take his prompting, but it was a silence born of terror, not defiance. As Peter Thomson saw it, this was Buckingham's 'play-within-a-play, not designed to convince but offered as a party-joke' (SS). No sooner had the agèd Mayor hailed Richard as king than the crowd fled, so fast that they flattened the old man underfoot.

In the 1980 production, Richard's rise was driven by resentment at his treatment by society, not by Buckingham's desire for power. It was poetic justice, therefore, that he played on this hypocrisy in duping the court. Richard would become the plague that everyone saw him as; a point made when Hands isolated his threat, 'A plague upon you all' (1.3.58), by cutting the remainder of the speech. Richard was an outsider, and from his earliest court appearance associated with other social undesirables, arriving in 2.1 with Tyrrel, the two murderers, and the unreliable, loose-living Hastings.

Textual changes turned Richard's conflict with the court into a personal vendetta, particularly against womankind. First he roused Elizabeth's anger by harping on Clarence's imprisonment (as a result of cuts this was now Richard's only accusation against her, and, as he knew, a false one). Then he unleashed Hastings's honest anger against the Woodvilles, watching as the Duke rushed headlong towards Rivers crying, 'And lessen'd be that *joy*, God *we* beseech *Thee*' (an altered version of the line spoken by Margaret, aside, at 1.3.111). This scattered the court and brought Barbara Leigh-Hunt's Margaret centre stage. Richard, who had moved to crouch in apparent fear beside the Bishop of Ely, made no comment on her arrival. It was the angry Hastings who shouted, 'Foul wrinkled witch, what mak'st thou in my sight?' (originally Richard's question: 1.3.164). As the outsider, Richard happily set events in motion and then quietly retreated to enjoy the spectacle.

Hastings's question and Ely's later comment, 'So just is God, to right the innocent' (originally Elizabeth's words: 1.3.182), identified Margaret as something outside and unholy. Driven by their condemnation to defend herself, she produced a knife and stabbed her hand with it, as in 1970. Now, however, smearing her blood on each of her subjects in turn, she turned the curse into a rite. When she came to Richard she grasped his hand, but he twisted it to catch her wrist so that, as she spoke the closing words, he wiped her blood across her face. The act implied that she had cursed herself, to the court's evident relief. But it also tied the outcast Richard into Margaret's ritual.

Richard's underplayed hypocrisy in 2.1, where he joined in the peacemaking with evident shyness and humility about whether he should shake hands with everyone, exposed Edward's double standards. After all (as Figure 22 shows) the King's mistress, Jane Shore, stood close behind him as he warned the court against empty vows:

> Lest He that is the supreme King of kings
> Confound your hidden falsehoods ...
>
> (2.1.13–14)

Richard's reference to the cripple who brought Clarence's reprieve too late then underlined this hollowness – 'Some tardy cripple bore the countermand' (2.1.90). Isolated by cuts, it hung in the air, exposing the court's dislike of disability.

Richard was not alone in recognizing hypocrisy. After Edward's death the court stood in silent tribute on the stage, each lord accompanied by his standard-bearer. When everyone dispersed, the standard-bearers, speaking the citizens' lines from 2.3, commented on the situation. As court retainers, and an onstage audience, they were well placed to see through the façade; although, as part of the performance, their silence was assured.

Richard's first act of revenge was on his apparent friend Lord Hastings, who had responded to Edward's request for reconciliation in 2.1 with an enthusiasm that seemed disloyal. The staging outlined this revenge process in detail, from the moment that Hastings knelt before the King, in 2.1, and Buckingham sent Catesby from the room – presumably to fetch Richard. Hastings next appeared in 3.1 with young York on his shoulders, an action which explained the boy's cheeky insistence that Richard do the same. When he then jumped on Richard's shoulder uninvited, Richard swirled round in a violent effort to throw him off, but the promptbook shows how 'Hastings stops R. by grabbing boy' – another sign of Hastings's altered loyalty in Richard's eyes.

Hastings as an apparent turncoat made Richard more suspicious of Buckingham. When, at the scene's close, the Duke thanked Richard for the promised earldom, the promptbook notes that 'Buck. offers hand to R. R goes to take it, finds dagger in it.' Disconcerted for a moment, they then shook left-handedly, with Buckingham putting 'his other hand on top' in affirmation. Richard's right hand, however, still held the dagger.

Hastings's arraignment was carefully prepared, the irony reinforced by his comfortable over-confidence in 3.2 as Jane Shore helped him to wash and dress (she was given some of Hastings's words to the messenger). Their jollity led to Hastings sprinkling Shore and Catesby with water in a pre-execution 'blessing' of Rivers, Vaughan and Grey, although he was in fact participating in his own last rites. The Priest, Sir John, arrived to warn him against Richard, but since the Pursuivant was here replaced by Catesby he had little chance to whisper anything before Catesby called in Buckingham, and any conversation ceased. The final lines of this scene were reassigned to give Hastings the invitation, 'Come, will you go', and Buckingham the reply, 'I'll wait upon your lordship' (3.2.121–2), a line which Buckingham repeated at several points in this production, and which always concealed a threat.

The sinister implications of 3.2 became explicit in the council scene (3.4), which was not played around a table, as in the previous four Stratford productions, but with each lord standing before his emblem in formal court. The panoply of the public setting suggested that Richard and Buckingham's plot sought to exploit the gap between the outward signs of authority and the source of power, just as Buckingham's plan had undermined the religious ritual of 2.1. This gap widened as Lovell and Ratcliffe slipped in to replace the official guards when Richard and Buckingham withdrew temporarily at 3.4.41. On his return, Richard took Hastings downstage and made his accusation of witchcraft in private, supporting the claim by stabbing a dagger into his left hand to show how dead it was. Once the peers had officially acquiesced in Hastings's arraignment and departed, he was unceremoniously dispatched by Lovell and Ratcliffe, who ran downstage to stab him in the back. The business differed from 1970, however, in that they quickly dragged his body off before the official guards returned.

The two scenes before the interval, 3.5 and 3.7, linked because the Scrivener's scene was cut, built on this violence and its mockery of court formality. Richard and Buckingham took costumes from a theatrical skip for the charade before the Mayor (3.5), as they spoke the same lines from *3 Henry VI* that Hands had added in 1970. Although the Mayor now took refuge in the skip during the mock fighting, the same game was played with Hastings's head as in the earlier production, and again the Mayor, briefly, passed out. He was still dazed, therefore, when he was made to accept their justification for the execution, with Catesby standing behind him and working his arms like a puppet on the words 'serve', 'seen', 'speak' and 'princes both':

> But, my good lord, your Grace's words shall serve,
> As well as I had seen and heard him speak;
> And do not doubt, right noble princes both,
> But I'll acquaint our duteous citizens
> With all your just proceedings in this cause
>
> (3.5.61–5)

Until now, emblems and offices had represented a spurious social structure. Here they were simply stage props.

The Baynard's Castle scene (3.7) continued the theatrical metaphor, with the staging provided by a travelling puppet show that the gang had commandeered. It was appropriate symbolism, therefore, that puppets of Adam, Eve and the Devil hung from Richard's platform. Details, such as Buckingham's distraction of the Mayor and citizens while he threw a prayer-book up to Richard, added to the scene's farcical theatricality, a 'broad comic-opera vein' which Peter McGarry saw as accentuating 'the play's in-built air of surrealism' (*Coventry E. Tel.*). As Buckingham 'persuaded' Richard, the citizens turned into a pantomime audience, responding, 'No! No!' and 'Do! Do!', or repeating Buckingham's 'Never! Never!' and 'Bigamy! Bigamy!' They were not intimidated – a major difference between the 1970 and 1980 productions – but seemed rather to enjoy being part of the show. It was public mockery, through imitation, of the fraudulent court, whose apathetic amorality, now mirrored in the crowd, had just as easily let Richard take revenge by taking over.

IV

Hands's 1970 production contrasted Buckingham's rise to power as Richard's unofficial Protector with the visible decline of female authority at court. Brenda Bruce's Elizabeth had once been strongly independent, despite the overtly patriarchal structure of Edward's court, but her position weakened with his death. Her grieving in 2.2, lengthened by the weary incantation of some words, was reprimanded by the Bishop of Ely for sounding like despair:

> God is much displeas'd
> That you take with unthankfulness His doing.
> In common worldly things 'tis call'd ungrateful
> With dull unwillingness to repay a debt
> Which with a bounteous hand was kindly lent:
>
> (2.2.89–93)

(In the original text, Dorset speaks these words to comfort and cheer his mother.) Further alterations reinforced the court's attempt to marginalize the women, and particularly to exclude them from state affairs, as in the discreet addition of 'my lord' with which Norman Rodway's Richard pointedly invited Rivers – but not his mother and sister-in-law – to discuss the princes' return to London:

> will you go
> To give your censure[s] in this business, *my lord?*
> (2.2.143–4)

Such details underlined the repositioning of the noblemen, and their silencing of the women and children present, that Edward's devoutly patriarchal legacy allowed.

Marginalization encouraged demonization, even by the women of themselves, in this 1970 production; a fact that showed itself in the growing sense of guilt felt by the Duchess for her son Richard's birth. Hands retained the dialogue between Clarence's children and their grandmother (2.2.1–33) – cut in all but four of the productions – where she first reveals her private sense of shame (2.2.29–30). He also combined 2.1, 2.2 and 2.4 into a single movement that foregrounded the women's belief in their innate responsibility for Richard's sin (2.3 was moved to the opening of Act 3). This culminated in the Queen and Duchess detailing Richard's unusual birth and childhood (2.4), while the many children present – including Princess Elizabeth, the Duke of York, and Clarence's son and daughter – played around them, their games causing one another to fall and cry. The women's demonizing of deformity was therefore offset by the petty cruelties engaged in by the so-called normal children, their instinctive fear blinding them to the fact that cruelty can be learned – as Richard's development, and Buckingham's influence over him, had shown.

That fear then underpinned the women's grieving in 4.4, a scene in which Hands showed them, and by extension society, turning Richard into a scapegoat for their overwhelming sense of guilt. The formal rhetoric of the scene was restructured as a ritualistic chorus, the women's speeches balanced by reassignment to present them as the Fates. Some lines were interwoven and some spoken simultaneously, with critics commenting on how difficult it was to decipher individual words. But the detail seemed to be less important than the sense of a ritualistic force, fed by a patriarchally inculcated sense of guilt, which the voices were invoking against Richard. It was an interpretation endorsed by programme extracts discussing the play's association of patterned language and ritual action with a belief system that makes Richard a scapegoat, 'so that in the end the ironist himself is subject to a greater irony, that he has functioned as an instrument of destruction in the world of guilt' (Brooke, 133) – a system that Richardson's arch-rationalist Buckingham soon recognized.

An indication that Rodway's Richard eventually saw the extent of Buckingham's ambition came, as it had in 1953, at the end of 3.5. After Richard had corrected the Duke's proposal to return in three hours by adding, '*Within the hour, cousin of Buckingham*', he waited for him to return. And, since the Scrivener's scene (3.6) was cut, the audience watched him waiting. He did so quietly at first until a shoulder cramp suddenly sent him into a screaming dance of pain, his pent-up anger and frustration erupting into furious self-disgust. Once Richard was King, therefore, he was less easily checked by Buckingham. For one thing he refused to remain seated on the throne, his unpredictable behaviour, forcing the court to rise and sit by turns, challenging the formality expected of him. This rejection of the codes and values that Edward had established was epitomized in Richard's request that the page find him a murderer, since here the page was but a child himself. And when Richard finally froze out Buckingham, he threw him a fob watch, the archetypal acknowledgement of service no longer required.

In contrast to this chaos, the coronation scene of Alan Howard's Richard in 1980 (4.2) was stately, with ranks of nobles, heraldic emblems and a band processing slowly down the stage, the music swelling from drumbeats to a brassy dissonance. Richard's request for Buckingham's hand (4.2.3) came as he turned back through this procession and lurched painfully towards the throne. Derek Godfrey's Buckingham, however, made no move. When the King then stumbled, therefore, it was left to Catesby and Lovell to offer help. Once Richard had reached the throne, the promptbook shows each member of the gang – Lovell, Catesby and Ratcliffe – stepping forward to clasp his hand as he offered them the thanks that is usually given to the Duke:

> Thus high, by thy advice
> And thy assistance, is King Richard seated.
>
> (4.2.3–4)

Signalling the end of the proceedings, Richard moved down to sit on the steps, pulling Buckingham down beside him in an apparent informality. But the camaraderie was superficial. He took Anne's wedding ring from her finger to give to Tyrrel as an assurance of free passage, and made Stanley approach the throne and back away several times like a dog responding to commands. And, even though Lovell, Catesby and Ratcliffe were trusted men, each was made to dance attendance on his favour and, the promptbook shows, moved only on his word.

Buckingham hesitated once again at this new frankness, particularly at the blunt request to kill the boys. He alone came and went from the scene at his own volition, and was duly ignored by the new king for such presumption. When Richard eventually acknowledged the Duke, the promptbook has him grasping the watch-chain around Buckingham's neck and swinging him violently, breaking the chain but retaining the watch. It was an inversion of the 1970 business with the fob watch, but the implication remained the same: time was now in Richard's hands. He then 'moves UL [upstage left] where he collects orb and sceptre', according to the promptbook, and in full majesty dismissed the Duke. With Richard gone, however, Buckingham 'looks at Stanley and Urs. [Sir Christopher Urswick], then exits pros. R. [proscenium right]. They exit UR [upstage right]', a visual suggestion that all three now propose to defect together.

Richard was right, therefore, to be suspicious. He had been so since he questioned the true source of young York's cheekiness, as the dagger in his hand to Buckingham had implied. And he was equally uneasy when Buckingham had vowed to woo the Guildhall citizens as if for himself (3.5). Here Hands repeated his 1970 adaptation – so that Richard waited for Buckingham's return 'within the hour' – but this time he occupied himself by painfully attempting to walk upright, just like Buckingham. He fell, however, just as the Duke's soldiers were returning and they laughed out loud. It was a more subtle example of the anger at his own inadequacy that Norman Rodway's character had shown, with the same implication that, despite his power over others, he remained unable to control himself.

The counter-force that signalled Richard's downfall in this 1980 production manifested itself immediately after the interval, when the women came to visit the princes at the Tower (4.1), each of them – the Duchess of York (Marjorie Yates), Anne, Princess Elizabeth and Clarence's daughter Margaret – carrying a large holdall containing home comforts for the boys. When they were denied entrance and told of Anne's coronation the women dropped the bags, littering their broken contents across the stage (an image also used by Adrian Noble in 1988), and the Duchess of York cried out, 'O my accursed womb, the bed of death!' (a line advanced from 4.1.53). If Richard's plan had been to let society know the fear and self-hatred that it had made him feel, he had succeeded with the women.

But Margaret, the other figure who had tried to make the court world feel her grief, proved more powerful. She entered 4.4 alongside Queen Elizabeth, whose heartfelt sighs as Margaret spoke established something of a bond of grief between them. This was then developed in the orchestration of their laments, using the same effect that Hands had experimented with in the 1970 production. The speeches in 1980 were more elaborately intertwined, with complaint answering complaint in an inter-weaving of opposition and support, so that their voices sounded more in harmony than their words. Finally, the promptbook shows, Elizabeth and the Duchess were seated on the ground with Margaret standing over them, her arms outstretched in the conventional pose of Justice, as if signalling that out of this grieving and apparent confrontation had come the resolve to act.

The women needed no decision to face Richard (that being the understood outcome of the scene with Margaret), so Hands cut the women's dialogue (4.4.126–35) and brought him on just after Margaret left. The women spoke in unison, addressing him as no one else had freely done, not even Buckingham. When the concatenation ended, Elizabeth's cry (transposed from 4.4.144 to 4.4.149) rang out: 'Tell me, thou villain-slave, where are my children?' Richard was more disturbed, however, by his mother's curse. As she spoke, the promptbook shows her dragging herself towards him, making him retreat to the other side of Elizabeth and hide himself, as he had done in 1.3. Moaning softly, she crawled slowly past him, and up and off the stage. Shocked into silence by this, he picked up the shawl that she had dropped and held it for a time, lost in contemplation. 'His mother's curse leaves him so shattered that he plays the next scene with Elizabeth in earnest, as though he might really find in her a new mother', as Julie Hankey observed (*TLS*).

Elizabeth was unwilling to be a surrogate, however, as she made clear when she attacked him with her nails. Ignoring this, Richard took the shawl and put it round her shoulders as if investing her with the Duchess's role (4.4.325). The promptbook then shows him delivering the speech describing himself as Caesar's Caesar (4.4.326–36) while standing on the throne, as if to show how upright and noble a son-in-law he could be. By cutting all references to the Garter, George and crown (4.4.366–73), Hands focused Richard's subsequent attempts to swear an oath on this heroic self, which, in turn, gave force to Elizabeth's response that his earlier acts and character had denied him the nobility he now professed. His growing desperation that she believe him was emphasized by moving the half-line, 'Myself, myself confound!', to the end of his self-curse:

> God and fortune, bar me happy hours!
> Day, yield me not thy light, nor, night, thy rest!
> Be opposite, all planets of good luck,
> Myself myself confound!
>
> (4.4.400–2; 399)

For a time Elizabeth seemed genuinely moved by this new earnestness, enough to take his hand as he pushed his face into her belly and called her mother: 'Therefore, dear mother – I must call you so' (4.4.412). And by cutting her ambiguous question, 'Shall I go win my daughter to thy will?' (4.4.426), Hands hinted that she was sympathetic to him by the end. She even let him kiss her in a complex, but honest, mixture of gratitude and attempted love. But when she had to force him not to drag her to the floor, her reaction changed. Breaking from him, she walked away, having decided to delay a decision. This sudden change of mind prompted Richard's angry aside, 'Relenting fool, and shallow, changing woman!' (4.4.431), delivered as if he knew that his last move had been a mistake. The scene was not, therefore, another exhibition of Richard's wordplay. He had, quite unintentionally, shown emotional vulnerability, even more than when he wooed Anne, and it had nearly won him another chance.

V

Richard's decline in the 1970 production was marked by his weakening control of time, the role that he had wrested from Buckingham. References to clocks, to a calendar and to the sun's refusal to shine were pointed up by pauses, or by selective cuts, and they showed Richard troubled by an adult world in which events were overtaking him. This movement of a wider wheel of time was epitomized in the women's curses (4.4), discussed earlier. By reassigning roles in the last two acts, Hands underlined the defection of the Bishop of Ely and Lord Stanley, both of whom had been prominent at Richard's court, and kept the same supporters, Catesby, Lovell and Ratcliffe, close to Richard. At the end, it seemed, he could only trust his gang. Their solidarity was underlined by the replacement of the verse found on Norfolk's tent (5.3.305–6), with the fifteenth-century poet Collingbourne's nursery rhyme,

> The cat, the rat and Lovell the dog,
> Rule all England under a hog,

sounding like a childish imitation of the women's incantation in 4.4.

As Richard, Rodway's response to this growing opposition was typically immature, and he lost direction at the end. News of Richmond's invasion disconcerted him because, unlike Goring's Richard, he was no warrior. He did not discuss battle tactics with his men – the lines were cut – nor did his oration make many references to fighting. He was terrified by the ghosts' visitation, which here became a unified attack as each moved forward to address first Richard and then Richmond (Peter Egan) while, behind them, the rest wound in and out in an 'Inferno-like dance' (*Times*). At the end, the promptbook shows, they lifted Richard shoulder high, with young York kneeling on his chest and pummelling him, until he woke, screaming for a horse, and they departed. It was a nightmare that stayed with him to the end, manifesting itself in his concern with superstition. The promptbook shows that Rodway broke Richard's conscience speech with several pauses, as if in terror, and that he twice repeated the words 'I fear. I fear' to Ratcliffe. Ratcliffe's words of encouragement were curtailed to emphasize his reference to the two cock crows (5.3.210–11) – recalling Christ's betrayal by Peter – and cuts in Richard's dialogue with his men reinforced the superstitious references to time, to the tearful morning dew, and the absence of the sun. An added line has Richard asking Ratcliffe if he saw the sun today, as if reassurance is all that childlike Richard needs.

The battle scene picked up 'the macabre, eerie ballet' of his nightmare (*E. Standard*). Richmond and Richard fought in a spotlit slow-motion 'light battle' (promptbook), the effect 'almost cinematic' (*S. Telegraph*), with Rodway in Richard's huge boar's head helmet and, as Figure 18 shows, disabled by a broken broadsword. The ghosts, who had 'swirled on' before the battle, lined up at the rear of the stage and then moved forward to encircle the two men and to stab Richard, as hunters might (*S. Telegraph*), while Christopher Gable, as a masked death figure, 'turns in a circle CS' (centre stage) to the sound of a flute (promptbook). There is some confusion as to who delivered the final blow. The promptbook and several reviews observe that 'Richard was killed, not by Richmond, but by Death' (*SS*), and the promptbook notes a lighting change 'As Death stabs and faces front'. Death then began the same serpentine *Totentanz* (Dance of Death) from Bosworth eve, leading the ghosts – and finally Richard – in a chain from the scene. Terry Hands himself, however, and John Kane, who played Lovell and also under-studied Richard, recall that Richmond killed Richard.[3] This may therefore be a detail which changed after the press night. The *Totentanz*, and much of the earlier stylized action, was choreo-graphed by Christopher Gable (a member of the Royal Ballet) and was based, according to John Kane, on the final moments of Ingmar Bergman's film, *The Seventh Seal* (1957), where death dances his victims away across the skyline. Here it not only took up the ghost-dance of the previous evening, but reflected the mad antics with which Richard's childlike gang frequently left the stage, and continued, in a controlled pattern, the wild chase that had opened the play.

As the dissonant sounds of the *Totentanz* gave way to 'a heavenly choir' (*S. Telegraph*), Richmond stood centre stage and spoke a closing prayer, consisting of fourteen lines taken from his final speech (23–6, 35–7, 29, 31–4, 40–1), in which he asked that God's 'fair ordinance' replace the fearful madness of internecine wars – 'The son, compell'd, been butcher to the sire' (5.5.26) –

with balanced family relationships, from which civil harmony would grow.

In the 1980 production, Alan Howard's Richard was clearly shaken by Elizabeth's physical rejection of him at the end of 4.4. After she left, he remained thoughtful, crouching close to the floor as he had when listening to his mother's curse. As in 1970, the extent of his desertion by his closest friends was emphasized by the restructuring of lines in 5.2. Words originally spoken by Oxford, Blunt and Herbert were assigned to Ely, Stanley and Brakenbury, all of whom now fought on Richmond's side. This left Richard with only Ratcliffe, Catesby and Lovell, the rat, the cat and the dog of Collingbourne's rhyme which was used once again in place of Norfolk's verse at 5.3.305–6.

The ghosts' visitation now echoed the chorus of female voices already united against Richard as, again speaking in unison, they circled behind each sleeper, with only 'Despair and die' and 'Live and flourish' clearly discernible to the audience. This time, however, they did not lift Richard. He awoke terrified, and the promptbook shows him clinging to Ratcliffe on 'I fear, I fear!' (5.3.215), just as earlier Howard had tried to hold on to Elizabeth (4.4). It was a picture of private anguish in direct contrast with the enemy camp (set side by side with Richard's across the stage), where Ely, Stanley, Brakenbury and Urswick, all former friends to Richard, were shown placing their hands on Richmond's shoulders in a public affirmation of support.

Hands's alteration of the order of events in this scene (5.3), though slight, underlined the logic of Richard's rapidly declining fortunes as a consequence of desertion and dissent. News of Stanley's treachery (5.3.343–7) was followed by Richard's battle oration (5.3.315–42), and then the discovery of Collingbourne's rhyme on Catesby's tent (5.3.304–14). Richard took the poem, spat on it, screwed it up and lobbed it at the audience, moving centre stage into the protective semicircle of Lovell, Catesby and Ratcliffe. On the line, 'Our strong arms be our conscience, swords our law' (5.3.312), he knelt, and the gang of three drew their swords, joining hands on what now became Richard's closing cry:

> March on! Join bravely. Let us to it pell-mell –
> If not to Heaven, then hand in hand to hell!
>
> (5.3.313–14)

'To hell with everything, my friends', Howard's Richard seemed to say – a very different response from Goring's heroic battle cry.

Turning upstage, the gang then broke through a line of four soldiers ranged across the rear of the stage. The soldiers moved forward to kneel centre stage in the same diamond configuration that Richard and his gang had just adopted. Four more soldiers came from each corner of the stage to fight them. It was a symbolic confrontation, which may have represented Richmond's soldiers attacking the gang of four. As these dispersed, Catesby joined Ratcliffe and Lovell centre stage to ask for 'Rescue!, *Ratcliffe, Lovell*, rescue, rescue!' (a version of 5.4.1), but the promptbook does not show their response. Finally Richard, for whom no entrance is indicated, 'collapses DC' (downstage centre) on the line, 'Slave! I have set my life upon a cast' (5.4.9).

Richard's death in 1980 was as unconventional as in the 1970 production. When he called for a horse (5.4.7), the ghosts materialized in a line across the back of the battlefield, and watched as Richmond arrived. Nothing in the promptbook indicates a fight between the protagonists. In its place came a sequence of movements, each accompanied by a lighting change and music, which suggests that the action was stylized. First the ghosts encircled Richard and divested him of various items: Anne took his sword, Clarence his calliper, Henry VI his jacket, Prince Edward his right shoe and Hastings his left glove. Richmond (Pip Miller), who was standing to one side, then stabbed him, and 'Alan falls to floor' (at some point he must have risen from the ground), and the ghosts danced upstage and off to an oboe solo.

The significance of the clothing here was not entirely clear. It may simply have represented the removal of all protection from

Richard. But individual items could be seen to represent his deformity in that they protected or, in theatrical terms, symbolized it. Like the pulley device, they were the means by which it was socially perceived. So the ghosts removed the emblems that defined him, socially and theatrically, as different and vulnerable, and, to some, made him unworthy of love. Richard died therefore as the individual he longed to be, neither physically disabled nor a figure wearing the mask that society's view of his deformity imposed – the whole man, in fact, that the audience had glimpsed briefly at the opening of the play.

This in turn had implications for Richmond's ritualistic stabbing of Richard. Either he killed his enemy as an innately evil man, a villain uninfluenced by the painful deformities represented by his clothing, or he executed a vulnerable and unprotected victim of the prejudice that society offers the outsider. Did Richard die a victim, or was he made to face his enemy as an equal? As in 1970, his death was symbolic, not realistic, and invited spectators to find meaning or meanings in it beyond the conventional triumph of virtue over evil. (A similar slipping of deformity, and a similar complication of the play's conclusion, marked the death of David Troughton's Richard in Steven Pimlott's 1995 production, discussed in chapter 3.)

The final scene consisted solely of Richmond's speech, longer than in 1970 but none the less shorn of its historical references and again restructured to conclude with the prayer that his and Elizabeth's heirs might bring 'smooth-fac'd peace ... smiling plenty, and fair prosperous days' (5.5.33–4) to heal the wounds. It was an interesting and slightly disturbing emphasis on the bodily perfection of peace, in that, like Richard's death, it brought to mind the production's opening moment. There, as an able-bodied man, Richard had given a similar description of Edward's sunshine court. The circularity prevented any neat and easy closure. It also challenged preconceptions by linking Hands's *Richard III* to his companion production of *Richard II*, with its opening image of another golden-haired, smooth-faced, smiling, whole – and thus symbolically good – king.

What I have labelled as psycho-social treatments of the play adopted the same broadly realist approach as the political interpretations discussed in the opening chapter. Where the political readings minimized Richard's physical eccentricity, however, the psycho-social responses used it to evaluate the social norms by which deviance is defined. Some productions extended this examination of what society considers deviant to the prejudices and taboos applied to women in a patriarchal world.

The emphasis on Richard's vulnerability in most of these productions had implications for that dimension of the play which relies on his sparkling intellect and cunning, particularly in verbal confrontation. Richard's interaction with the audience and his comic wit were modified by directors' cuts, and his ironic commentary transferred to the staging itself, with the same loss of metadramatic counterpoint as in the political productions. What appears as a weakening of Richard's role had the effect of turning Buckingham, overtly or by implication, into the real power behind Richard's rise, with audiences and critics alike attracted to him as the Machiavellian manipulator. Once again, the non-realist aspects of both Richard and the play proved resistant to a single interpretation of Richard's otherness.

NOTES

1 Critics noted how far Hands's production of *Coriolanus* diminished the political implications of the play. See Berry (1981, 33).
2 Terry Hands, letter to the author, 10 June 1999.
3 Terry Hands, letter to the author, 10 June 1999; John Kane, conversation with the author, 24 February 2001.

3

METATHEATRICAL
RICHARDS

ealist interpretations of *Richard III* have had a long and
successfully varied history on Stratford's main-house
stage. In the last two decades, however, a few directors
have stepped outside this framework in order to explore the play
as a self-conscious piece of theatre. Such productions have made a
feature of apparent inconsistencies in the play's construction
which disrupt attempts to read it as real, as for example in the
interplay of the chronicle past with the dramatic present, or the
divided focus on Richard and historical account. And, by offering
alternative, sometimes contrasting, ways in which to read the
play, these directors have actively engaged their audiences in the
question of interpretation.

This chapter discusses five productions of *Richard III*. Two
began life at The Other Place studio: the first an experimental
production directed by Barry Kyle in 1975, the second directed by
Sam Mendes as the RSC's 1992 touring production, which returned
to the Swan Theatre in early 1993. The third, and most recent,
Richard III was the final play in Michael Boyd's presentation of the
unadapted first tetralogy at the Swan Theatre in 2001. The
directors' preference for more intimate playing spaces freed them
from the spatial, visual and acoustic requirements of the scenic
stage, and, without the realist frame, each could determine the
conventions within which his production would be played. With
the sightlines in these smaller spaces working against a single,

universal point of view, the audience's reading of the staging was, however, less easy to control. The minimalist approach adopted in all three productions exposed, and exploited, the play's structure rather more than those discussed in earlier chapters. Queen Margaret, for example, chronicled retributive justice and delineated dramatic form in a double role which focused attention on the director's interpretation of that form.

The other two productions, directed by Bill Alexander in 1984 and Steven Pimlott in 1995, faced the challenge of conveying the play's self-conscious artifice on the main picture-frame stage. Although superficially very different, these productions attempted to reflect the rich texture of linguistic, literary and dramatic allusion in *Richard III*, and to disclose those depths in the play's design that are conveyed in images and conventions less familiar to a modern audience. Both directors extended this web of allusion by reference to the play's own theatrical past, thereby drawing its textual interplay of artistry and history into the present moment of production. Pimlott's staging in particular made the audience conscious of their role as active interpreters, in a production that presented itself as one among many interpretations of Richard's tale.

BARRY KYLE, 1975, AND
SAM MENDES, 1992

I

Barry Kyle's 1975 production at The Other Place was designed to play alongside *Perkin Warbeck*, John Ford's drama set in the subsequent reign of Henry VII, because Kyle and John Barton, who directed *Perkin Warbeck*, felt that both plays dramatized a conflict between the glamour of politics and the force of good government. Each interpretation 'examined political repression and dictatorship in contemporary political terms', according to Kyle, with his *Richard III* offering a 'Gulag Archipelago production

... partly Tudor and partly Solzhenitsyn and Stalinism'. The diabolism of Richard was modified in order to create parallels between the 'palpable politicians' Richard and Richmond/Henry VII, and so Richard became an intelligent but understated protagonist; 'an excellent and astute government politician who knows how to deal with his own image', as Kyle put it.[1]

Ian Richardson played Richard, having appeared in Gaskill's 1961 production as Catesby, and in 1970 as Buckingham. On both occasions his performances drew the critics' praise, and his appearance as Richard was much anticipated. The few reviews of the production (not all productions at The Other Place were widely reviewed at this point) admired his performance of Richard as 'a man of genius who has chosen to be brilliantly evil rather than brilliantly good' (*Birm. Post*), but, despite a cast which included Barbara Leigh-Hunt as Elizabeth, Bob Peck as Hastings, George Baker as Clarence, and Charles Dance as Catesby and as a murderer, the production as a whole was considered to have smothered the play with directorial invention inspired by 'other thinkers than Shakespeare – Brecht, Peter Weiss, Peter Brook and so on' (*D. Telegraph*). Richardson himself described it as 'a directorial showpiece' which proved a 'ghastly failure' (Cook, 42).

The set design by John Napier portrayed England as a mental asylum, a sterile but sinister institution lit by fierce white light and dominated by a lighting-rig tower, on which, as Figure 24 shows, sat the throne (a covered armchair). Ratcliffe and Catesby became hospital workers, with Margaret, played by Brenda Bruce, in attendance throughout as an official, who acted at times as stage manager. An iron hospital bed, wheelchair and primitive wooden furniture were the main stage props (as shown in Figure 24), with a swing used for the young Duke of York, and as Clarence's 'prison'. In the opening moments of the play, pieces of armour were raised over the stage as memorials to a civil war that had plunged England into the decline now represented by the mental ward. (Peter Nichols's play, *The National Health*, at the Old Vic in 1969, was based on the same metaphor.)

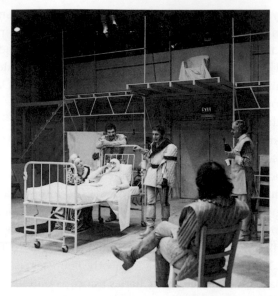

FIGURE 24 England as a sick nation was suggested at The Other Place (1975), by a hospital ward setting for the court (2.1), with Edward IV (Jeffery Dench) surrounded by his nouveau-riche family – Queen Elizabeth (Barbara Leigh-Hunt), Rivers (Christopher Saul) and Richard (Ian Richardson) – with Buckingham (Tony Church – who later became Richmond) and Hastings (Bob Peck).

The costumes overlaid modern with medieval, each figure wearing a shirt or long dress of the same pinstriped ticking beneath tabards or jackets, as the photograph reveals. Elizabeth, and Richard once King, wore leopard-skin fur-fabric, her coronet set awkwardly around a pharaoh-style hat, his crown shaped like the St Edward's Crown worn at present coronations. No attempt was made to conceal the anachronisms. The impression was of children dressed up for play, and of a parallel between the business pinstripe and the madhouse gown.

Tim Hatley's stage set for the 1992 production at The Other Place shared the economy (but not the specificity) of Napier's 1975

FIGURE 25 The final image of Mendes's 1992 production at The Other Place (and later in the Swan) shows shafts of hazy sunlight silhouetting the figure of Richmond (Mark Lewis Jones) as he holds the crown high, while Richard (Simon Russell Beale) lies in the earth exposed beneath the wooden stage floor, his dead eyes staring upwards at the light (5.5).

design, which allowed the play 'a fizzing sharpness and speed of presentation' (SQ). A rectangular thrust stage of plain wooden boards was backed by a wall of similar size and shape made up of grey wooden panels, most of which opened as narrow doors or windows (seen in the background of Figures 25, 27 and 28). When the apertures were open to reveal lighted space behind, this wall seemed as thin as a punch-card, but, when closed up, the blank wall reinforced the claustrophobic interiority of the stage space. After Bosworth, smoke-filled golden light filtered through the gaps on to the front-stage gloom, outlining the frame as a weak scaffold against the sun (as Figure 25 reveals).

The set was matched by lighting that in the early scenes outlined the interiority of the action, throwing squares and hard-edged rectangles of light on to the stage floor as if through high windows or skylights. Natural light was circumscribed therefore

FIGURE 26 Richard (Simon Russell Beale) woos Anne (Annabelle Apsion) across the panels of daylight allowed into the claustrophobic dark world of the 1992 staging (1.2).

by the darkness that defined it, as in the photograph of Anne and Richard, Figure 26.

A consistent feature was a single yellow light bulb hanging low over the stage (seen in Figure 27). Mendes's emphasis on light under the control of darkness appeared in the opening image of Richard standing centre stage beneath it, his mockery sun. The extinguishing of the light, in a repeated ritual depicted in Figure 27, marked the executions of Richard's victims. And only at the end, as Richard lay in a pit of dark earth, his face turned upwards towards the hazy sun, could the audience glimpse, beyond the open doors, a world of space and light over which he had never had control (Figure 25).

The costumes invited a similarly representational reading. Apart from Kate Duchêne's Queen Elizabeth, who wore a long, close-fitting red dress, all wore varying shades of black, grey and white in a uniformity that sustained the monochrome design. The style was

FIGURE 27 Queen Margaret (Cherry Morris) looks down, intoning part of her curse from 1.3 (1992), as Rivers (Michael Packer) and Grey (Mark Lewis Jones) face execution (3.3). The bespectacled Ratcliffe (Simon Dormandy) waits patiently behind them, before he signals death by closing each victim's eyes and switching off the overhanging bulb.

eclectic, drawing more on symbolic detail than period authenticity. Trenchcoats represented cloaks and gowns, beneath which the men wore modern black trousers and white shirts or vests with different symbols of office. The women wore long robes, and the princes' modern school uniform, as Figure 28 shows, indicated youth.

Certain figures were entirely representational, such as the Aldermen of London who became modern City businessmen with

FIGURE 28 Richard (Simon Russell Beale) conceals his anger in the role of jolly uncle (3.1), with the Duke of York (Annabelle Apsion) on his back. Prince Edward (Kate Duchêne) and Buckingham (Stephen Boxer) laugh. The minimalist setting, and the doubling of Anne and Elizabeth as the royal children, emphasized the symbolism in Mendes's 1992 interpretation.

briefcases and bowler hats. They struck a contrast with Cherry Morris's Margaret, who, with her wild grey hair and shapeless cardigan, suggested an eccentric senility quite opposite to the self-contained rationality of Richard's pinstriped men.

The structural emphasis in the clean-cut lighting and simplicity of staging drew attention to the patterns made by the action and actors. Parallels in and between scenes were reinforced by stage blocking, especially in the death ritual delivered to Hastings, Rivers and Grey – the figure of Vaughan was cut – and Buckingham by Ratcliffe, a tall, thin, bespectacled and boney-fingered executioner. The moment (from 3.3) is shown eerily in Figure 27. He extinguished life by closing the victim's eyes and then, as the light dimmed, clicking off the overhead bulb. At each death Margaret stood framed in an overhead window, quietly intoning the curse she had called down on them all in 1.3.

The play's spare 'architectural' (*SS*) patterning was further underlined by conflation and doubling – a cast of seventeen actors in twenty-three of a possible forty-three roles. Kate Duchêne and Annabelle Apsion, who played Queen Elizabeth and Anne respectively, doubled as the two young princes, seen in Figure 28, and several roles were conflated into the figure of Ratcliffe, played by Simon Dormandy, among them that of Richard's executioner, pictured in a dark suit behind the prisoners in Figure 27. Dormandy also played Clarence, so this appearance at each execution brought with it a ghostly reminder of the spiritual and physical pain of Clarence's death. This echo neatly reinforced the structural relationship between the play's first conscience speech (1.4.9ff.) and its reiterated deaths. The doubling, reminiscent of that in Jane Howells's 1983 BBC television productions of the *Henry VI* plays and *Richard III*, required the audience to modify their character identification by recognizing each figure's place in a narrative full of parallels and counterpoint. They had to move, therefore, between modes of reading.

II

Ian Richardson was an understated Richard in Kyle's 1975 production. Much of his theatrical self-reference was removed from the text, including the soliloquy 1.3.324–38, and asides to the audience reduced. Lines from *3 Henry VI* (3.2.165, 168–71), in which Richard views the world as hell, were added to his opening speech, but this now made no mention of villainy. And he was particularly restrained in his delight at winning Anne. Richardson's suave elegance delineated a quietly calculating, ruthlessly intelligent but single-minded politician who kept his own counsel. He did not ask for audience sympathy, but commanded their collusion with a charm that never let them feel at ease.

Other figures became more politically astute. Buckingham (Tony Church) saw Richard solely as a means to power. A line taken from John Barton's text for the 1963 production was added at Richard's entrance in 1.3, where Buckingham advised his friend, 'See where they come; I pray, speak friendly to them' (Barton, scene 56), indicating an alliance which predated the play's events. Informing Richard of his failure at Guildhall, Buckingham paused long enough to give the impression that all was lost, before announcing that the citizens were ready to hear Richard speak. The joke was not well received by Richard, who saw in it an unwelcome hint of Buckingham's power. The Earl of Hastings colluded more overtly in Richard's early plots, knowing in advance of the Pomfret executions. And Lord Stanley (Griffith Jones) was made politically prominent, as he had been in the Hall–Barton *Wars of the Roses*, voicing uncertainty as to his true political master in pastiche Shakespeare taken from that adaptation (see discussion in Chapter 1, pp. 54–5). The production's emphasis on realpolitik and ambitious jostling for power recalled much of Hall and Barton's history cycle.

The theatre space itself reinforced the intimidating realism of this asylum world. Open windows allowed outside sounds, such as the citizens' voices in the Baynard's Castle scene (3.7), to encircle the audience, who sat on mattresses at the edge of the playing area. When Richard, dressed in a surplice, bade farewell to his 'gentle friends' at 3.7.246, he swung incense over these spectators and dismissed them to the interval. But when Ratcliffe and Catesby flung the theatre doors wide, members of the audience recall that it was several minutes before anyone dared move.

Mendes's formal blocking, the punctuation of the action with ritualized executions, together with the representational costuming and the geometrical lighting design, reinforced the play's 'structural shapeliness' and underlined its rhythm (*SS*). The staging also delineated the frighteningly logical process of Richard's acts, which began with his arrival. The eerie opening music, a squealing clarinet and trumpet, softened first to a drumbeat and then to the tapping of Richard's stick as he approached the still-black stage. As in 1975, when Richard's footsteps had sounded on the staircase, the audience heard and sensed him before they saw him – an effect achieved in subsequent entrances by the sound of barking dogs as he approached. Eventually the yellowing bulb illuminated a shaven-headed lump of man dressed quite simply in a modern long grey leather coat, black trousers and white collarless shirt, and leaning forward on a cane (seen in movement in Figure 28). The appearance was monolithic, inflexible and toad-like, recalling both Mussolini and Churchill, as Figure 29 suggests. As Richard, Beale stared at the audience for some time before speaking, and then delivered the first thirteen lines in a tone of barbed cynicism which hinted that his image of the sunshine court was false. Lengthening the sneer on the word 'lute' with every vowel sound that he could muster, he slowly twisted sideways to show why he did not fit the happy picture, the enlarged shadow now thrown by footlights on to the rear wall revealing the hump that turned him from statesman to reptile.

Richard's control of light represented his control of the stage in these early scenes, a command enhanced by the reassignment of lines in 1.1 so that he not only introduced Clarence's and Hastings's arrivals, but led both conversations as if he alone triggered events. Beale's performance inspired unease much more than laughter, his departure through the audience stifling with a goggle-eyed stare any temptation to applaud. This distancing was reflected in the cutting of certain theatrical self-comparisons, as in 1975, particularly his allusion to the Vice-figure (3.1.82–3). Much to the surprise of some reviewers, therefore, Beale did not play to the audience; 'rather, you are privileged to overhear him as he conducts an expert and complacent self-analysis' (S. Times). Others noted his 'cool, legalistic tone' (Indep. Sun.).

Richard's move towards the throne, however, introduced splashes of colour to the stage, such as the red balloons that he gave the princes in welcoming them to London, which qualified this impression of contained control. Because adult actors played the princes, their size implied that they had long outgrown

FIGURE 29 'Off with his head!' Simon Russell Beale's Richard (1992) vents mock-fury on Hastings (Christopher Hunter) at the coronation council (3.4). When that same head, parcelled neatly in a box, is presented to Richard in the following scene, he spears it with his cane, seen here lying across the table.

balloons, which they held on to rather self-consciously, as seen in Figure 28. It was the first sign of Richard's misjudgement. Later, at his enthronement, he appeared, lumbering through the audience and on to the stage, in a vast purple satin and fur cloak and golden version of a paper crown, as if he had raided the dressing-up box. Here too the colour stood out garishly against the grey surroundings, lending the event an air of childish farce. But the farce was also frightening. His entrance through the theatre brought with it a chill draught of air, while ahead of him, behind the rear-wall openings, parts of a huge black-and-white reproduction of his face stared out at the audience; for this moment Richard seemed to dominate inside and beyond the playing space. All the same, the colour, his costume and his behaviour – when, falling as he stepped on to the stage, he rejected all offers of assistance like an angry child, and would only accept Buckingham's support to reach the throne, 'Cousin of Buckingham! ... Give me thy hand' (4.2.1, 3) – pinpointed an emotional immaturity, and aroused 'horror, contempt, pity, disgust, [and] fear' in his audience (*SQ*).

III

In 1975, Kyle set the all-pervasive influence of the past, represented in what his production saw as the absurdist figure of Brenda Bruce's Queen Margaret, against the frighteningly realistic present of his Richard's rise to power. Made more prominent here than in any other RSC *Richard III*, Margaret assisted at the deaths of Edward, Rivers and Grey, Hastings, Buckingham and Richard himself, and, when not on stage, observed the action from the watchtower. Appearing as a madwoman in 1.3, she spread out a childish painting of the royal family and, in cursing them, put pennies over the eyes of Edward and his sons. Then, addressing Rivers, Grey and Hastings (as in 1992 the figure of Vaughan was cut), she gave each a coin. At this point most of her subjects tried to ignore her, distracting themselves by flicking through hospital magazines.

But this Margaret was no mad inmate. Her presence at each death underlined the completion of her curse and the repeated pattern of history. And her physical participation in those deaths linked her closely with Richard's aspiring management. When Edward died on stage at the end of 2.1, she cleared a route for the stretcher-bearers, speaking the stage directions as she did so, and reset the scene for events to continue. The promptbook shows her pinning up a child's drawing of Edward on the Tower wall, as she did for all the other victims. Later, when Rivers, Grey and then Hastings face execution, Margaret was on hand to blindfold them and watch as each found her coin in his pocket. By lurking slyly in corners she seemed the embodiment of the nemesis she called on, and Richard an actor in her play. Indeed she surprised Richard on her first appearance by sitting in his chair like Banquo's ghost. Observers did not feel that she instigated events, however. Her role was to stage-manage rather than direct. But, for a time at least, the power of the past that she represented actively allied itself with Richard's plans.

That partnership was dissolved when Margaret incited Elizabeth to revenge herself on Richard in 4.4. The women's words, redistributed here between Margaret and Elizabeth (because the Duchess of York was cut), were delivered adversarially and at speed, creating a conflict which seemed to strengthen and unite them. They faced Richard together, therefore, at 4.4.136. Margaret spoke his mother's curse (4.4.184ff.) as if resuming sole control of asylum-England, and relegating Richard to his inmate role. Likewise, Elizabeth's growing recognition of the vicious cycle linking past and present inspired her to outface Richard's argument. In an absurdist world, Richard's linear logic proved a weakness, and realpolitik a kind of insanity. This Margaret did not retire to France. The cyclical power of the past that she represented would always be in control.

The design and direction of Mendes's production also underlined the drama's sequential and consequential structure, the 1992 set acting as a template, picking out the drama's patterning in a clearer version of the shape that Kyle tried also to define. But as events disclosed Richard's emotional immaturity, breaking into the austere colouring of set and costume, so this visual severity became specifically identified with an unemotional and calculatedly rational interpretation of the world.

It was a rationale displayed at first only by Richard, in the clear-sightedness of his soliloquies, or in outwitting Anne and his other victims. But the careful restructuring of 2.1, 2.2 and 4.4 cast this cold logic in a different light. As in 1975, Clarence's children were omitted and 2.1 elided with 2.2 so that Edward died immediately on leaving the scene. This alteration was not original, but the further transposition of the Duchess of York's criticism of her surviving son, Richard, from 2.2.51–4 to the end of 2.1, and of her blessing (from 2.2.107–8) to follow that critique, was new. Now at Elizabeth's news of her husband's death (2.2.34ff.), Ellie Haddington's Duchess of York crossed to her, lamenting the loss of two princely sons and the survival of her 'one false glass' in lines advanced from 2.2.51–4. These words are not spoken publicly in the text, where they are female confidences voicing fear of Richard and for the future. Here they were heard by all. Richard's request for his mother's blessing followed (taken from 2.2.104–6), prompted by his need to correct the impression left by this public condemnation of him. By combining blessing with condemnation – a combination repeated at 4.4.184–96 – Mendes linked Richard's mistrust of emotion to the inheritance of hatred and withheld love etched in the collective memory. The unfinished blessing, therefore, became a pivotal moment in a scene that began with an ill-accepted peace between opposing sides.

The court's denial of emotion was indicated early in the play. Richard's tone had mocked the image of Edward's amorous court in his opening speech, implying that it was a façade. Moments later, when he hugged Clarence, burying his head in his brother's chest and promising him freedom (1.1.110), Clarence was obviously amazed. Richard was acting, of course, but Clarence plainly had no idea how to take such unexpected intimacy. His family avoided physical contact, including between mothers and children, even in grief. And Richard had himself become 'a man alone because he refused help' (SS), as Peter Holland observed. Later, when he received proof of the princes' deaths in the form of tiny pyjamas, he sniffed them in a gesture that was at once horrific and wistful, as if he was fascinated by the smell of something lost or never known. Not surprisingly, when Richard described his submission to Buckingham's direction as like that of a child (2.2.153), the Duke stared quizzically at him, uncertain what he meant by such an unlikely image.

The divisive impact of the court's insensitivity was evident in Mendes's intercutting of 2.2 with 2.3, where the discussion between Queen Elizabeth, her young son and the Duchess of York was played alongside the citizens' concern at England's instability. The groups were separated by darkness. The royal women and the prince sat in a small square of window light on the stage floor, front left. The three other undefined figures were silhouetted in the upper windows, and spoke chorally to the audience. Lighting and music switched attention sharply between the two, a 'cinematic' (SS) cutting which counterpointed the women's domestic fears for selves and children with the citizens' public concern for a land governed by a child; shared fears, but different viewpoints. The scene closed on the Duchess in soliloquy, grieving her experience of unquiet and wrangling days in lines taken from 2.4.55–65. As in her earlier public condemnation of Richard, here her voicing of the future had about it something of Margaret's vengeful cataloguing of the past.

The citizens' place in 2.2/2.3 was taken by Margaret in 4.4, her figure picked out against the rear wall in a diagonal shaft of light, while Queen Elizabeth and the Duchess of York sat imprisoned in the same square of light as earlier, the two areas once more separated by darkness but now illuminated simultaneously.

Invited to teach the women how to curse, Margaret sprinkled a circle around herself, and smeared her face with dust (as she had in 1.3), representing, perhaps, the ashes of those whom she memorialized. Standing in the same place as in 1.3, she finished the curse that Richard had earlier interrupted. Her need to do so was emphasized in Cherry Morris's pleading delivery of 'Bear with me: I am hungry for revenge, / And now I cloy me with beholding it' (4.4.61–2). This was not a bitterly ironical Margaret. Selective cutting had removed many of her mockingly derisive lines, and emphasized instead her need to conclude the logic of revenge to silence her own ghosts; an interpretation very like that of Peggy Ashcroft in 1963. And, as then, it was this shared need that eventually united the women against Richard. The Duchess was following Margaret's example, therefore, when she turned the 'butt-end' of her earlier blessing into her curse (4.4.184ff.).

The parallels formed by the adaptation of the text here and in Act 2 defined one source of Richard's calculating and unforgiving logic in the inflexible rationalization of the past that permeated the court world. In 1975 a similar ritualistic patterning of events, marked by Margaret's presence, had signalled the inevitable and yet apparently absurd hold that history has upon the present. But in 1992 Margaret's rigid patterning of history did not seem inevitable. It was her chosen, self-destructive way of relating the present to the past.

IV

Margaret's opposition to Richard in Kyle's production was epitomized by her role in Buckingham's death. As at the earlier executions, she helped him to remove his jacket and shirt, and watched as he discovered the coin that she had given him in 1.3. This time, however, the victim did not leave the stage once 'dead', but knelt before Margaret, who dressed him as Richmond and kissed him on his line, 'Remember Margaret was a prophetess!' (5.1.27). He then turned to address his 'troops', made up of Richard's ghostly victims, Mistress Shore, Elizabeth, Ely and Oxford.

The Buckingham/Richmond metamorphosis gave an ambiguity to the final scenes, with Richard's death heralding not liberation but a subtler version of the same political manipulation, controlled by Margaret as history's cynical and cyclical force. The ghosts did not appear to Richard but possessed him as he spoke their lines, magnified eerily around the auditorium, as if he were now mad. Death came as he was about to stab Richmond, at which point his body was hooked on to a rope and hauled aloft in a repetition of the play's opening business. From overhead on the tower, Margaret watched him become another battle trophy. And Richmond stood finally beneath the body, in the same position, and surrounded by the same choirboys, as Richard had been in the Baynard's Castle scene (3.7). At the close of his speech, the choirboys blew out their candles, the organ music ceased, and Richmond/Buckingham's 'Amen' (5.5.41) sent the audience out of the small theatre in exactly the same way that Richard had closed the first half. It seemed that the only difference between this administration and the last was that Richmond/Buckingham was even less concerned than Richard that his audience recognised his duplicity.

Mendes's production drew more subtle parallels between Richard's remorselessness and the retributive justice that condemns him than the interpretative extremes of Kyle's asylum world allowed. The patterns that Mendes saw in the text did not play out an inevitable cycle; rather they defined the circumscribed thinking in each figure's recollection of, or response to, the past.

The staging of Richard's interchange with Elizabeth in 4.4 showed how she recognized and harnessed the circularity of that logic, and successfully turned it against Richard himself. The stage furniture, a camp chair and folding table, which Richard knocked over at one point in his rage, reflected the instability of his position. As the protagonists skirted one another, much as Richard had once stalked Anne, he retreated to this writing table and to state affairs. But Elizabeth refused to let him keep things business-like. Scrawling his victims' names across the maps and documents, she challenged his plan to regenerate the family tree by showing him how many roots were dead, 'the remorseless logic of her answers giving not an inch' (SQ).

Richard's earnestness to put this past behind him revealed itself in his inability to sustain a counter-argument. Frustrated by failure, he grasped Elizabeth round the neck, forcing his words upon her, and showing how far the political had become personal by cursing himself. In 'Myself myself confound', Richard says, 'if I lie, let me defeat myself in argument'. But from the way in which

Elizabeth left the stage it was clear that he had already done so: 'The scene ended because she had found a way of leaving the stage. . . . Richard was found to be devastatingly imperceptive, caught out by the inflexibility of grief' (*SS*). Kate Duchêne began this departure from the close of Richard's desperate speech (4.4.397–417), delivering her apparent capitulation (4.4.418–29) as she walked slowly downstage away from him. Richard's missive of a kiss to her daughter was not matched, therefore, by any physical contact. She simply paused before moving on, her refusal to turn implying that the kiss would be as fruitless as his letter. She left the scene in the direction that he was originally to have gone, preceding him in this as she had throughout their argument.

After Elizabeth's departure, the promptbook shows how Simon Russell Beale's Richard became quite static on the stage, as if he had lost the initiative. He sat back in the chair and paused for some time before dismissing her with 'Relenting fool, and shallow, changing woman!' (4.4.431), although the hesitation of 'sh-shallow' betrayed his disbelief in these words. He had been outwitted by the same rational coldness that he had used on others, and he knew it.

This sense of defeat was reinforced in the staging. On entering, Ratcliffe unfurled a huge map of England centre stage, so that for the rest of the scene Richard stood on an image of the land that he was defending. But the map dwarfed him. Suddenly the stage space that he had once easily commanded became too huge for him, a symbol of his political and moral defeat that neatly underscored the play's design. (In Strurua's production at the 1979 Edinburgh Festival, Richard and Richmond fought beneath and through a vast map of England.)

The conference table reappeared for the scene on Bosworth eve (5.3), Richard's and Richmond's camps set at each end to ease the rapid intercutting. Figure 30 shows the ghosts gathered at the table with wine and party balloons, indulging now in pleasures so plainly absent (despite Richard's opening description) from Edward's court. They include Mike Dowling, who, although he

FIGURE 30 The 1992 ghosts joined Richmond (Mark Lewis Jones) and Richard (Simon Russell Beale) at the council table, which represented the opposed camps on Bosworth Eve (5.3). Lit eerily from below by their own light, which outshone that from Richard's overhanging bulb, the ghosts of Hastings (Christopher Hunter), Rivers (Michael Packer), Edward IV/Prince Edward (Michael Dowling), Buckingham (Stephen Boxer), Anne (Anna-belle Apsion) and Clarence (Simon Dormandy) toasted the protagonists with the promise of victory or defeat, while Margaret, watching from the doorway overhead, quietly tapped out the rhythm of their words.

played Edward IV, was present either as a representation of his murdered son, Prince Edward, or as an amalgam of the two figures, and who spoke only to Richmond with the blessing, 'Live, and beget a happy race of kings' (5.3.158). The text was rearranged at this point so that everyone addressed first Richard and then Richmond, giving them a powerful unity in the scene as the protagonists faced each other and listened. And, while the ghostly revellers spoke, Margaret, framed in an overhead window, tapped out the rhythm of their incantation.

Richard's conscience speech (5.3.178–207) was spoken in semi-darkness, his figure illuminated again by the single yellow bulb in a dim echo of his opening words. It too was delivered entirely rationally, without hesitation and 'with a brilliant clarity, emotionless and stark' (*SQ*), the cold calculating summary of the situation that had characterized this Richard. He was indeed a villain and a murderer. Richard may have loved Richard at the start of the speech, but by the end he reasonably concluded that he found nothing in himself to pity. So he joined the ranks of the revengers and condemned himself. This conclusion was reinforced by Margaret's insistent tapping, quieter now and hidden behind the wall, which recalled Richard's tapping at the opening of the play, and reminded us that he and Margaret had shared their logic from the start.

By the close of the speech, Richard was drained of hope. His final battle began, in effect, with the orations, underscored with drumbeats that took up Margaret's tapping. Each protagonist stood in spotlight, alternately illuminated, to deliver the battle orations, which were intercut to allow the fraternal spirit of Richmond's argument to counteract Richard's self-centred cynicism, an effect 'there in embryo' in Shakespeare's text, according to Peter Holland (*SS*). This gave the figure of Richmond a greater presence, as he seemed to take on his opponent in argument before doing so in battle. The fight itself took place exactly where the map had lain, the stage floor removed to reveal a brown peat-filled pit – 'a place for children's games' (*SQ*) – in which the two fought, at first with swords and then wrestling in the dirt. Richard was exhausted, but by no means defeated, when Margaret suddenly appeared, circling the edge of the stage. He froze on seeing her, seemingly mesmerized, and the pause gave Richmond time to regain balance, spin Richard over and stifle him. This death appeared to satisfy the retributive logic of the past, recalled by Margaret, and ushered in the collaborative future, voiced by Richmond. But some critics found this shared responsibility for Richard's death confusing in its implication that Richard was 'finally overwhelmed by conscience' rather than the force of good; a 'controversial and un-worked out' idea, according to Nicholas de Jongh (*E. Standard*). As Kirsty Milne observed, 'since

Margaret is more than a trifle parti pris, she is an odd choice as moral arbiter' (*S. Telegraph*) – the same question that was raised by her presence at the close of Moshinsky's 1998 production.

Richmond delivered his final speech, slowly and calmly, from the pit, the hazy glow of backlighting and smoke now penetrating the rear-wall openings but not quite reaching him. He prayed for rather than commanded sunshine, in a welcome contrast to Richard's absolute control. Stanley brought the crown in, but tossed 'this prize toy' 'casually, even rather contemptuously' (*SQ*) at Richmond's feet. And though the new king picked it up, he by no means gloried in it. Eventually he held it above himself, his figure arching backwards towards the light which had yet to reach him, a final image captured in Figure 25. The play concluded, therefore, in exhaustion, its filtered light offering hope and anticipation far more than victory.

MICHAEL BOYD, 2001

This most recent RSC production of the play is discussed here as work in progress, since both text and performance changed daily during the twelve Stratford previews, and some of the following detail may be contradicted by the London promptbook and first-night reviews. Performance aspects notwithstanding, the roots of the interpretation lay in the sequence of *Henry VI* plays which preceded it, and with which it played in repertoire at the Young Vic Theatre later in the year. The director himself saw the play as *Henry VI*, 'part 4',[2] and with a limited number of performances at the Swan Theatre in Stratford, most of which sold out in advance to mailing list members, he could reasonably expect most members of the audience to have attended all four plays. In London, however, it was likely that more theatregoers would see *Richard III* as a solo production (indeed more performances of this play than of the other three were scheduled) and so miss something of the larger picture that Boyd's staging patterns worked towards, particularly in his re-introduction of ghostly figures from *3 Henry VI* into this final play. It was 'a breathtaking achievement' that, as Michael Billington observed, 'needs to be taken whole' (*Guardian*), even though, according to Susannah Clapp, *Richard III* was 'the culmination but not the crown' of the cycle (*Observer*).

As part of a four-play cycle, this *Richard III* obviously had structural elements in common with the trilogy adaptations discussed as 'political Richards' in chapter 1. However, Boyd's production responded to the play in terms of archetypal patterns in relationships and events rather than as a realist political history. And his decision to stage the action in the round (necessitating changes to the Swan's audience/stage configuration) reinforced this non-realist approach in ways and with effects very similar to the metatheatrical interpretations discussed in this chapter. Not for the first time in this volume, therefore, a production challenges a single definition. However, Stratford audiences were invited to derive more meaning from the production's self-conscious theatricality and allegorical patterning than from its specific account of political history, and for that reason it is considered here.

I

Tom Piper redesigned the Swan Theatre auditorium for these productions, bringing the audience around a central playing area, or 'courtyard-like oblong' (*Scotsman*), from which seven ground-level walkways fanned out 'like the fingers of a hand through the audience' (*Observer*), which turned the stage into 'a dynamic crossroads' (*Indep. Sun.*, 17 Dec 2000) for the fast-paced action of the *Henry VI* plays. Figure 31 shows five of the entrances, with the central metal doorway (or hell-mouth, as it was called in rehearsal) framed by a black-clad balcony and curved 'pock-marked' (*Times*) bronze doors (seen closed in the background in Figure 33). This was used for ceremonial entrances, such as Richard's appearance after his coronation in 4.2 (to sit on the step/throne pictured), and as the closed impassive portal of the Tower in the preceding scene. Their heavy clanging punctuated the action with the same sinister

FIGURE 31 The set for the 2001 production, described by its designer, Tom Piper, as a 'splayed-out body with a trap for guts', is seen here at the opening of 4.2, with the central 'hell-mouth' doors open, the balcony above it shrouded in black curtains, and the step/throne waiting for Richard. Four of the entrances through the audience are visible, as is the larger of the two trapdoors. The smaller trap was positioned immediately in front of the throne.

effect as John Bury's metal setting in 1963, the designers sharing the same 'notion ... about truth to materials.... If you paint wood, you should still be able to see that it's wood' (Piper, quoted in *Indep. Sun.*, 10 Dec 2000). The princes, and later York, made posthumous appearances on the balcony above this entrance, and Margaret watched the court from the first gallery to the left-hand side of the picture. At the opposite end of the space and below the musicians' gallery, a metal walkway let Richard's army pass over the stage, and the ghosts look down on the final action. (The photograph has been taken from this walkway.) A large off-centre trap, visible in the foreground, gave access to the execution chamber from which the victims' ghosts later appeared. A smaller trap (not visible but situated immediately in front of the step/throne) disclosed the malmsey wine for Clarence and, later, Richard. The effect, as Tom Piper saw it, was of a 'splayed-out body with a trap for guts' (*Indep. Sun.*, 10 Dec 2000).

The simplicity of this setting allowed Boyd to draw the 'metaphysical landscape' (*Scotsman*) of the action in morality-play terms, blending 'text-based' and 'visual theatre' (*Guardian*) into patterns that extended across all four plays; although Susannah Clapp in the *Observer* felt more aware of 'a procession of separate scenes' rather than the seamless unfolding of events that the staging might have allowed. With the minimum of staging and of props – Clarence's bed, the step/throne, a sack of bones carried by Margaret – the eye was drawn to figures. The court wore rich brocades cut in clean, elegant lines (the clothes were influenced by current fashion designers, such as Alexander McQueen), the noblemen in doublet, breeches and boots, sometimes with high-collared coats, the women wearing long, full-skirted dresses that trailed slightly, and jewels not seen in the *Henry VI* plays. Higher collars and more heavily textured materials than those seen in the earlier productions gave the court an air of hauteur and of constraint, a stiffness evident in Queen Elizabeth's appearance in the background of Figure 33. As she grieved for her husband's death, in 2.1, the Queen was held from falling by this heavy brocade gown, as if the private identity was struggling against the public role.

The blocking of scenes and the reintroduction of characters from *Henry VI* into *Richard III* invited audiences to see parallels with moments in the earlier plays. Heather Carson's lighting did the same, the sickly green-gold haze flooding the early court scenes in a sour contrast to the golden glow on which *3 Henry VI* had closed. Moments of revelation, whether Margaret's predictions or Richard's awakening conscience, were played not in the chiaroscuro of some other productions, but in a cold white light, as if the past had bleached all colour from the present. James Jones's music, largely percussion and saxophone, underscored Richard's satanic plotting with a maraca rattle that grew neatly into salsa rhythms at his coronation ball.

Boyd's interpretation offered a morality-style reading of parent–child relationships and inherited hatreds in the play. His *Henry VI* productions had shown patriarchy aligning itself with patriotism, and Englishness degenerating into a conventionally masculine, retrospective and self-interested concept that was passed, usually by irresponsible example, from real or surrogate fathers to their sons, and from leaders to the led. This pattern was established primarily through doubling, delineating the moral inheritance of key figures, and outlining cycles of virtue and viciousness across the four plays (as Jane Howells had done in her 1983 BBC television productions of the plays). The doubling, for instance, of Richard Cordery as Humphrey, Duke of Gloucester, Henry VI's honourable Lord Protector, and as Buckingham, king-maker to Richard III, showed the latter sharing the astuteness of the former, but using it dishonourably to pursue self-serving ends. Joan of Arc and Margaret of Anjou were warrior women mocked, feared and, in Joan's case, sexually abused by the English for their foreign subversion of gender roles. Fiona Bell's doubling of the parts underlined this gender bias in English selfhood. Her subsequent return as Margaret in *Richard III* reactivated a cycle of revenge that predated the Roses conflict, and grew out of gender politics as much as dynastic loyalty.

Boyd's conflation of other roles concentrated on Richard's action in the present. His henchman Catesby (James Tucker), for example, secretly gathered information as the second citizen (2.3), and then as a messenger in Elizabeth's household (2.4), where he arrived in time to overhear the Archbishop resign the authority of the Great Seal to the Queen. The conscience-stricken second murderer, who finally took no part in killing Clarence (1.4), was the third citizen (2.3), who now warned others against Richard as he fled capture himself. Having left this scene in Catesby's company, he was next seen bound and gagged at Pomfret, walking to his death behind Rivers and Grey. The first citizen in 2.3 was the Scrivener-monk in 3.6, who, mistrusting the 'ill-dealing' Richard (3.6.14), became Stanley's secret messenger to Richmond (Sam Troughton) in 4.5.

The assignment of roles therefore established two distinct narrative threads: one focused, through doubling, on the historical past – 'the winter of our discontent' (1.1.1) – and the other focused, though conflation, on the present – the 'now' in which bustling Richard plots his play. And a major achievement of this interpretation was the clarity with which they were shown to intertwine.

II

Aidan McArdle's Richard arrived in his own play with the same cheeky – 'puckish, bustling, cerebral' (*Guardian*) – demeanour that he had shown as the French Dauphin, then as the informer-monk John Hume, and finally as Richard in the *Henry VI* plays: 'With his shaggy beard and white face, he looks like a blend of Rasputin and Chaplin and has the ruthless humour to go with that image' (*Times*), although this was 'much more Trickie Dickie than the hound of hell. The self-admiring humour is separated from the evil' (*S. Times*). Figure 32 shows the mad monk Richard, wearing the same functional slate-grey coat-gown over black breeches that he had worn in the *Henry VI* plays, his left arm strapped to the coat, and a small-sized hump on the left shoulder resembling a body-backpack. Although his left boot was raised slightly and formed part of a calliper, none of his slight deformities hindered his movement and he used his left arm quite freely later in the play. With black curls and a chin edged neatly with a beard, his face recalled Antony Sher's Richard (1984), although Sher conveyed none of the same wide-eyed openness of youth. McArdle spoke the first thirteen lines in softly mocking tones, exaggerating the accents of the 'grown-up' court, and mimicking their dancing measures. When he voiced frustration with these effeminate pursuits, however, he strode across the stage, haranguing each side of the

FIGURE 32 With his tousled hair and neatly trimmed beard, Aidan McArdle's Richard (2001) recalled both Rasputin and Chaplin. The cape collar of his grey coat-gown provided some support for his disabled left arm, although his hand was not too weak to grasp a sword. His right hand threatens Margaret (Fiona Bell) with a dagger.

audience like a child prevented from going out to play. His desire to win Anne, it seemed, derived in part from his need for titles – 'her husband and her father' (1.1.156) – that would establish him as adult in what now passed for the patriarchal world.

He showed little grasp, though, of what wooing required. The approach was daring, but neither skilful nor premeditated, and enforced with physical threats. When Anne slapped his face, he pushed her head violently against the hell-mouth doors and then praised her beauty. Not surprisingly, she took Richard's dagger in self-defence, bringing his men, Lovell and Ratcliffe, who were accompanying the cortège, out of the shadows to assist him; but Richard's quick thinking turned the moment to advantage as he bared his breast and invited her to stab. McArdle played up Richard's physical rather than verbal resourcefulness, suggesting that he rarely spoke to women other than with the biting anger shown to Margaret in the earlier plays. Although Aislin McGuckin's Anne did not fully understand him, she seemed to pity the violence of his emotion, reading it as troubled repentance and capitulating almost to quiet him as one might give in to a fractious child. Concerned, however, that he should learn some self-control, she pointedly denied him a farewell kiss.

Richard's bond with Buckingham came close to that of father and son in this production, an impression enhanced by the physical contrast between them. Richard Cordery's Buckingham was a towering figure, easily able to dominate the playing space, and with a warm, full voice that combined authority with 'an emollient nastiness – all perfunctory smiles and prelate-like sanctimoniousness' (*Observer*). Richard's description of their partnership, delivered without irony, confirmed this fatherly role: 'I, as a child, will go by thy direction' (2.2.153). He then kissed his mentor's hand in deference. However, when Richard later reinforced the bond by promising the earldom of Hereford (3.1), the Duke offered to shake hands as equals, but Richard presented his hand for Buckingham to kiss. Although the Duke playfully submitted, it was a sign that Richard did not intend to share power once he had grown up into king.

III

The incorporation of Richard's action in the wider retributive pattern began with Margaret's intervention in 1.3. A figure in a mud-splattered grey robe, her short, blond hair caked with grime (as seen in Figure 33), her pale face and rotting teeth not aged but seemingly decayed by death, Margaret (Fiona Bell) first stood and watched in silence from the gallery (on the left-hand side of Figure 31). Her apparent return from the grave was nothing strange to those who had seen the *Henry VI* productions, where ghost-figures such as the Talbots, Duke Humphrey and Suffolk had lingered on to swell the ranks of rebel citizens and fighting troops. Margaret's return likewise tied the ugly past into the present, embodying as she did the disease that the high-collared and ambitious peers were so afraid of. As the reaction of Queen Elizabeth and Buckingham in Figure 33 suggests, Margaret's arrival seemed to bring a nasty smell into the room. It also silenced the rhetoric as she hurled a weighty sack into the centre of the gathering, and followed it with her own brutal words. She then took offensiveness a step further when she tipped out the contents of the sack to reveal the bones of her murdered son, Edward. As she cursed Richard, she assembled these into a skeleton, seen in Figure 33, kissing each bone in turn and finally cradling the skull in her lap just as, in *2 Henry VI* (4.4), she had cradled the head of her lover, Suffolk, and, at the end of *3 Henry VI* (5.5), she had held her boy. Finally, she turned his death's head towards Richard, the picture capturing this chilling moment from Richard's point of view.

The bones were a central image in Boyd's interpretation and invited various readings. As the remains of a dead child, they symbolized the future of both dynasties, destroyed by civil war. As *memento mori*, they showed the corrupting rationale of vengeance on which Margaret fed, and which lay just below the surface of Edward's court. As totems of the past, they were another parent–child relationship corrupted by a war pursued in the child's name; and, as burdens on the present, they showed the mother continuing the abuse. The vicious consequence of this was made plain in Margaret's last appearance, in 4.4. By this time she wore the sack of bones tied across her body, and as she spoke she crawled over the ground towards the grieving women, her movements and her snarling words now those of the 'hell-hound' (4.4.48) that she saw in Richard.

FIGURE 33 Having assembled the skeleton of her murdered son, Queen Margaret (Fiona Bell) turned his death's head towards Richard to conclude her curse, in 1.3 (2001). Queen Elizabeth (Elaine Pyke) and Buckingham (Richard Cordery), watched in horror as Margaret held centre stage, their stiff formality challenged by the intrusive offensiveness of her words and action.

The palimpsest of death images on the 'splayed-out body' (*Indep. Sun.*, 10 Dec 2000) of the stage was striking, particularly when viewed from above – first King Henry's corpse (1.2), then the skeleton of his son (1.3), and finally Clarence, who was sprawled across a prison bed (1.4), asleep as the scene opened and dead at its close. The court's response to this, and to King Edward's death, fed the incestuous conflict, with Boyd's inclusion of Clarence's offspring (2.2.1–78, last seen at Stratford in 1984) underlining the adults' irresponsibility. In their anger and their scheming no one comforted the children. This neglect gave resonance to young York's fascination with his uncle's weapons in 3.1. Taking the dagger, he limped around the stage, exaggeratedly aping Richard's gait and humped appearance, the clever caricature showing how quickly, and how dangerously, the young learn to imitate their elders.

IV

These two movements – Richard's linear advance and Margaret's wheel of retribution – came together in the Baynard's Castle and coronation scenes (3.7 and 4.2), where Boyd required the audience to recognize the play's conflicting frames. In fact the first scene drew on all of the roles in which this production had already cast its audience; as Richard's confidants, as the Scrivener's fellow citizens, and as omniscient readers of its staging patterns and theatrical frames. It was a show within a show, with footlights on the stage and balcony, but with the house lights coming up on Buckingham's reference to 'the Mayor and *these good friends*' (3.7.65). The alteration from 'aldermen' let Cordery's Buckingham indicate the theatre audience as citizens, and characterize their response as 'vehement instigation' by waving the arm of a front-row spectator to prove his point. Having persuaded Richard to take the crown, he then encouraged the same audience to join in his acclamation, 'God save Richard the Third' (replacing 3.7.239). But Buckingham's appeal, with its invitation to the audience, as moral arbiters, to condone or condemn Richard's villainy, brought their roles, and the scene's frames, into conflict (an effect similar to that achieved at the close of Steven Pimlott's 1995 staging of the play). In most of the Stratford performances the audience laughed, but still said nothing; a reaction which Buckingham read as the citizens' rejection of his artifice, and so, turning to Richard, he quickly asked, 'Tomorrow may it please you to be crowned?' (3.7.241). But, once the Mayor, Lovell, Ratcliffe and Catesby had departed, he, at ground level, and Richard, on the balcony, turned back to share a private smile, now quite unconscious of those 'gentle friends' the audience, whom they thought they had dismissed. Still illuminated by the house lights, however, the watchers knew that none of them had obeyed Richard's farewell words (a contrast with the 1975 production, where Richard released them to the interval). The final moments of the scene therefore reinforced the division between the partners, held within the false security of their play-world, and the audience, who saw more than Richard knew.

A similar multilayered response was invited by Richard's coronation scene (4.2). He entered, robed and crowned, through the same metal gates to which Elizabeth had just appealed for her sons' safety (in 4.1). Standing centre stage, he kissed and then dismissed Queen Anne, and turned to receive the fealty of his court. The Mayor, then Buckingham and Stanley, followed by Lovell, Ratcliffe and Catesby, and finally his mother, advanced to kneel and kiss hands. They then ranged themselves behind the ground-floor audience as the procession continued, to Richard's obvious delight, with those dead courtiers whose support or enmity he had encountered on his journey to the throne: Rivers, Grey and the second murderer; Hastings; Clarence; Warwick; Edward IV; and Queen Margaret and her son, each of whom kissed hands and then stood on either side of Richard. Henry VI (David Oyelowo) knelt and, instead of kissing hands, prostrated himself at Richard's feet, and finally Richard of York (Clive Wood) stepped forward to complete the circle. Looking directly at his son, he proclaimed, 'God save Richard, of that name the third.'

Only Richard and the audience seemed conscious of these individuals. Richard's response changed from pleasure to bemused uncertainty as he began to wonder what this attendance meant. The audience, on the other hand, saw figures from the past welcoming Richard into the retributive cycle, now that the father's ambitious title – Richard the Third – had been established in the son.

V

Boyd's third pattern, the moral counter-argument against this vicious retribution and Richard's role in it, began with the second murderer's stand against the deed in 1.4, and against Richard in 2.3. His principled stance was then taken up by Stanley, who voiced exactly the same fears about Richard to Lord Hastings in 3.2. Stanley was even more central to Boyd's design than he had been in the 1963 *Wars of the Roses* adaptation, where Barton's text had turned him into a conscientious politician. By reassigning lines, Boyd raised him into a figure of virtue and justice who worked, under the eyes of Richard's henchmen, to bring Richard down. His significance in this respect built on the actor, Keith Bartlett's, roles in the earlier plays. In *1 Henry VI*, Bartlett had been paired with Sam Troughton (who also played Richmond) as the English warrior hero Talbot and his son, and they returned as the ghosts of the Talbots to swell Jack Cade's rebels in *2 Henry VI*. In *3 Henry VI* they were together again as a boy who kills his father and a father who kills his son; an inspired doubling which depicted with stark simplicity the corruption of human virtue as a result of civil war. Many in the Stratford audience, therefore, saw their father–son relationship as Stanley and Richmond growing out of these earlier incarnations, their mutual respect standing out clearly against York and Lancaster's corrupt inheritance. Their role as moral watchmen was reinforced when they acted as Henry VI's pallbearers in 1.2, and observed, with some concern, as Richard deceived Anne. Forced to fight on Richard's side, Stanley gave wise, fatherly advice to Richmond and then, as an afterthought, offered the valiant youth his sword. This then became Richmond's emblem, balanced on the palms of both hands as a sign of even-handed justice, and the cross-hilt his crucifix in prayer.

By alternating the action in the Bosworth camps (5.3), instead of staging it concurrently, Boyd drew a contrast between each protagonist's control of stage space and audience attention. Richard's uneasy issuing of orders was countered by Richmond's concern that his men, now also the theatre audience, understood the principles for which he was to fight. Dismissing their seconds, the protagonists finally faced each other down the stage, Richard laughing as he sipped a cup of wine, while Richmond, holding a stone and a white feather up to heaven, asked a blessing on the 'bruising irons of wrath' (5.3.111). It was unclear exactly what these objects represented. They suggested cannon stones and arrow feathers, but they also recalled moments in the earlier productions, such as when York had used a sack of stones to map out his claim to the throne (2 Henry VI, 3.2), and when feathers charted the ensuing conflict, red for a Lancastrian loss, white for a Yorkist, drifting downwards in the fickle wind. Originally the stones of violence were grounded in moral certainty, and feathers marked its loss in what ensued.

As Richmond's prayer ended, Richard drained his wine-bowl and fell straight to sleep. Immediately the hell-mouth doors flew open and Anne, in coronation robes, stepped forward to take her sleeping husband in her arms. When she spoke of his 'edgeless sword' (5.3.164) falling, her hand moved down toward his genitals as if signalling impotence, at which moment the princes appeared on the balcony, each staring silently ahead while raising a pillow before his face as more white feathers fell. Anne then looked across at Richmond and promised him well. As she left, the large trapdoor opened and, rising through smoke, a series of ghosts arrived to take revenge on Richard. Rivers, Grey and the second murderer advanced with daggers drawn and stabbed him. Clarence then 'drowned' his brother in malmsey wine (concealed under the small trap), before Edward, Prince of Wales, hooded him and stabbed him in a reprise of his own murder. All spoke separately to Richmond as they descended once again into the smoking underworld. Finally Henry VI appeared, removed the hood and turned Richard's face towards the balcony, as Margaret had earlier turned her son's skull towards him. For the first time, Richard was made to look at the dead boys. Falling to his knees at the sight, he held on to Henry as if begging forgiveness and, in an addition for the London performances, 'produce[d] the self-same stones' (*Guardian*) with which his father had illustrated his claim to kingship – pathetic proof, as Michael Billington observed, that Richard had 'grown up in a corrupt ethos of insatiate crown hunger' (*Guardian*). But Henry pushed him aside and, closing the trapdoors, defined the entirely selfless, Christian philosophy of kingship that Richmond espoused:

> *Thy* pity *shall be* balm to heal their wounds.
> *Thy* mildness *shall allay* their swelling griefs.
> *Thy* mercy *dry* their water-flowing tears
> *Be not* forward of revenge, though they much *err.*
> Virtuous and holy, be thou conqueror.[3]
>
> (*3 Henry VI*, 4.8.41–3, 46; *Richard III*, 5.3.129)

This speech, adapted from lines referring to the King himself, bestowed on Richmond the Christian principle of merciful justice that he, Henry VI, had tried, and failed, to rule by. Thus it initiated a regenerative action that moved beyond the vicious cycle of revenge, as Henry's closure of the hell-trap signified.

Finally Henry led Richmond from the scene, leaving Richard to wake alone and terrified. As white light flooded the stage, McArdle spoke the conscience speech in dialogue with the audience, just as, in his opening lines, he had used them to 'assist' his case. Their silent voices now became the 'thousand several tongues' (5.3.194) which proved his villainy; and, in effect, their answer to Buckingham's earlier request (3.7).

The closing battle was stylized in a series of emblematic actions, the entire company – Lancastrians, Yorkists and Tudors together – advancing in a phalanx from hell-mouth with weapons drawn, and moving into an anticlockwise circle around Richard, who sat above them on the shoulders of the blindfolded Buckingham. This circle represented all the internecine turmoil as much as Bosworth Field itself, the swirling mêlée raising a combined shout as it broke into individual factions who then ran from the stage. In its place, six pairs of long-swordsmen faced each other across the stage, their weapons flailing in rhythmical movement as Richard walked up and down between them, clashing swords. They ran off, to be replaced by the exhausted Catesby, who looked up to the balcony and called out to Richard's father, York, for assistance, 'Rescue! My lord of *York*, rescue, rescue!' (5.4.1). (The role of Norfolk was cut in this production.) York then appeared on the balcony, and stared down at his kneeling son, who called out to him for a horse (5.4.7). His father's reply was to open his arms to reveal the two young princes. The action was a silent accusation of child-murder from one who had himself been brought to his knees by the evidence of his youngest son Rutland's death (in *3 Henry VI*, 1.4), and whose own death at Margaret's hands was avenged by the murder of her son, Edward. York – as ghostly head of the Yorkist faction – broke the vicious cycle by accusing his own son.

Rising to his feet again, Richard turned to face Richmond. But, before he could move, York and his Duchess advanced down the stage and, standing either side of their son, removed his crown while intoning the Duchess's condemnation:

YORK
Bloody thou art; bloody will be thy end.
DUCHESS
Shame serves thy life and doth thy death attend.
YORK AND DUCHESS
Despair and die!

(4.4.195–6; 5.3.128)

Thus the parents took responsibility, making Richmond's success also the conclusion of the family's revenge. A brief, stylized encounter between the protagonists brought Richmond's final blow, accompanied by martial music and by the company (dispersed amidst the audience on the first gallery and at the rear of the stalls) in a united shout. It sounded as if the entire auditorium joined in. With the ghostly audience still watching, Richmond recovered and received the crown from his father Stanley, holding it in his hands until he had ascertained the welfare of his brother, George.

When Richmond enquired the names of the dead nobles, however, Tyrrel (Jake Nightingale, who also played the rebel Cade in *2 Henry VI*), now one of Richmond's soldiers, stepped forward to shout the words, 'Hew *him* to pieces! Hack *his* bones asunder!' (adapted from *1 Henry VI*, 4.7.47), at which point all the ghosts moved forward. But Richmond's angry response ordered respect, not revenge:

> *No!* Inter *his body* as becomes *his birth*.
> Proclaim a pardon to the soldiers fled
> That in submission will return to us.
>
> (5.5.15–17)

The new order would start afresh, and so the ghosts stepped back. The altered first-line reference here to Richard reinforced Boyd's characterization of Richmond as Henry VI's inheritor, a blend of Talbot's loyalty and leadership with the dead king's compassion and desire for harmony; the mix of valour and holiness, in fact, to which the Ghost of Henry VI had earlier referred. This was borne out in the rest of Richmond's speech, delivered with conviction by Sam Troughton.

The company then left, Richard rising last and turning briefly to face an uncrowned Henry (who now stood at the opposite end of the stage) before the blackout. This coda, witnessed only by the audience, qualified the virtuous and balanced sentiments of Richmond's closing speech in several different ways. It represented the morality play conflict between goodness and evil, or self-lessness and self-interest, in the world (although such an unexpectedly simplistic conclusion overlooked the role of Henry's passive goodness in creating the vacuum for chaos). On a human level, this 'perverse kinship' (*Guardian*) drew parallels between the child king and the child villain, both cheated of natural development by family conflict. And in terms of history, the resemblance between Richard and the Dauphin, both boyishly played by McArdle, brought the action of the plays full circle, as France again faced England, and York out-stared Lancaster, ready to begin the dramatic conflict all over again.

BILL ALEXANDER, 1984, AND
STEVEN PIMLOTT, 1995

I

Not all the metatheatrical interpretations of *Richard III* exploited the simplicity of Stratford's newer playing spaces. Both Bill Alexander and Steven Pimlott used the Royal Shakespeare Theatre's picture-frame stage as a foil for the play's theatricality and its allusion to dramatic convention. Yet this was not always easy to detect from the stage sets alone. William Dudley's medieval setting for the 1984 production was praised by some for reviving the sort of pictorial realism not seen in a Stratford *Richard III* since before the war. His design was based on the chancel of Worcester Cathedral, with high stone walls rising to clerestories on both sides, and, across the rear of the stage, large wooden doors surmounted by coats of arms. In the centre space four large tombs with effigies faced down towards the audience in a configuration that situated the unseen high altar in the auditorium itself. Figure 34 shows this in the Bosworth eve setting, with two flag-bedecked tents, described by Antony Sher, who played Richard, as 'like the mouths of Heaven and Hell in morality plays' (Sher, 169). Thus the audience was omniscient, except when a 'stone' screen was flown in at the proscenium to close off the chancel from the front stage. This had the effect of turning the set through 180 degrees, and so placing the forestage action in the nave beyond the screen, with the audience looking through the screen towards, instead of away from, the altar.

Some critics noted that the setting was much closer to the Victorian romantic revival than to anything authentically medieval. Nicholas Shrimpton, who described the production as a 'comic melodrama' (*TES*), criticized it as a highly technical form of Victorian scenic illusion, and Robert Shaughnessy was reminded of the sort of pastiche realism fostered by the modern heritage industry. Both he and Shrimpton were uneasy with this

FIGURE 34 William Dudley's set for the 1984 production, dressed with tents, on opposite sides of the proscenium, for Bosworth Eve (5.3). Four royal tombs dominated the centre stage, with large double doors to the rear surmounted by swords and heraldic shields. The ghosts emerged and departed through traps behind the front tombs. At either side, the clerestory allowed shafts of sun, or moonlight, to filter across the chancel. A carved front screen could be flown in across the proscenium to close off the forestage.

'reassurance of solidity, hierarchy and tradition: history set in stone, or in the simulacrum of stone' (Shaughnessy, 123).

In fact the audience was not required to be as unconscious of the production's artifice as Shaughnessy suggests. Although the set appeared realistically monolithic, it was also ironic in its parody of Victorian architectural staging. History may have dominated the stage in stone, but spectators could see that this was not realistic because, unlike pictorial staging, the ecclesiastical setting remained unchanged, even for Bosworth. And what change there was – the 'stone' front screen flying in and out very fast and in full view, or the battlefield tents appearing in the side aisles (shown in Figure 34) – reinforced the artifice. The production represented the historical past, but proclaimed the fact that the representation was itself a construct.

Steven Pimlott's 'daringly bizarre and experimental' (*E. Standard*) 1995 production shared Bill Alexander's acknowledgement of ambiguities in *Richard III*. Both Pimlott and David Troughton, who played Richard, spoke in interview about a number of opposed worlds, or elements, in the play,[4] and seemed happy for their production not to seek to reconcile the differences. This came across in Tobias Hoheisel's permanent 'expressionistic' (*E. Standard*) set design, which defined a variety of ways of looking at the play. Using a colour-coded division of the stage into performance areas, it outlined in spatial terms the text's collage of dramatic styles.

The variety of these performance areas means that illustrating the design is something of a challenge. Figure 35 shows the set with the inner stage, set here as an inner room, deployed over the forestage and the balcony above, but, as the following description shows, this is only one of the configurations that Hoheisel's design allowed. The main stage was divided horizontally into three: a front-stage brick-edged wasteland, painted lurid green and dominated by a *Godot*-esque tree, stage left; a central wooden wall with sliding box-car doors and a flight of open stairs attached stage right; and, above this, a black metallic walkway, sloping slightly downwards from stage left to right. The walkway was linked by colour to a proscenium-front space, stage far right (not illustrated), where the ghosts of Richard's victims gathered as the play advanced. These last two sections formed a black half-frame that acted as a background to the more classically tragic elements of the narrative. It was, for example, across the walkway that the grief-stricken Elizabeth bewailed her children's loss, as their ghosts writhed in sympathetic agony below.

The front arena was a public space in which the onward action of the drama, mostly in progress from stage right to left, took place. Here we watched Richard's colloquial interruption of that action – such as Clarence's departure for the Tower, Hastings's

FIGURE 35 Tobias Hoheisel's set for the 1995 production, the central inner stage deployed for the court scene (1.3). This also served as a prison cell (with metal doors), and as Hastings's bedchamber. When closed, it slid back into the wooden rear wall. To the front a green, rock-edged space, with a blasted sapling, was initially Richard's and Margaret's territory. Steps led up to a black-clad balcony, linked by colour to the proscenium side space (stage right, not shown) where the ghosts gathered as the play advanced.

departure from it and the funeral procession of Henry VI. For some scenes, the sliding doors of the central wall opened and a small mobile platform was temporarily suspended over part of this front arena, as illustrated. Named 'the tongue' in the promptbook, its deployment imitated the disc tray of a CD player. This temporary stage extended back into an inner room with four doors, where the private court and imprisonment scenes were played.

Only Margaret (played, as in 1992, by Cherry Morris), Richard and his victims after death moved directly from the temporary platform to the front-stage area. This created a spatial symbolism not unlike Richard's flexibility of movement on the Elizabethan stage, between the *platea*, or non-specific side-stage area close to the audience, and the *locus*, or specific location represented in the centre of the stage. Here it signalled the figures' movement outside the present time-frame of events on the inner stage. The separation of arenas also emphasized Richard's physical control of both the public forestage world and the inner court affairs on the platform. It was thus a visual correlative of Richard's verbal dexterity.

Whereas Alexander's, like Olivier's, production moved between the two dramatic styles that each identified in the play, Hoheisel's staging allowed Pimlott to represent a range of dramatic modes concurrently. The set represented a collage of the genres – tragedy, comedy, existentialist, morality and realism – in which history has been structured, underlining some of them through allusions to other fictional world-views, such as Eliot's *The Waste Land* and Beckett's *Waiting for Godot*. It 'all seemed to militate against the cohesion of the drama', complained the *Oxford Times*, while, looking back as usual to 1963, Michael Billington regretted Pimlott's lack of emphasis on the play's 'political intricacy' (*Guardian*, 1995). Pimlott and Hoheisel were certainly inviting audiences to read on a range of non-realist levels, by revisiting the play's dramatic and historical conventions, and by translating its narrative structures, more than its narrative content, into modern staging terms.

II

The Alexander production offered two ways of looking. And that ambiguity was evident in the appearance of Antony Sher's Richard. He was dressed in a black body-suit of tight-fitting silk material, seen to good effect in Figure 36, which emphasized the thinness of his legs, in contrast with an overdeveloped neck and torso, and incorporated a huge scoliotic hump which extended from the centre of his back up to his head. This bent the figure forward, requiring Richard to support himself on two leather-covered crutches. He also wore a black silk tunic, the sleeves of which tapered at the elbows into two hanging strips of cloth.

FIGURE 36 Crutches, elongated sleeves and a torso enlarged by a scoliotic hump helped Antony Sher to create an image of Richard as the 'bottled spider', in 1984 (1.1).

These extended almost to the ground and completed the image of a six-legged creature, as the illustration shows.

The exaggerated medieval costume made him into an insect, and the crutches provided his agility. These, however, were far too sophisticated – initially lightweight aluminium with elbow grips – to be authentically medieval. Ostensibly required to assist movement, they were essentially Richard's instruments. He could appear helpless without them, his legs splaying out behind, weak and useless, but he was also quite capable of mounting a horse unaided, and of walking unsupported around his victims. He did not need the crutches. But they let him dominate the stage. Sher, a physically small actor, was able to propel himself across the proscenium with considerable speed, his character controlling the action simply by agility. He launched himself into a spiralled leap of glee at major achievements. He could stand on the spindly legs to wave the crutches delightedly in the air, slowly at times, fast at others, or rub them together in sexual innuendo. The strength of Richard's legs clearly varied with his intention, so that the deformity became another act that he could turn on at will.

Sher's Richard merged medieval symbolism and modernity. As the setting played with images of history, so he played with ways of imaging Richard: from the authentic hump, which we saw in the interpolated coronation scene, to the symbolic six-legged insect who opened the play. The sheer physicality of Sher's acting, assisted by the crutches, led to a memorable performance, described by Milton Shulman as 'audacious and bravura' (*Standard*) and by Michael Billington as 'a landmark performance that captures a role for a generation' (*Guardian*, 1985) – praise worthy of Olivier or Irving. Thus, just as the set invoked nostalgic images of history, so this Richard found himself filtered through other famous performances, not least the picture-stage's legendary Richards that Sher sought resolutely to avoid.[5]

One or two critics had problems with the interpretation. Milton Shulman pointed out that the performance 'begins at a histrionic top and stays there'. A Richard 'who gives a literal physical impression to phrases that the Bard meant only to be taken metaphorically' (*Standard*) makes us wonder why no one else in the play sees what a demon he is. The problem may have arisen unexpectedly because Alexander played far more of Shakespeare's text than did the barnstorming productions to which Sher's performance and the set referred. Victorian Richards could look overtly sinister because the medieval world which watched them was silenced by textual cuts; Margaret was missing, Elizabeth rarely met Richard on the way to Bosworth, and his victims and the citizens went unheard. Rejecting Cibber's structural cuts, the 1984 production allowed these figures almost all of their curses and condemnation. And, since this Richard already fulfilled the metaphors that they threw at him, the effect was to reinforce the theatrical irony surrounding his image. When the production went on tour to Australia in 1986, however, the role of Queen Margaret, played by Patricia Routledge, was cut, taking the text closer to that of Cibber and the Victorian actor-managers.

Steven Pimlott's production, on the other hand, established very clearly the double-sided way in which he wanted Richard to be seen. As the action opened, David Troughton, clad in a red doublet and very unmedieval schoolboy shorts, slid open the wooden doors and limped towards the audience, his stiffened left leg lending him an exaggeratedly jaunty air that was hard to read as wholly benign or threatening. For several seconds he eyed the audience, and was about to speak when, on the overhead gantry, the court appeared in grotesquely pantomimic procession, moving in rhythm to a garish pavane. Richard scurried back inside, to emerge, as Figure 37 reveals, dressed in a jester's cap, bells and white ruff, and carrying a Janus-faced miniature of his head on a fool's stick, 'like some latter-day Dick Tarlton' (SQ, 1996). He began again, this time the expected 'Now is the winter of our discontent' prologue, performing the first thirteen lines to the assembled spectators above, as illustrated. A follow spot and their applause confirmed it as a show. On 'But I', however, the onstage audience froze and Richard turned downstage to address the rest of the speech to us, his other audience, in a tone devoid of merry obsequiousness. It was not clear whether he spoke the words that he would have delivered earlier. Those reviewers who assumed so already knew Shakespeare's text. But audience foreknowledge, or even jadedness, about the text and Richard's history was an element on which this production traded. And its false opening teased us with the possibility of quite another play. The effect of this double-take was to identify the texted history as

FIGURE 37 Edward IV's pantomimic coronation procession across the balcony, in 1995, pauses to hear Richard (David Troughton), dressed as a court jester, perform the opening thirteen lines (1.1), his Janus-faced fool's head on a stick hinting that he was a more dangerous joker than he appeared.

itself an artifice, and Richard as a performer 'determined to prove a villain' in that play.

Troughton's image as Richard made as striking a statement as Sher's, but in a different way. Like Sher, his appearance played on one of Richard's metaphors, in this case one that he uses to describe himself, the Vice-figure, translated into the jester or Punch-Richard. The production notes reveal an initial intention that he should also have had a tail and a big Punch nose, an echo both of morality play and of the later pantomimic tradition of *Richard III* productions. Like Sher's, therefore, Troughton's Richard incorporated elements of the figure's performance history, but in a more self-conscious way. And he fitted into, and mocked, a stage-play world that was also artifice.

Troughton's decision to create Richard's deformity without elaborate prostheses assisted his portrayal of the figure's ambiguity:

the man and the performing devil. Working on chronicle description of a breech birth, he assumed a hip deformity that gave Richard a stiff leg and a rolling gait. The withered right arm was simply held beneath the costume in the elbow of a T-shirt, and a small left-shoulder hump completed the transformation. In rehearsal, this minimalist approach allowed Troughton to drop the physical disabilities and address his soliloquies to the audience without deformity. It suggested that there were two 'perceived Richards in the play – the one he presents to the audience and the other to the court', as Troughton put it (Troughton, 75). Although in performance Richard only threw off the deformity at the moment of his death, this divided perception was implicit in the opening business, and in the fact that his degree of disability varied according to the scene he played.

III

The stage set's domination of the action in Alexander's production made the establishment of a court world in opposition to Richard rather difficult. Each court scene was automatically overlaid with symbols of the monarchy's spiritual significance. Moreover, these scenes were pushed forward on to the front third of the stage because four tombs took up most of the central acting space. It led to a predominantly linear blocking whenever a large number of characters were on stage, particularly in the court scenes. Taken together, these effects denied the court a sense of separate identity, both physically within the stage setting and metaphorically in the play. Richard and his victims shared the same symbolic world.

Even Patricia Routledge's Queen Margaret offered a somewhat impotent opposition to Richard, her curses – 'bottled spider', 'bunch-back'd toad' (1.3.242, 246) – all too clearly there in Richard's shape. Her words upset him less than his reply, and the subsequent attack of the assembled court injured her and forced her to the ground. In fact the emptiness of any opposition to Richard identified the past, represented by the flag-draped

Margaret, as an irrelevance which belied its architectural domination of the stage. This was reflected in the token deference to religion and the rituals of monarchy shown by a court focused on more worldly and self-interested concerns. And that was evident in the characterization of Queen Elizabeth.

Frances Tomelty's Elizabeth was politically astute. She pointedly took her husband's place at the council table when Richard arrived in 1.3, and her grief after Edward's death was obviously fear for her own position. Even when mourning her sons at the opening of 4.4, her words were more bitterly ironical than rhetorical, emphasizing the self-reference in '*my* poor Princes ... *my* tender babes ... *my* unblow'd flowers' (4.4.9–10; my emphases). Her decision to remain and hear Richard's suit in 4.4, therefore, was a political one.

Traditionally the scene sees Elizabeth voicing moral condemnation of Richard's crimes, refusing to let him turn the language of past guilt into the words of future courtship. But here the body language between Tomelty's Elizabeth and Sher's Richard spoke loudly of their separate ambitions for power. Instead of voicing judgement, Elizabeth's words were cunningly intended to manoeuvre him into a deal. This was clear as she moved around the throne, her hands upon it, or speaking head to head with Richard across it, until, on the line 'What were I best to say?' (4.4.337), she sat down in it, delivering the words, as her face in Figure 38 suggests, as if she were really asking how she might sell the agreement to her daughter.

But the apparent capitulation was complicated by Elizabeth's growing sexual attraction to Richard. Promising to endow the Queen with grandchildren, Richard had used the only tactic left to him, sexual persuasion, something which had already proved successful with Anne (Penny Downie). There, sliding a crutch beneath her dress, he had intimated penetration. Now, holding Elizabeth close, he reached down to rub her belly in rhythm with the lines:

FIGURE 38 Richard (Antony Sher, 1984) finds his throne, and his argument, usurped by Queen Elizabeth (Frances Tomelty) in 4.4, as she deceives him into thinking that she is interested in a political match between the crippled King and her daughter.

> But in your daughter's womb I bury them,
> Where, in that nest of spicery, they will breed
> Selves of themselves, to your recomforture.
>
> (4.4.423–5)

Both Tomelty and Downie admitted that they found the idea of 'portraying women as *per se* falling like ninepins for violence, evil and ugliness' (*Observer*) somewhat disturbing. And Sher's defence of this, by suggesting that women 'in the safety of the auditorium' could allow themselves to be similarly 'seduced by him' (*Observer*), only added to the unease. Tomelty dealt with this dilemma by showing that Elizabeth submitted to his sexual persuasion in order to turn it immediately to her advantage. She implied acceptance of the deal in 'Write to me very shortly, / And you shall understand from me her mind' (4.4.428–9) – an acceptance confirmed by the removal of 4.5, in which Derby reveals Elizabeth's agreement to marry her daughter to Richmond. Yet on 'Bear her my true love's kiss' (4.4.430) she leaned forward and kissed Richard's lips as he tried to kiss her hand. (Pimlott used the same business, but with Richard stealing the kiss.) The act elicited surprise from Richard. It implied that she read more personal commitment, perhaps even power-sharing, from him in this agreement than he had anticipated. It was his unease, therefore, which prompted the comment, 'Relenting fool, and shallow, changing woman!' (4.4.431).

This was an unconventional reading of the scene. Elizabeth's was not the voice of moral judgement. She appeared as another of the new order who, like Malcolm Storry's Buckingham, saw the value to themselves of Richard's vulnerability, playing on the demon image that as king he sought to throw aside. It was an instance of the way in which the production muddied moral absolutes and compromised providential history's domination of events, particularly in the play's second half.

The inner court world of the 1995 production was defined quite clearly by the platform on which it was first presented. Self-consciously performative, as in the opening scene, the figures of Elizabeth (Susan Brown) and her Woodville family slid out like waxworks on the mobile stage; 'there is no sense of history or pageantry', complained the *Birmingham Post*. The men's costumes were Tudor style, their pastel shades and decorative jewels, ribbons and embroidery, along with formal hats and gloves, signalling a dandified narcissism. The exaggerated, carnivalesque quality of their costumes can be seen on the walkway in Figure 41. The restrictions of the inner stage added to this ridiculous appearance, so overdressed were they for the small space they occupied. The metaphor was written larger in Elizabeth herself, who wore a striking costume in black and yellow, her farthingale out of proportion both with her chair and with the stage. She can be seen in the background to Figures 37 and 39. A white turban headdress surmounted by a jagged, party-style crown enhanced the pantomimic kitsch of the costume, creating altogether Margaret's 'queen in jest' (4.4.91). The fact that this restricted space was suspended above the stage floor gave an edge of insecurity to the court, their conceit leaving them hedged in and vulnerable to external influences such as Richard.

The significance of stage space continued when Margaret appeared. Dressed in the black robes of tragedy that eventually all the other women would take on, she moved from the ghost space stage right to enter through the front 'fourth wall' of the mobile platform. But she delivered her curses from the forestage. Behind her, and eerily lit by cold blue footlights, her victims writhed in agony as the world of tragedy, past and to come, cut through the pantomime. The moment when she curses Richard, with the court in pain behind her, is shown in Figure 39.

The set's patterning of space and action invited criticism, similar to that of the 1984 production, that the staging was too restrictive of the play and made 'other characters no more than puppets in the private shadow play taking place in Richard's imagination' (*Guardian*, 1995). But Pimlott deliberately broke down these rigid divisions in the second half. When Elizabeth and the Duchess of York met Margaret on the front stage in 4.4, enmity turned towards solidarity, with Margaret eventually cradling Elizabeth in her arms. Instead of rehearsing empty curses, Elizabeth's second meeting with Margaret redirected her rhetoric into wordplay subtle enough to outwit Richard in the confrontation that followed. It was clear that physically and verbally the codes were integrating.

So long as Richard could trust each of his audiences to remain exactly where he wanted them – the court, the onlookers above stage, the passing traffic of public life – then he could keep his performances under control. But when the watchers answered back by breaking through the stylistic conventions, Richard's own performance began to slip.

FIGURE 39 As Queen Margaret (Cherry Morris) curses Richard (David Troughton, 1995), the court writhes in agony behind them on the inner platform stage (1.3).

IV

Given the similarity between Richard's appearance and his metaphoric significance in Alexander's interpretation, it was not until the production's second half that any difference between the two became clear. Then the developing distinction between the bottled spider and the deformed man was reinforced by the altered dynamic of the play; a reversal signalled immediately after the interpolated coronation on which the first half closed. This added scene drew very different descriptions according to whether it was read as realistic and unnecessary – 'superficially documentary' (Richmond, 120) – or as a symbolic, 'phantasmagoric' (*Guardian*, 1985), anti-communion, representing Richard's evil inversion of all that Christianity holds good. Some elements were surreal; the ceremony was watched, from atop the tombs, by what Figure 40 suggests are Clarence's children and the two princes, all of whom are alive at this point in the play. In the procession

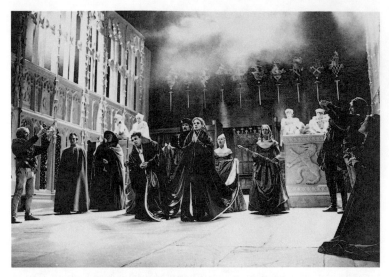

FIGURE 40 In the 'phantasmagoric' coronation scene, interpolated midway through the 1984 production, Richard (Antony Sher) and a terrified Anne (Penny Downie) process down the stage. The murderers (Brian Parr and Sion Probert) hold the crowns high on either side of the scene, as Queen Elizabeth (Frances Tomelty), kneeling in mourning on the right-hand side, looks on. So do her young sons and Clarence's children, illuminated eerily in white light as they sit atop the tombs.

Clarence's murderers carried the two crowns (they can be seen holding them up on either side of the picture), and whores, previously seen in Hastings's company, bore Anne's train and the sceptre (also visible behind Anne in the photograph). Behind the clerics and the murderers came Anne, obviously terrified, and an exultant Richard, both swathed in robes of velvet and ermine. They knelt facing upstage to receive the coronation sacrament from the Archbishop, with heavy organ chords underscoring the horror when Anne's smooth shoulders and Richard's huge spinal deformity were exposed for the anointing. Grasping the sceptre in his eagerness to end the ceremony, Richard kissed Anne roughly and then shoved her aside before lurching upstage, his long robe swaying like a reptile as he mounted the steps and installed himself triumphantly in the throne. This was then raised shoulder-high by soldiers as the lights dimmed, leaving Richard's grinning face picked out in spotlight, commanding applause.

The scene following the interval, now 4.2, opened with a clarinet solo, in a strikingly hollow contrast to the orchestral fullness of the earlier score. Richard now occupied the throne down centre stage, with his supporters and Anne seated, facing the audience, on either side of him. Their mood was muted. Having dragged himself grotesquely towards the throne in the coronation scene, he now sat with his legs curled neatly to one side, looking almost childlike in this very large version of King Edward's chair. He no longer had his crutches and, even as the King, no longer filled the stage. Once Buckingham had departed, a page called to fetch Tyrrel kissed Richard's proffered hand but sat down uninvited, and with little deference to the King. The tone of the new regime was thus established: a mood of fearlessness in a court no longer entirely under Richard's control.

Alexander underscored the suddenness of this reversal by transposing 4.1 – the women visiting the princes at the Tower – and 4.2, Richard's first scene as King. Theatrically 4.1 can seem an anticlimax, particularly if it follows the interval, because directors find it a difficult scene with which to revive the play's momentum. If the scene is followed by the interval, however, then the first half closes on an uneasy note, as the audience is left to speculate on the princes' fate. Alexander wanted neither. Given that the interpolated coronation made Derby's announcement of the ceremony at 4.1.28–30 redundant, 4.1 could be moved. Shakespeare's text delays Richard's decline until 4.2, a scene which opens with him 'thus high' enthroned and ends with him facing his first defection. So Alexander's transposition, his only major textual alteration, allowed him to depict devil-Richard's zenith before the interval, in the added coronation scene, and instantaneously reverse that image by opening the second half with an already vulnerable man.

As King, Sher's Richard used no crutches. They may have helped him to the throne but he would make his way now as man, not monster. Yet, as a man, this Richard exerted little power. His sudden weakness was demonstrated in the scenes that followed, when Richard stayed close to the throne and was all the more vulnerable away from it; particularly in his confrontation with Queen Elizabeth and his mother (Yvonne Coulette) en route to Bosworth Field (4.4). Richard's entourage had entered church to ask for blessing, the King on a throne-litter carried shoulder high by soldiers down towards the unseen altar. When the women placed themselves on either side of him, the soldiers, turning left and right on Richard's signal, found themselves unable to escape. Richard was imprisoned in the throne by the attack, his physical inability to depart matching now his verbal inability to stem the women's words.

When he moved away from the throne and knelt beside his mother, she took his hand and began to curse. Anticipating something far more innocuous, another blessing perhaps, Richard, surprised, tried to pull his arm away, but the Duchess held fast, pinning him down so that he could not command the stage. The throne was his sole haven, from where he dominated events only when held aloft by others, a metaphor of his need for support. But, as both Buckingham and the Duchess revealed, this was something that he could no longer rely on.

Some critics found the suddenness of this reversal hard to take. Milton Shulman (*Standard*) commented that the performance became thin, and Nicholas Shrimpton disliked the fact that the 'cinematic style' broke down in the second half. He felt that this was too late to change the code for an audience 'which had spent the previous two hours adjusting to a different set of scenic assumptions' (*TES*). Both comments bespeak a preference for the dramatic consistency and uniformity offered by the realist productions discussed in the first two chapters.

In fact the play breaks its own code at this point. It reverses the pattern established in the first three acts by revisiting earlier situations but presenting them within what might be termed 'a different set' of assumptions. And these inverted parallels signal the reversal of Richard's fate: his arrangement of the princes' deaths goes less smoothly than that of Clarence; the same wooing tactics that he used on Anne meet obstacles at every turn when he attempts to win Elizabeth's daughter; and even in deploying men to counter Richmond he is less efficient than when he organized his mock-election campaign. As the dramatic landscape widens from localized London to the heart of England, so the dramatic action overtakes him, and the mapping of political events moves out of his control. All of this introduces a fresh perspective that refocuses the dramatic viewpoint from first person narrative to chronicle account. Even Richard begins to wonder if there is a larger pattern, as he recalls Henry VI's prediction about Richmond (4.2.104–5), and observes that the glorious 'fair sun' no longer shines out on his side.

Olivier's film identified these two perspectives very clearly, as the action moved from patent artifice in the pseudo-medieval interiors of the court scenes to the locational reality of Bosworth Field. The contrast was different in Alexander's production because Richard played both morality figure and psychologically destroyed man within the same pastiche-medieval frame. Hence the critics' unease. He could sit atop the tombs but, unlike Olivier's Richard, he was never able to move above or outside the chronicle history frame and mock the values represented in the morality figures – saint, devil, Vice – that he plays. In the later acts it was harder to see why the chronicle history world would set itself against him, since he was so evidently part of it.

But, as I suggested earlier, this staging was not necessarily to be read as authentically medieval. The critics' own reactions reveal that, the more realistic the action became in tracing the historical events of Richard's fall, the more anachronistic and emblematic the setting appeared; particularly when the opposing tents of Richard and Richmond (5.3) were pitched before the high altar: Bosworth 'taking place in Poets' Corner', Shrimpton joked (*TES*).

This was seen as an error, but it was also an interesting point. By playing the later scenes against the same architectural setting, itself pseudo-medieval 'simulation and nostalgic pastiche' (Shaughnessy, 123), Alexander focused attention on divisions in the play and on Richard as a divided subject. He now featured in at least three narratives. One of these was the morality history of the chronicles' account that the setting and his appearance symbolized. Underlying this was the realist narrative of Richard's final days. And a third was the image of Richard conveyed through the play's performance history, represented here in terms of Victorian pictorial illusion and barnstorming melodrama. The production revealed that the altered focus of the play was not entirely Richard's doing. And so, intentionally or otherwise, Alexander identified the same ambiguous awkwardness in that change that Olivier's film had done, by not altering his setting at all.

David Troughton maintained the ambiguity of his Richard throughout. The set design reinforced his skills as self-appointed jester, switching between performance styles in a world obsessed with show. It showed how often Richard plays to onstage audiences: the court; the Mayor and citizens; the coronation council; and the monks who watch him wooing Anne. (This time Troughton's Richard also played one of those monks and the role of Sir John, the priest whom Hastings meets in 3.2.) Even his march to Bosworth (4.4) was theatrical, with Richard as carnival king leading a brass band, not an army.

In all this his auditorium audience, to whom he confided as 'a theatrical extension of his own self' (Troughton, 95), remained omniscient, as Pimlott illustrated in the Baynard's Castle scene (3.7). From the front arena, John Nettles's Buckingham, the warm-up man, addressed the citizen audience ranged across the walkway overhead, while Richard and his henchmen hurriedly set the stage below them in the inner room. The *Birmingham Post* complained at this reversal of 'the natural focus of the stage'. But exposing convention by 'pushing ideas to a self-conscious extreme' (*Independent*) was fundamental to this interpretation. The theatre audience therefore witnessed both sides of the charade as the mobile stage slid forward and presented 'Richard at prayer' to the citizens' view. Figure 41, photographed after Buckingham had joined the citizens on the walkway, shows the theatricality of the inner scene from the omniscient viewpoint of the theatre audience.

Some in Richard's audience were entirely duped; others – the onstage ghosts, the silent citizens and the auditorium audience – saw the deception. This point was made immediately after Richard's coronation when, in private, he presented himself as king to the theatre spectators (4.2). When no acclamation came, he called angrily for Buckingham to re-seat him in the throne. As in 1992, the citizens in 2.3 became a watchful chorus which addressed the audience directly, and simultaneously, from the walkway. Their costumes here, and in the Baynard's Castle crowd (3.7), were drawn from both the sixteenth and twentieth centuries (seen in Figure 41) in apparent references to the timelessness of tyranny, and to the play's ongoing audiences. Their words and watchful silence seemed to indicate that same fascination with, and collusion in, public fictions that the presence of later theatre audiences also signified.

Richard's mother was the one audience that Troughton's Richard could neither fool nor please. And many of his other performances seemed to be attempts to compensate for this. Richard's first meeting with her in the play was emphasized by its transposition from the beginning of 2.2 to the end of 2.1, where it allowed him to be caught by her, alone, as he tried on the crown left behind by Edward's sudden departure. He hid it behind him like a naughty child, while she rebuked him with the requested blessing, in what was obviously not their first uneasy moment together. When they met for the second and last time (4.4), and he again submitted to her, the moment triggered Richard's psychological decline. Responding to what seemed a motherly welcome as she knelt on the ground, he took off the crown, as he

FIGURE 41 In 1995, the inner stage slid forward to present Richard (David Troughton), seemingly at prayer, to his audience of citizens who, led by Buckingham (John Nettles), watch from the overhead balcony (3.7). Moments earlier Richard and his 'bishops' had taken their costumes and props from the theatrical skip now doubling as an altar.

had done earlier, and crawled towards her, curling into the foetal position in her lap. The moment is captured in Figure 42. He clearly expected another blessing, but, calmly and gently, she delivered the worst of curses, wishing her love on the enemy side. At this, Richard's mouth opened slowly in a silent scream, a serious echo of his mock scream as Margaret cursed him in 1.3, and a response quite opposite to Sher's anger. It was at this point, Troughton said, that his human Richard started to despair.

Once he had been decisively rejected by his mother, several other audiences began to reject his control, a reversal which was physically reinforced by groups and individuals beginning to outplay Richard in Richard's *platea* space. Elizabeth had already moved out from the confines of the inner stage to the black-edged walkway. Now, in 4.4, she met Richard in the front-stage arena.

FIGURE 42 Richard (David Troughton) expects a blessing (4.4), but the Duchess of York (Diana Coupland) gently curses her unsuspecting son as he lies, like a sleeping child, in his mother's lap. The throne is empty, and the crown lies at his feet (1995).

Susan Brown records that Pimlott had spoken of the women as 'the emotional and intuitive heart of the play – the antithesis of the conspiring men' (Brown, 102). Playing now an 'altogether wiser, more humane, less posturing creature' (111) than the Elizabeth of the early scenes, and with a good deal of her lamentation cut to allow this, Brown showed the Queen out-manoeuvring Richard with every turn of what was now a tightly focused argument: 'there is a life-or-death political game to be played to keep her daughter, and probably herself, alive. It is a game I think Elizabeth plays brilliantly' (111).

From her position on the ground, where her apparent vulnerability led Richard to assume her powerlessness, Elizabeth eventually moved to sitting on the throne, where, like Frances Tomelty in 1984, she seemed to be seriously considering Richard's offer of a return to power as Queen Mother. For a moment Richard was fooled by this, and by her gentle enquiry, 'What were I best to say?' (4.4.337). But heavy cuts in the following exchange took her from apparent capitulation to angry attack as she rebuked his efforts to swear by 'the time to come!' (4.4.387). Rising from the chair, she pointed out to Richard that the future would be filled with the surviving relatives of his victims. It was a key line in this interpretation of the scene, and Richard was taken entirely by surprise. He had clearly never thought about the collective memory, that audience of the bereaved who would remain his enemy. Troughton staggered back, and stared out at that other collective memory, the theatre audience, whom Richard had once considered his 'confident alter ego' (Troughton, 89) but who had begun to appear 'questioning and disapproving' (92), with the same look of shock as when his mother damned him.

Seeming to capitulate, Elizabeth left the stage, only to be called back by Richard's request that she bear his kiss to her daughter. Obviously drained by their lengthy dialogue, she returned and offered her hand, but Richard pulled her to him and kissed her lips, forcefully and obviously to her disgust. Susan Brown's Elizabeth took this, and the dismissive 'Relenting fool, and shallow, changing woman' (4.4.431), which she overheard, as evidence that she had deceived him, and she wiped the kiss from her lips as she left the scene.

After the ghosts had emerged from their side-stage limbo (from where they had watched parts of the preceding action) to infiltrate his sleep, Troughton addressed Richard's conscience soliloquy to his only remaining listeners, the auditorium audience. At 5.3.180, he moved his chair from the mobile platform, where he and Richmond had met the nightmare apparitions, into a front-stage spotlight, and spoke calmly and rationally to the theatregoers, voicing 'their' responses as if in dialogue with them. It was a moment that Troughton read as Richard's psychological rejection by the audience within himself. But for Richard the performer it was also a vital debate. He had successfully played the villain role assigned to him – 'I am determined to prove a villain' (1.1.30) –

and yet he was rejected for proving such a success. Troughton's calmly rational delivery of the speech, beginning 'I *shall* despair' (5.3.201–04, my emphasis), setting out the problems facing both sides of the figure – the fictional player and the historical man – neatly clarified the ambiguity in the role.

V

Given the pseudo-morality framework and the manner in which the later scenes played with it, several moments in the second half of the 1984 production invited an ironic interpretation of what is often regarded as the completion of the providential plan. In particular, moments such as Richard's second meeting with his mother and confrontation with Elizabeth (4.4), discussed earlier, his soliloquy (5.3.178ff.), his oration to his troops (5.3.315ff.) and his death (5.5) focused attention more on what was now Richard's search for self and for a role than on any awakening conscience.

The growing division in Richard's role was clear in the playing of his conscience speech in 5.3. Sher dropped to his knees in front of the throne in which he had been sleeping and addressed most of the soliloquy (5.3.178–207) to his shield, which had been laid ready for the next day's fight. In answer to the question, 'What do I fear?' (5.3.183), a sharp overhead light illuminated the shield, making it appear mirror-like. Richard looked into this mirror and, in a different voice, replied, 'Myself' (5.3.183). It seemed a voice conjured, like the light, by external agency, and the word was not delivered as a question but as a fact. The rest of the dialogue speech was delivered in these two distinct voices, as a 'doppelganger soliloquy' (*Times*), but without any naturalistic hesitation, in a style which emphasized the balanced pattern of the words as much as their meaning. Some critics considered the effect an acting failure. But it conveyed a sense of the figure's enforced ambiguity at this point. Richard's debate appeared to involve the intervention of providential determination, represented by one voice and the light: the same force which imposed the morality-style patterning of history epitomized in the monolithic setting. And it was that force, or voice, in himself that Richard seemed to fear.

The naturalistic effects of panic and lost confidence, which actors often invest in the conscience speech, Sher transferred to the battle oration (5.3.315ff.). Unable at first to find the words, Richard looked around at his followers as if seeking a prompt, or to be excused a role which now he feared. His voice dissolved repeatedly into tired sighs, as the divided Richard of the conscience speech returned. Part of him – the voice of patterned Providence – composed the words, but another stifled all his efforts to deliver them sincerely. The focus was again on the pattern of the rhetoric, this time broken and ineffective. Although he eventually found voice enough to complete the speech, the implication seemed to be that Richard could not play the scene because he was in despair not only with himself but with the role that providence required of him.

The death that this Richard recognized as inevitable was played entirely emblematically; the chaos of battle replaced with 'the right image for a ritualistic slaughter', as Alexander saw it (Sher, 188). Scene 4 opened on an empty stage and Richard's cry of 'A horse! A horse! My kingdom for a horse!' (5.4.7) amplified round the auditorium. He then entered alone through the rear doors, his figure outlined against white light and smoke. Slithering exhausted to the front, he offered his coronet up to God in exchange for escape, so it was clear that we were inside a church, not in the battle, and that Richard had fled to sanctuary. As he knelt in prayer, holding the crown above him, Christopher Ravenscroft's golden Richmond, visor down and sword reversed, processed forward and speared him through the hump. The moment before death is captured in Figure 43. Immediately Richard's figure became a grotesquely rocking object, held upright by the sword that pinned it; a sword, crossed at both hilt and base, which could not have been a fighting implement. Richard's death as he knelt in sanctuary was thus an act of judgement executed by a figure of Providence, and an apt closure to the morality

FIGURE 43 Armoured in gold, and lit by a blaze of light from the cathedral doorway, Richmond (Christopher Ravenscroft) raises his double-crossed sword before plunging it into Richard (Antony Sher). In the same moment, Richard lifts the crown towards the unseen high altar, and the audience, so that the golden halo seems to hang, symbolically, between the figures of the holy avenger and the devil king (1984).

dimension of the play. At the same time, the absence of a fair fight, and the spectacularly theatrical slaughter of the praying figure by a Darth Vader-like Richmond, with full orchestral underscoring, sustained this production's increasing ambiguity. In both theatrical and moral terms, therefore, Richmond's closing speech of peace provided only a half-convincing climax.

The sense of Richard caught finally in an unwilled performance was conveyed more clearly in the closing scene of the 1995 production. As in 1984, there was no attempt to stage a battle, realistic or stylized. Here it became a battle of words. Richard and Richmond confronted each other with their orations, the shared rhetorical style delivering quite different points of view; Richmond looking to the future from the overhead walkway, and Richard facing his theatre audience from the stage below. Their speeches were initially intercut, as in Mendes's 1992 arrangement, although they eventually overlaid each other, Richmond rising to a crescendo as Richard gasped for words, in what became a battle for the stage, and for the belief (or suspended disbelief) of the audience.

By cutting the dialogue about George Stanley's son (5.3.343–7) and Catesby's request that Richard be rescued (5.4.1–6), Pimlott skipped straight from the orations to the end of the battle with neither protagonist moving. Richard's cry for a horse, therefore, was addressed to the audience, as if he were asking them to retain belief in him sufficient to continue his version of the tale. But, as he did so, the opening pavane struck up, and the ghosts of Richard's victims processed across the walkway. Standing in spotlight, Richard turned towards them, repeating his opening lines, 'Now is the winter of our discontent / Made glorious summer...' (1.1.1–2), followed by 'And all the clouds that lour'd upon our House / In the deep bosom ...' (1.1.3–4). Finding no response, Richard turned to the auditorium audience with 'But I, that am not shap'd for sportive tricks' (1.1.14) and, on video, 'I, that am ...' (1.1.16) (the promptbook has 'I am I' from the conscience soliloquy – 5.3.184 – so Troughton's choice of words here may have varied with performances). Finally he used the image of the thorny wood from *3 Henry VI*:

> And I, – like one lost in a thorny wood,
> That rents the thorns and is rent with the thorns,
> Seeking a way, and straying from the way;
> Not knowing how to find the open air,
> But toiling desperately to find it out –

> Torment myself to catch the English crown:
> And from that torment I will free myself,
> Or hew my way out with a bloody axe.
>
> (*3 Henry VI*; 3.2.174–81)

Each time his words trailed off into silence as he received no recognition from above or from the auditorium. Placing first his sword and then the crown, which he removed with obvious distress, on the ground, he looked out into the audience. Then, closing bitterly with 'all the world to nothing!' (1.2.242), he returned his figure to physical wholeness by standing upright and relaxing his left arm. After this he turned and walked slowly and with ease to the ghosts' side-stage area (stage right), his follow spot dimming as he left the stage.

When Richard had left, the ghosts continued on their way across the balcony, this time in silence. Behind them, Richmond turned, alone and in spotlight, and announced, 'The day is ours; the bloody dog is dead' (5.5.2). He then descended the front stairs as Stanley entered and moved towards the front-stage crown and sword, the scene now half lit as if by a cold dawn light. Dismissing Stanley with 'Proclaim a pardon to the soldiers fled / That in submission will return to us' (5.5.16–17), Richmond stood alone for the closing speech, which he delivered, slowly and clearly with a rising crescendo, from the same front-stage space that Richard had just vacated. Kneeling to lift the crown, he stood upright and held it above his head before lowering it in silence as the light began to fade. As he did so, Richard, watching from his side-stage space, began a slow handclap.

Troughton saw the moment when he lost Richard's deformity as the figure's death. He 'ceases to be' (Troughton, 99) because the audience fails any longer to believe in him. Having lost control of his script, the jester Richard 'dies' theatrically. Having been defeated by his ghostly conscience, the psychological Richard gives up in despair, 'registering an inner defeat quite at odds with the usual picture of the tyrant fighting to the end like a cornered rat' (*Independent*). Others saw in it, and in the later handclapping, the implication that Richard, and potentially Richmond, were merely players of an unchanging role, that of the tyrant. Such figures were watched 'powerlessly, by their dupes and their victims', as Richard had been by his growing onstage audience of ghosts, and earlier by citizens from across the centuries, 'as the theatre of history rolls on' (*SQ*, 1996).

Some in the auditorium audience were uncertain how to read this closure, particularly Richard's cynical applause for Richmond. Had the play ended? Was the applause inside or outside 'the play'? Was the figure applauding still Richard, or was he now Troughton himself? Should they join in? Breaking the conventional closure in this way clearly disturbed the audience's place in the performance. The side-stage presence either of a Richard liberated from myth-history, or of the actor freed now from the villain role, invited alternative readings of the formal end. As Troughton saw it, the opposition between the play as 'true' History or 'true' Tragedy came to the fore (Troughton, 100). Applause here might signify collusion in chronicle history, or endorse the player-Richard's seeming scepticism at that narrative. Either way, the dramatic artifice of the play's own multilayered framework was exposed, as the unconventional ending opened up the possibility of other versions of the tale – even, perhaps, the one which we were denied at the opening. For a moment the audience faced the need to distinguish between reality and fiction. And, for that moment at least, they recognized the difficulty of doing so, despite, or perhaps because of, the diversity of fictional forms made manifest in Pimlott's account.

The diversity of *Richard III*'s fictional forms, recognized by Pimlott, is also acknowledged in the range of responses represented in this book. Productions have moved away from the blood and thunder melodramas of the early twentieth century, where star actors would fit their performances of Richard into the 'usual moves'. Directors now embrace the historical dimension that Cibber and

Irving so disliked, presenting its moral pattern as a political or social tragedy in which Richard has a serious role to play. And they have been thanked for clarifying medieval history, and for making the work relevant to the present, as Peter Hall intended the RSC should do. All the same, the text has to be adapted to sustain this focus, which means that Richard's 'disturbing vitality' (Brooke, 124), which attracted Cibber, Irving, Olivier and Sher to the role, often disappears amidst the moral seriousness. It is as if some directors share Cibber's fear that the play's structural inconsistencies and 'contrasting linguistic and dramatic modes' (124) would make it unintelligible to modern audiences. The fact that Stratford has staged a third of its post-war productions of the play in the last ten years confirms that it is still good box office, and might even suggest its increased popularity, if only as an examination text. It has been performed in all three theatres, in a variety of theatrical styles and with quite different company structures and directorial concepts – all further proof of the play's diversity. Indeed, three of these four productions (the exception being that in 1998) presented original and challenging inter-pretations of the play's dramatic structure, exploring its theatrical artifice and acknowledging the audience as interpreters in some way. And each treatment trusted to some extent in the audience's knowledge, either of Shakespeare's play or of its subject's legendary status as a consequence of *Richard III*. During the same period the play has featured in two films – Richard Loncraine's *Richard III* (1996) and Al Pacino's *Looking for Richard* (1996) – neither of which played the text in what might be considered a 'straight' or conventional way. Pacino used its structure as a metaphor, to 'allegorize his own experience of playing Richard' (Boose and Burt, 15), and Loncraine viewed the action through the frame of recent history and the lens of popular film.

Could it be that these ambitious responses play to audiences already experienced in the various interpretations of, or allusions to, the text on film and video, or in cycle sequences and as a solo drama at Stratford and elsewhere? Maybe audiences are, or always were, more willing to accept the drama's structural complexities than directors have allowed? Or perhaps, in a decade that has seen political and social upheaval, and the evidence of tyranny on a vast scale, the dislocation and irresolution of an ambivalent reading make more sense. Certainly, if the last half-century is anything to go by, theatre practitioners and audiences alike will look forward with keen interest to the ways in which this play shapes itself to innovative, challenging and no doubt controversial interpretations at Stratford, and beyond, in the present millennium.

NOTES

1 Barry Kyle in conversation with the author, 29 November 1989.
2 Sarah Esdaile, associate director of *Richard III*, in conversation with the author, 25 February 2001.
3 The Stratford promptbook has this speech in the past tense, but David Oyelowo, who played the ghost of Henry VI, confirms that he used the future tense.
4 Steven Pimlott discussed this in an interview with Robert Smallwood published in the programme for *Richard III*.
5 Sher's book *Year of the King* details his preparation for the role, particularly his work on the physical disability scoliosis, and on the psychopathic state of mind, both of which took him away from performances of monstrous Richards, such as that of Laurence Olivier which haunted him throughout the rehearsal period.

PRODUCTION CREDITS AND CAST LISTS

Unless otherwise stated, all the productions were staged at the Royal Shakespeare Theatre (known in 1953 as the Shakespeare Memorial Theatre).

1953

Director	Glen Byam Shaw
Designer	Motley
Music	Leslie Bridgewater
Lighting	Peter Streuli
Fights	Michael Warre

RICHARD	Marius Goring
DUKE OF CLARENCE	Michael Warre
SIR ROBERT BRAKENBURY	Bernard Kay
LORD HASTINGS	Tony Britton
LADY ANNE	Yvonne Mitchell
QUEEN ELIZABETH	Rachel Kempson
LORD RIVERS	Donald Eccles
LORD GREY	Dennis Clinton
MARQUESS OF DORSET	William Peacock
DUKE OF BUCKINGHAM	Harry Andrews
STANLEY, EARL OF DERBY	John Bushelle
QUEEN MARGARET	Joan Sanderson
SIR WILLIAM CATESBY	Powys Thomas
TWO MURDERERS	Michael Hayes, Alan Townsend
KING EDWARD IV	Noel Howlett
SIR RICHARD RATCLIFFE	Mervyn Blake
DUCHESS OF YORK	Margot Boyd
BOY – CLARENCE'S CHILD	James Morris

DUKE OF YORK	Robert Scroggins
PRINCE EDWARD	Anthony Adams
LORD CARDINAL BOURCHIER	Philip Morant
LORD MAYOR OF LONDON	Peter Norris
HASTINGS, A PURSUIVANT	Nigel Davenport
PRIEST	Michael Hayes
SIR THOMAS VAUGHAN	Peter Duguid
BISHOP OF ELY	Michael Turner
DUKE OF NORFOLK	Philip Morant
LORD LOVELL	Jerome Willis
SCRIVENER	Peter Duguid
PAGES	Richard Martin, David O'Brien
SIR JAMES TYRREL	James Wellman
EARL OF RICHMOND	Basil Hoskins
EARL OF OXFORD	Denys Graham
SIR JAMES BLUNT	Michael Turner
SIR WALTER HERBERT	Cavan Malone
EARL OF SURREY	Peter Johnson
SIR WILLIAM BRANDON	Alan Townsend
GHOST OF EDWARD, PRINCE OF WALES	Richard Martin
GHOST OF KING HENRY VI	James Wellman

GUARDS, HALBERDIERS, GENTLEMEN, LORDS, CITIZENS, ATTENDANTS, SOLDIERS, LADIES, MONKS, ALDERMEN, MESSENGERS:
Diana Chadwick, James Culliford, John Glendenning, Charles Gray, George Hart, Charles Howard, Gareth Jones, John Kilby, David King, John Roberts, Raymond Sherry, Mary Watson, Jean Wilson

Number in company	47
Press night	24 March 1953

1961

Director	William Gaskill
Designer	Jocelyn Herbert
Music	Marc Wilkinson
Lighting	Richard Pilbrow
Fights	John Barton

RICHARD	Christopher Plummer
DUKE OF CLARENCE	Peter McEnery
SIR ROBERT BRAKENBURY	Clifford Rose
LORD HASTINGS	Colin Blakely
LADY ANNE	Jill Dixon
TRESSEL	James Kerry
BERKELEY	Brian Wright
QUEEN ELIZABETH	Elizabeth Sellars
LORD RIVERS	Michael Murray
LORD GREY	Gareth Morgan
MARQUESS OF DORSET	Peter Holmes
DUKE OF BUCKINGHAM	Eric Porter
STANLEY, EARL OF DERBY	Redmond Phillips
QUEEN MARGARET	Edith Evans
SIR WILLIAM CATESBY	Ian Richardson
TWO MURDERERS	Gordon Gostelow, Russell Hunter
KING EDWARD IV	Tony Church
SIR RICHARD RATCLIFFE	James Kerry
DUCHESS OF YORK	Esmé Church
GIRL – CLARENCE'S CHILD	Rosemary Mussell
ARCHBISHOP OF YORK	Roger Jerome
DUKE OF YORK	Adrian Blount
PRINCE EDWARD	Michael Lewis
LORD CARDINAL BOURCHIER	Julian Battersby
LORD MAYOR OF LONDON	William Wallis
HASTINGS, A PURSUIVANT	Eric Flynn
PRIEST	Ronald Scott-Dodd
BISHOP OF ELY	Clifford Rose
DUKE OF NORFOLK	Gordon Gostelow
LORD LOVELL	Paul Bailey

SCRIVENER	Terry Wale
PAGE	Michael Warchus
SIR JAMES TYRREL	David Buck
EARL OF RICHMOND	Brian Murray
EARL OF OXFORD	David Buck
SIR JAMES BLUNT	Russell Hunter
EARL OF SURREY	Julian Battersby

GUARDS, HALBERDIERS, GENTLEMEN, LORDS, CITIZENS, ATTENDANTS, SOLDIERS, MOURNERS, MESSENGERS: Paul Bailey, Richard Barr, Michael Blackham, Sebastian Breaks, Eric Flynn, Peter Holmes, Roger Jerome, Bruce McKenzie, Gareth Morgan, Ronald Scott-Dodd, Terry Wale, Michael Warchus, Brian Wright

Number in company	36
Press night	24 May 1961

1963

Directors	Peter Hall with John Barton and Frank Evans
Text adaptation	John Barton
Designer	John Bury
Music	Guy Woolfenden

RICHARD	Ian Holm
DUKE OF CLARENCE	Charles Kay
SIR ROBERT BRAKENBURY	Robert Jennings
LORD HASTINGS	Hugh Sullivan
LADY ANNE	Janet Suzman
QUEEN ELIZABETH	Susan Engel
LORD RIVERS	Roy Marsden
DUKE OF BUCKINGHAM	Tom Fleming
STANLEY, EARL OF DERBY	Jeffery Dench
QUEEN MARGARET	Peggy Ashcroft
SIR WILLIAM CATESBY	Ian McCulloch
TWO MURDERERS	Clifford Rose, Philip Brack
KING EDWARD IV	Roy Dotrice
SIR RICHARD RATCLIFFE	John Hussey
DUCHESS OF YORK	Madoline Thomas
CITIZENS	Marshall Jones, Brian Jackson, John Normington
DUKE OF YORK	Peter Gatrell
PRINCE EDWARD	Anthony Gatrell
PRINCESS ELIZABETH	Valerie Cutts
LORD MAYOR OF LONDON	Ken Wynne/John Corvin
LORD MAYOR'S WIFE	Penelope Keith
BISHOP OF ELY	Jolyon Booth
DUKE OF NORFOLK	Philip Brack
SIR JAMES TYRREL	Brian Harrison
MESSENGERS	Peter Geddis, Ronald Falk, Henry Knowles, Tim Wylton
EARL OF RICHMOND	Derek Waring
EARL OF OXFORD	Michael Murray/Brian Jackson

GHOST OF EDWARD, PRINCE
   OF WALES   James Hunter
GHOST OF KING HENRY VI   David Warner

GUARDS, HALBERDIERS, GENTLEMEN, LORDS, CITIZENS,
ATTENDANTS, SOLDIERS, SERVANTS:
Barbara Barnett, Anthony Boden, Shaun Curry, Valerie Cutts, Ronald
Falk, James Falkland, Peter Geddis, David Hargreaves, James Hunter,
Robert Jennings, Marshall Jones, Roger Jones, Henry Knowles,
Caroline Maud, Rhys McConnochie, Lee Menzies, Tim Nightingale,
David Rowlands, John Steiner, David Walsh, Tim Wylton

Number in company	47
Press night	20 August 1963
Transfer	London, Aldwych Theatre, 11 January 1964
National Sound Archive recording of 1964 Stratford revival	31 October 1964
BBC TV recording	22 April 1965

1970

Director	Terry Hands
Designer	Abdul Farrah
Music	Michael Dress
Lighting	John Bradley
Movement	John Broome

RICHARD	Norman Rodway
DUKE OF CLARENCE	Terrence Hardiman
SIR ROBERT BRAKENBURY	Allan Mitchell
LORD HASTINGS	Barry Stanton
JANE SHORE	Sara Kestelman
LADY ANNE	Helen Mirren
QUEEN ELIZABETH	Brenda Bruce
LORD RIVERS	William Russell
LORD GREY	Peter Harlowe
MARQUESS OF DORSET	Richard Jones Barry
DUKE OF BUCKINGHAM	Ian Richardson
STANLEY, EARL OF DERBY	Philip Locke
QUEEN MARGARET	Sheila Burrell
SIR WILLIAM CATESBY	Trader Faulkner
TWO MURDERERS	Peter Egan, Anthony Langdon
KING EDWARD IV	Patrick Stewart
SIR RICHARD RATCLIFFE	Ben Kingsley
DUCHESS OF YORK	Eileen Beldon
BOY ⎱ CLARENCE'S CHILDREN	Matthew Sim
GIRL ⎰	Kate Sim
CITIZENS	Allan Mitchell, Gaye Rorke, Ted Valentine
DUKE OF YORK	Colin Mayes
PRINCE EDWARD	David Allen
PRINCESS ELIZABETH	Mary Rutherford
LORD MAYOR OF LONDON	Terrence Hardiman
SIR THOMAS VAUGHAN	Michael McGovern
BISHOP OF ELY	Patrick Barr
LORD LOVELL	John Kane
PAGES	Kieran Healy, Gregory Kahn

SIR JAMES TYRREL	Christopher Gable
CHRISTOPHER URSWICK	Ted Valentine
EARL OF RICHMOND	Peter Egan
SIR JAMES BLUNT	Anthony Langdon
Number in company	31
Press night	15 April 1970
London venue	Roundhouse, 7 December 1970

1975

Director	Barry Kyle
Designer	John Napier
Music	James Walker

RICHARD	Ian Richardson
DUKE OF CLARENCE	George Baker
SIR ROBERT BRAKENBURY	Gareth Armstrong
LORD HASTINGS	Bob Peck
JANE SHORE	Ann Hasson
LADY ANNE	Celia Bannerman
QUEEN ELIZABETH	Barbara Leigh-Hunt
LORD RIVERS	Christopher Saul
LORD GREY	Gareth Armstrong
DUKE OF BUCKINGHAM	Tony Church
STANLEY, EARL OF DERBY	Griffith Jones
QUEEN MARGARET	Brenda Bruce
SIR WILLIAM CATESBY	Charles Dance
TWO MURDERERS	Charles Dance, Terence Wilton
KING EDWARD IV	Jeffery Dench
SIR RICHARD RATCLIFFE	Terence Wilton
DUKE OF YORK	Neil Surman
PRINCE EDWARD	Wayne Morris
LORD MAYOR OF LONDON	George Baker
BISHOP OF ELY	Christopher Saul
SIR JAMES TYRREL	Jeffery Dench
EARL OF RICHMOND	Tony Church
EARL OF OXFORD	Gareth Armstrong

Number in company	16
Stratford venue	The Other Place
Press night	7 October 1975

1980

Director	Terry Hands
Designer	Abdul Farrah
Music	Guy Woolfenden
Lighting	Terry Hands with Clive Morris
Fights	Ian McKay

RICHARD	Alan Howard
DUKE OF CLARENCE	Richard Pasco
SIR ROBERT BRAKENBURY	David Bradley
LORD HASTINGS	Bruce Purchase
JANE SHORE	Catherine Riding
LADY ANNE	Sinead Cusack
QUEEN ELIZABETH	Domini Blythe
LORD RIVERS	Brett Usher
LORD GREY	Rob Edwards
MARQUESS OF DORSET	Sion Tudor-Owen
DUKE OF BUCKINGHAM	Derek Godfrey
STANLEY, EARL OF DERBY	Trevor Baxter
QUEEN MARGARET	Barbara Leigh-Hunt
SIR WILLIAM CATESBY	Tom Wilkinson
TWO MURDERERS	James Hazeldine, Joe Melia
KING EDWARD IV	David Suchet
SIR RICHARD RATCLIFFE	John Bowe
DUCHESS OF YORK	Marjorie Yates
BOY ⎫ CLARENCE'S CHILDREN	Hayden Parsey/Oliver White
GIRL ⎭	Joanna Dukes/Martha Parsey
DUKE OF YORK	Andrew O'Brien/Charles Rendall
PRINCE EDWARD	Paul Davies-Prowles/Jason Smart
PRINCESS ELIZABETH	Julia Tobin
LORD MAYOR OF LONDON	Raymond Llewellyn
PRIEST	Timothy Walker
SIR THOMAS VAUGHAN	William Armstrong
BISHOP OF ELY	John Carlisle
LORD LOVELL	Bille Brown
SIR JAMES TYRREL	Arthur Kohn
CHRISTOPHER URSWICK	Michael Fitzgerald

EARL OF RICHMOND   Pip Miller
GHOST OF EDWARD, PRINCE
  OF WALES   Jonathan Tafler
GHOST OF KING HENRY VI   John Darrell

GUARDS, HALBERDIERS, GENTLEMEN, LORDS, CITIZENS,
ATTENDANTS, SOLDIERS, MONKS:
John Darrell, Felicity Dean, Kilian McKenna, Abraham Osuagwu,
Jonathan Tafler, Sion Tudor-Owen, Ned Vukovic

Number in company	42
Press night	4 November 1980
Transfer	Newcastle, Theatre Royal,
	17 March 1981
	London, Aldwych Theatre,
	24 November 1981
National Sound Archive recording	
of Aldwych Theatre transfer	8 December 1981

1984

Director — Bill Alexander
Designer — William Dudley
Music — Guy Woolfenden
Lighting — Leo Leibovici
Fights — Malcolm Ranson

RICHARD	Antony Sher
DUKE OF CLARENCE	Roger Allam
SIR ROBERT BRAKENBURY	Paul Gregory
LORD HASTINGS	Brian Blessed
LADY ANNE	Penny Downie
TRESSEL	Andrew Jarvis
BERKELEY	Charles Millham
QUEEN ELIZABETH	Frances Tomelty
LORD RIVERS	Adam Bareham
LORD GREY	Andy Readman
MARQUESS OF DORSET	Andrew Hall
DUKE OF BUCKINGHAM	Malcolm Storry
STANLEY, EARL OF DERBY	Peter Miles
QUEEN MARGARET	Patricia Routledge
SIR WILLIAM CATESBY	Simon Templeman
TWO MURDERERS	Brian Parr, Sion Probert
KEEPER OF THE TOWER	Guy Fithen
KING EDWARD IV	Harold Innocent
SIR RICHARD RATCLIFFE	Ian Mackenzie
DUCHESS OF YORK	Yvonne Coulette
BOY } CLARENCE'S CHILDREN	Stephen Denby/Dominic Wilson
GIRL }	Charlotte Williams/ Hannah Winters
ARCHBISHOP OF YORK	Andrew Jarvis
DUKE OF YORK	Timothy Luckett/ Reuben Purchase
PRINCE EDWARD	Rupert Finch/Daniel Wilson
LORD MAYOR OF LONDON	Norman Henry
HASTINGS, A PURSUIVANT	Hepburn Graham
BISHOP OF ELY	Donald McKillop

DUKE OF NORFOLK	Andrew Jarvis
SCRIVENER	Hepburn Graham
PAGE	Charles Millham
SIR JAMES TYRREL	Jim Hooper
MESSENGERS	Hepburn Graham, Steven Pinner, Jonathan Scott-Taylor
EARL OF RICHMOND	Christopher Ravenscroft
EARL OF OXFORD	Steven Pinner
SIR JAMES BLUNT	Jonathan Scott-Taylor
SIR WALTER HERBERT	Guy Fithen
EARL OF SURREY	Andy Readman
SIR WILLIAM BRANDON	Charles Millham
GHOST OF KING HENRY VI	Jim Hooper

GUARDS, HALBERDIERS, GENTLEMEN, LORDS, CITIZENS, ATTENDANTS, SOLDIERS, MONKS, ALDERMEN, LADIES: Guy Fithen, Hepburn Graham, Charles Millham, Liz Moscrop, Steven Pinner, Alison Rose, Jonathan Scott-Taylor, Sarah Woodward

Number in company	39
Press night	19 June 1984
Transfer	Newcastle, Theatre Royal, 19 March 1985
	London, Barbican, 30 April 1985
Tour	Adelaide, Melbourne, Brisbane, 8 May to 5 July 1985
Video recording	9 January 1985
National Sound Archive recording of Barbican transfer	11 June 1985

1988

Director	Adrian Noble
Designer	Bob Crowley
Music	Edward Gregson
Lighting	Chris Parry
Fights	Malcolm Ranson
Sound	Paul Slocombe

RICHARD	Anton Lesser
DUKE OF CLARENCE	David Morrissey
SIR ROBERT BRAKENBURY	Roger Watkins
LORD HASTINGS	Edward Peel
LADY ANNE	Geraldine Alexander
TRESSEL	Jeffrey Segal
QUEEN ELIZABETH	Joanne Pearce
LORD RIVERS	Edward Harbour
LORD GREY	Kevin Doyle
MARQUESS OF DORSET	Jo James
DUKE OF BUCKINGHAM	Oliver Cotton
STANLEY, EARL OF DERBY	Darryl Forbes-Dawson
QUEEN MARGARET	Penny Downie
SIR WILLIAM CATESBY	Patrick Robinson
KING EDWARD IV	Ken Bones
SIR RICHARD RATCLIFFE	Richard Bremmer
DUCHESS OF YORK	Marjorie Yates
CITIZENS	Cissy Collins, Trevor Gordon, Candida Gubbins, Roger Watkins
DUKE OF YORK	Lee Broom/Guy Newey
PRINCE EDWARD	Lee Barton/Paul Curran
LORD MAYOR OF LONDON	Raymond Bowers
BISHOP OF ELY	Jeffrey Segal
DUKE OF NORFOLK	Jason Watkins
LORD LOVELL	Mark Hadfield
SIR JAMES TYRREL	Raymond Bowers
MESSENGERS	Anthony Dixon, Kevin Doyle, Mark Hadfield, Kenn Sabberton, Jason Watkins

EARL OF RICHMOND   Simon Dormandy
GHOST OF EDWARD, PRINCE
  OF WALES   Lyndon Davies
GHOST OF KING HENRY VI   Ralph Fiennes

GUARDS, HALBERDIERS, GENTLEMEN, LORDS, CITIZENS,
ATTENDANTS, SOLDIERS:
Denise Armon, Kathleen Christof, Cissy Collins, Lyndon Davies,
Anthony Dixon, Kevin Doyle, Trevor Gordon, Jaye Griffiths, Candida
Gubbins, Caroline Harding, Kenn Sabberton, Jason Watkins

Number in company   36
Press night   22 October 1988
Transfer   Newcastle, Theatre Royal,
                             February 1989
                             London, Barbican, 1 April 1989
Video recording   6 January 1989

1992

Director	Sam Mendes
Designer	Tim Hatley
Music	Paddy Cunneen
Lighting	Paul Pyant
Fights	Terry King
Sound	Tim Oliver

RICHARD	Simon Russell Beale
DUKE OF CLARENCE	Simon Dormandy
SIR ROBERT BRAKENBURY	Sam Graham
LORD HASTINGS	Christopher Hunter
LADY ANNE	Annabelle Apsion
QUEEN ELIZABETH	Kate Duchêne
LORD RIVERS	Michael Packer
LORD GREY	Mark Lewis Jones
MARQUESS OF DORSET	Mark Benton
DUKE OF BUCKINGHAM	Stephen Boxer
STANLEY, EARL OF DERBY	Sam Graham
QUEEN MARGARET	Cherry Morris
SIR WILLIAM CATESBY	Daniel Ryan
TWO MURDERERS	Mark Benton, Christopher Hunter
KING EDWARD IV	Mike Dowling
SIR RICHARD RATCLIFFE	Simon Dormandy
DUCHESS OF YORK	Ellie Haddington
DUKE OF YORK	Annabelle Apsion
PRINCE EDWARD	Kate Duchêne
LORD MAYOR OF LONDON	Mike Dowling
BISHOP OF ELY	Mark Benton
SIR JAMES TYRREL	Michael Packer
CHRISTOPHER URSWICK	Christopher Hunter
EARL OF RICHMOND	Mark Lewis Jones

GUARDS, HALBERDIERS, GENTLEMEN, LORDS, CITIZENS, ATTENDANTS, SOLDIERS:
Members of the cast

Number in company	14
Stratford venue	The Other Place
Press night	11 August 1992
Tour	England and N. Ireland, September–December 1992; Tokyo, February–March 1993; Rotterdam, March 1993
London venue	Donmar Warehouse, January–February 1993
Stratford revival	Swan Theatre, March–May 1993
Video recording of Swan Theatre revival	29 April 1993

1995

Director	Steven Pimlott
Designer	Tobias Hoheisel
Music	Jason Carr
Lighting	Hugh Vanstone
Fights	Malcolm Ranson
Movement	Liz Ranken
Sound	Paul Slocombe

RICHARD	David Troughton
DUKE OF CLARENCE	Michael Siberry
SIR ROBERT BRAKENBURY	Robert Lister
LORD HASTINGS	Paul Bentall
JANE SHORE	Rachel Sanders
LADY ANNE	Jennifer Ehle
QUEEN ELIZABETH	Susan Brown
LORD RIVERS	Robert Arnold
LORD GREY	Justin Shevlin
MARQUESS OF DORSET	Simon Chadwick
DUKE OF BUCKINGHAM	John Nettles
STANLEY, EARL OF DERBY	Clifford Rose
GEORGE STANLEY	James Richard/Markland Starkie
QUEEN MARGARET	Cherry Morris
SIR WILLIAM CATESBY	Mark Bazeley
TWO MURDERERS	Anthony Hannan, Paul Hilton
KING EDWARD IV	Robin Nedwell
SIR RICHARD RATCLIFFE	Lionel Guyett
DUCHESS OF YORK	Diana Coupland
CITIZENS	Don Gallagher, Joanna Hole, William Whymper
ARCHBISHOP OF YORK	Victor Spinetti
DUKE OF YORK	Ivor Hill/Simon Pollard
PRINCE EDWARD	William Belchambers/ Matthew Hopkins
LORD MAYOR OF LONDON	Robin Nedwell
SIR THOMAS VAUGHAN	David Frederickson
SIR JAMES TYRREL	Don Gallagher

MESSENGER   Ralph Birtwell

EARL OF RICHMOND   Paul Bettany

GUARDS, HALBERDIERS, GENTLEMEN, LORDS, CITIZENS, ATTENDANTS, SOLDIERS:
Members of the company and citizens of Stratford-upon-Avon

Number in company	33
Press night	6 September 1995
Transfer	Newcastle, Theatre Royal, 19 March 1996
	London, Barbican, 27 June 1996
Video recording	30 September 1995

1998

Director	Elijah Moshinsky
Designer	Rob Howell
Music	Corin Buckeridge
Lighting	Peter Mumford
Fights	William Hobbs
Sound	John A. Leonard

RICHARD	Robert Lindsay
DUKE OF CLARENCE	Kevin McMonagle
SIR ROBERT BRAKENBURY	Charles Baillie
LORD HASTINGS	Robert East
LADY ANNE	Rachel Power
QUEEN ELIZABETH	Siân Thomas
LORD RIVERS	Dickon Tyrrell
LORD GREY	Jo Stone-Fewings
MARQUESS OF DORSET	Jon Fenner
DUKE OF BUCKINGHAM	David Yelland
STANLEY, EARL OF DERBY	David Killick
QUEEN MARGARET	Anna Carteret
SIR WILLIAM CATESBY	Tom Bowles
TWO MURDERERS	Russell Gomer, David Semark
KING EDWARD IV	Benny Young
SIR RICHARD RATCLIFFE	Frank Kovacs
DUCHESS OF YORK	Dilys Hamlett
CITIZENS	Charles Baillie, Victoria Davar, Paul Leonard, Patricia Leventon
DUKE OF YORK	James Robinson/Sam Wood
PRINCE EDWARD	Gwilym Lee/Dominic Vizor
LORD MAYOR OF LONDON	Paul Leonard
PRIEST	Jon Fenner
BISHOP OF ELY	Russell Gomer
DUKE OF NORFOLK	David Semark
SCRIVENER	Benny Young
SIR JAMES TYRREL	Dickon Tyrrell
MESSENGERS	Russell Gomer, David Semark
EARL OF RICHMOND	Jo Stone-Fewings

EARL OF OXFORD	Charles Baillie
SIR WALTER HERBERT	Benny Young
EARL OF SURREY	Dickon Tyrrell

GUARDS, HALBERDIERS, GENTLEMEN, LORDS, CITIZENS,
ATTENDANTS, SOLDIERS:
Members of the company

Number in company	25
Press night	28 October 1998
London venue	Savoy Theatre, 18 January 1999
Video recording	10 November 1998

2001

Director	Michael Boyd
Designer	Tom Piper
Music	James Jones
Lighting	Heather Carson
Fights	Terry King
Movement	Liz Ranken
Sound	Andrea J. Cox

RICHARD	Aidan McArdle
DUKE OF CLARENCE	Rhashan Stone
LORD HASTINGS	David Beames
LADY ANNE	Aislin McGuckin
QUEEN ELIZABETH	Elaine Pyke
LORD RIVERS	Richard Dillane
LORD GREY	Robert Barton
MARQUESS OF DORSET	Sarah D'Arcy
DUKE OF BUCKINGHAM	Richard Cordery
STANLEY, EARL OF DERBY	Keith Bartlett
QUEEN MARGARET	Fiona Bell
SIR WILLIAM CATESBY	James Tucker
TWO MURDERERS	Nicholas Asbury, Geoffrey Streatfeild
KEEPER OF THE TOWER	Edward Clayton
KEEPER'S ASSISTANT	Neil Madden
KING EDWARD IV	Tom Beard
SIR RICHARD RATCLIFFE	Gavin Marshall
DUCHESS OF YORK	Deirdra Morris
BOY ⎫ CLARENCE'S CHILDREN	Oliver Gallant/Ross McDermott
GIRL ⎭	Georgia Greene/Lily Milton
ARCHBISHOP OF YORK	Jerome Willis
DUKE OF YORK	Rupert Carter/Charlie Samuda
PRINCE EDWARD	George Clarke/Danny Earles
LORD MAYOR OF LONDON	Philip Brook
BISHOP OF ELY	John Kane
LORD LOVELL	Geoffrey Streatfeild
SIR JAMES TYRREL	Jake Nightingale

MESSENGER	Owen Oakeshott
CHRISTOPHER URSWICK	Christopher Ettridge
EARL OF RICHMOND	Sam Troughton
EARL OF OXFORD	Owen Oakeshott
GHOST OF EDWARD, PRINCE OF WALES	Neil Madden
GHOST OF KING HENRY VI	David Oyelowo
GHOST OF EARL OF WARWICK	Geff Francis
GHOST OF RICHARD, DUKE OF YORK	Clive Wood

GUARDS, HALBERDIERS, GENTLEMEN, LORDS, CITIZENS, ATTENDANTS, SOLDIERS: Members of the company

Number in company	34
Stratford venue	Swan Theatre
London venue	Young Vic, 4 April 2001
Press night	25 April 2001
Tour	Ann Arbor, University of Michigan, March 2001

REVIEWS CITED

1953

Birmingham Post, 25 March 1953
Daily Herald, 25 March 1953
Daily Telegraph, 25 March 1953, Patrick Gibbs
Daily Worker, 27 March 1953
Leamington Spa Courier, 27 March 1953
Manchester Guardian, 25 March 1953
Observer, 29 March 1953, Ivor Brown
Scotsman, 28 March 1953
Shakespeare Quarterly 12 (1953), 461–6, Clifford Leech
Sunday Mercury, 29 March 1953
Time and Tide, 4 March 1953, Roy Walker
Times, 25 March 1953

1961

Daily Mail, 25 May 1961, Robert Mullar
Guardian, 26 May 1961, Michael Wall
John O'London, 8 June 1961, Caryl Brahms
Morning Advertiser, 5 June 1961, Geoffrey Tarran
New Statesman, 2 June 1961, V.S. Pritchett
Observer, 28 May 1961, Irving Wardle
Scotsman, 27 May 1961, Charles Graves
Shakespeare Quarterly, 12 (1961), 425–41, Robert Speaight
Spectator, 2 June 1961, Bamber Gascoigne
Stratford-upon-Avon Herald, 26 May 1961, Edmund Gardiner
Sunday Telegraph, 28 May 1961, Alan Brien
Tablet, 5 July 1961, Robert Speaight
Times, 25 May 1961
Tribune, 2 June 1961, Mervyn Jones

1963

Evening News, 21 August 1963
Guardian, 21 August 1963, Gerard Fay
Guardian, 13 January 1964, Philip Hope-Wallace
Queen, September 1963
Shakespeare Quarterly 15 (1964), 377–89, Robert Speaight
Stratford-upon-Avon Herald, 23 August 1963, Edmund Gardiner
Theatre World, 59 (465), October 1963
Times, 23 August 1963
Times Educational Supplement, 24 January 1964, Peter Hall
Western Mail, 15 August 1963

1970

Birmingham Post, 16 April 1970, J.C. Trewin
Daily Telegraph, 16 April 1970, John Barber
Evening Standard, 16 April 1970, Milton Shulman
Financial Times, 16 April 1970, B.A. Young
Guardian, 16 April 1970, Gareth Lloyd Evans
Listener, 23 April 1970, D.A.N. Jones
Morning Star, 17 April 1970
New Statesman, 24 April 1970, Benedict Nightingale
Observer, 19 April 1970, Ronald Bryden
Shakespeare Quarterly, 21 (1970), 439–49, Robert Speaight
Shakespeare Survey, 24 (1971), 117–26, Peter Thomson
Sunday Telegraph, 19 April 1970, Frank Marcus
Times, 16 April 1970, Irving Wardle

1975

Birmingham Post, 10 October 1975, Keith Brace
Daily Telegraph, 9 October 1975, Eric Shorter

1980

Coventry Evening Telegraph, 5 November 1980, Peter McGarry
Daily Mail, 5 November 1980
Glasgow Citizen, 8 November 1980

Guardian, 5 November 1980, Michael Billington
Listener, 13 November 1980, John Elsom
Review Special, 31 November 1981, Lucy Hughes Hallett
South Wales Argus, 5 November 1980
Sunday Times, 9 November 1980
Times Literary Supplement, 14 November 1980, Julie Hankey

1984

Guardian, 19 June 1984, Colin Sherman
Guardian, 20 June 1984, Michael Billington
Guardian, 2 May 1985, Michael Billington
Observer, 28 April 1985, Suzanne Lowry
Shakespeare Quarterly, 36 (1985), 630–43, R. Chris Hassell, Jr
Shakespeare Quarterly, 36 (1985), 79–87, Roger Warren
Standard, 1 May 1985, Milton Shulman
Stratford-upon-Avon Herald, 29 June 1984, Gareth Lloyd Evans
Times, 1 May 1985, Irving Wardle
Times Educational Supplement, 13 July 1984, Nicholas Shrimpton

1988

Daily Telegraph, 24 October 1988
Daily Telegraph, 3 April 1989, Charles Osborne
Financial Times, 24 October 1988, Michael Coveney
Financial Times, 3 April 1989, Martin Hoyle
Independent, 24 October 1988, Paul Taylor
Independent, 3 April 1989, Peter Kemp
International Herald Tribune, 26 October 1988
Morning Star, 26 October 1988
Observer, 30 October 1988, Michael Ratcliffe
Shakespeare Quarterly, 40 (1989), 83–94, Robert Smallwood
Shakespeare Survey, 43 (1991), 171–81, Lois Potter
Sunday Telegraph, 9 April 1989, John Gross
Times, 3 April 1989, Jeremy Kingston
Times Literary Supplement, 4 November 1988, J. Pearce

1992

Evening Standard, 12 August 1992, Nicholas de Jongh
Independent, 13 August 1992, Paul Taylor
Independent on Sunday, 16 August 1992, Irving Wardle
Shakespeare Quarterly, 44 (1993), 343–62, Robert Smallwood
Shakespeare Survey, 46 (1994), 159–89, Peter Holland
Sunday Telegraph, 16 August 1992, Kirsty Milne
Sunday Times, 16 August 1992, John Peter

1995

Birmingham Post, 8 September 1995, Richard Edmonds
Evening Standard, 7 September 1995
Guardian, 8 September 1995, Michael Billington
Independent, 8 September 1995, Paul Taylor
Oxford Times, 8 September 1995, Don Chapman
Shakespeare Quarterly, 47 (1996), 326–9, Robert Smallwood

1998

Daily Mail, 29 October 1998, Michael Coveney
East Anglian, 10 October 1998
Eastern Daily Press, 12 October 1998
Evening Standard, 29 October 1998
Guardian, 31 October 1998, Michael Billington
Shakespeare Survey, 52 (1999), 229–53, Robert Smallwood
Sunday Times, 1 November 1998, John Peter

2001

Guardian, 27 April 2001, Michael Billington
Independent on Sunday, 10 December 2000, Marcus Field
Independent on Sunday, 17 December 2000, Kate Bassett
Observer, 29 April 2001, Susannah Clapp
Scotsman, 20 December 2000, Joyce McMillan
Sunday Times, 6 May 2001, John Peter
Times, 27 April 2001, Benedict Nightingale

ABBREVIATIONS

Birm. Post	*Birmingham Post*
Coventry E. Tel.	*Coventry Evening Telegraph*
D. Herald	*Daily Herald*
D. Mail	*Daily Mail*
D. Telegraph	*Daily Telegraph*
E. Anglian	*East Anglian*
E. Daily Press	*Eastern Daily Press*
E. News	*Evening News*
E. Standard	*Evening Standard*
FT	*Financial Times*
Glasgow Cit.	*Glasgow Citizen*
Indep. Sun.	*Independent on Sunday*
Int. Her. Trib.	*International Herald Tribune*
John O'L.	*John O'London*
Leam. Spa Cour.	*Leamington Spa Courier*
Man. Guardian	*Manchester Guardian*
Morn. Adv.	*Morning Advertiser*
Morn. Star	*Morning Star*
New States.	*New Statesman*
Rev. Special	*Review Special*
SQ	*Shakespeare Quarterly*
SS	*Shakespeare Survey*
S. Wales Arg.	*South Wales Argus*
SA Herald	*Stratford-upon-Avon Herald*
S. Mercury	*Sunday Mercury*
S. Telegraph	*Sunday Telegraph*
S. Times	*Sunday Times*
Theatre W.	*Theatre World*
TES	*Times Education Supplement*
TLS	*Times Literary Supplement*

BIBLIOGRAPHY

BOOKS AND ARTICLES

Addenbrooke, David, *The Royal Shakespeare Company: The Peter Hall Years* (London, 1974)

Barton, John, 'The making of the adaptation', in John Barton with Peter Hall, *The Wars of the Roses, adapted for the Royal Shakespeare Company from William Shakespeare's 'Henry VI, Parts I, II, III' and 'Richard III'* (London, 1970), xv–xxv

Barton, John, with Hall, Peter, *The Wars of the Roses, adapted for the Royal Shakespeare Company from William Shakespeare's 'Henry VI, Parts I, II, III' and 'Richard III'* (London, 1970)

Bate, Jonathan, and Jackson, Russell (eds), *Shakespeare: An Illustrated Stage History* (Oxford, 1996)

Beauman, Sally, *The Royal Shakespeare Company: A History of Ten Decades* (Oxford, 1982)

Berry, Ralph, *Changing Styles in Shakespeare* (London, 1981)

Berry, Ralph, *On Directing Shakespeare* (London, 1989)

Boose, Lynda E., and Burt, Richard (ed.), 'Totally clueless? Shakespeare goes to Hollywood in the 1990s', in Lynda E. Boose and Richard Burt (eds), *Shakespeare the Movie: Popularising the Plays on Film, TV, and Video* (London, 1997), 8–22

Brooke, Nicholas, 'Reflecting gems and dead bones: tragedy versus history in *Richard III'*, *Critical Quarterly*, 7, 2 (1965), 123–34

Brown, Susan, 'Queen Elizabeth', in Robert Smallwood (ed.), *Players of Shakespeare 4* (Cambridge, 1998), 101–13

Bury, John, 'The set', in John Barton with Peter Hall, *The Wars of the Roses, adapted for the Royal Shakespeare Company from William Shakespeare's 'Henry VI, Parts I, II, III' and 'Richard III'* (London, 1970), 237

Calvert, Charles, *'The Life and Death of Richard III', arranged for Representation from the Text by Charles Calvert* (Manchester, 1870)

Cerasano, S.P., 'Churls just wanna have fun: reviewing *Richard III'*, *Shakespeare Quarterly*, 36 (1985), 118–29

Cibber, Colley, *An Apology for the Life of Mr Colley Cibber written by Himself*, ed. Robert W. Lowe, 2 vols (London, 1889)

Cibber, Colley, *The Tragicall History of King Richard III*, in *Five Restoration Adaptations of Shakespeare*, ed. Christopher Spencer (Urbana, Ill., 1965), 274–344

Cook, Judith, *Shakespeare's Players* (London, 1983)

Day, Gillian, 'Determination and proof: Colley Cibber and the materialisation of Shakespeare's *Richard III* in the twentieth century', *Proceedings of the Fifth Biennial Conference of the Australian and New Zealand Shakespeare Association* (Newark, Del., forthcoming)

Dollimore, Jonathan, and Sinfield, Alan (eds), *Political Shakespeare: Essays in Cultural Materialism* (Manchester, 1994)

Downie, Penny, 'Queen Margaret', in Russell Jackson and Robert Smallwood (eds), *Players of Shakespeare 3* (Cambridge, 1993), 114–39

Fiennes, Ralph, 'Henry VI', in Russell Jackson and Robert Smallwood (eds), *Players of Shakespeare 3* (Cambridge, 1993), 99–113

Gaskill, William, *A Sense of Direction* (London and Boston, Mass., 1988)

Goodwin, John (ed.), *Royal Shakespeare Company 1960–1963* (London 1964)

Guthrie, Tyrone, *Theatre Prospect* (London, 1932)

Hall, Peter, 'Shakespeare and the modern director', in John Goodwin (ed.), *Royal Shakespeare Company 1960–1963* (London, 1964), 41–8

Hall, Peter, 'Introduction', in John Barton with Peter Hall, *The Wars of the Roses, adapted for the Royal Shakespeare Company from William Shakespeare's 'Henry VI, Parts I, II, III' and 'Richard III'* (London, 1970), viii–xiv

Hammond, Antony (ed.), *King Richard III*, Arden Shakespeare (London, 1981)

Hankey, Julie (ed.), *Plays in Performance: Richard III* (Bristol, 1988)

Hassell, R. Chris, Jr, 'Context and charisma: the Sher–Alexander *Richard III* and its reviewers', *Shakespeare Quarterly*, 36 (1985), 630–43

Hassell, R. Chris, Jr, *Songs of Death: Performance, Interpretation and the Text of 'Richard III'* (Lincoln, Neb., 1987)

Hodgdon, Barbara, '*The Wars of the Roses*: scholarship speaks on the stage', *Deutsche Shakespeare-Gesellschaft West Jahrbuch* (1972), 170–84

Holderness, Graham, *Shakespeare Recycled: The Making of Historical Drama* (Hemel Hempstead, England, 1992)

Holland, Peter, 'Shakespeare performances in England, 1992', *Shakespeare Survey*, 46 (1994), 159–89

Howard, Jean E., 'Shakespearean counterpoint: stage technique and the interaction between play and audience', *Shakespeare Quarterly*, 30 (1979), 343–57

Howard, Jean E., and Rackin, Phyllis, *Engendering a Nation: A Feminist Account of Shakespeare's English Histories* (London, 1997)

Irving, H., and Marshall, F.A. (eds), *The Henry Irving Shakespeare* (1890)

Jackson, Sir Barry, 'On producing *Henry VI*', *Shakespeare Survey*, 6 (1953), 49–52

Jackson, Russell, and Smallwood, Robert (eds), *Players of Shakespeare 3* (Cambridge, 1993)

Jessner, Leopold, notes to his unpublished 'Theaterbuch', cited in H. Müllenmeister, 'Leopold Jessner: Geschichte eines Regiestils', D.Phil. dissertation (Cologne, 1958)

Kott, Jan, *Shakespeare Our Contemporary*, trans. Boleslaw Taborski (London, 1964)

Leech, Clifford, 'Stratford 1953', *Shakespeare Quarterly*, 4 (1953), 461–6

Lesser, Anton, 'Richard III', in Russell Jackson and Robert Smallwood (eds), *Players of Shakespeare 3* (Cambridge, 1993), 140–59

McKellen, Ian, *William Shakespeare's 'Richard III'* (London, 1996)

Noble, Adrian, introduction to Royal Shakespeare Company, *The Plantagenets, adapted from William Shakespeare's 'Henry VI, Parts I, II, III' and 'Richard III' as 'Henry VI'; 'The Rise of Edward IV'; 'Richard III, His Death'* (London, 1989), vii–xv

Pearson, Richard, *A Band of Arrogant and United Heroes* (London, 1990)

Potter, Lois, 'Recycling the early histories: "The Wars of the Roses" and "The Plantagenets"', *Shakespeare Survey*, 43 (1991), 171–81

Rackin, Phyllis, *Stages of History: Shakespeare's English Chronicles* (London, 1991)

Richmond, Hugh, *Shakespeare in Performance: King Richard III* (Manchester, 1989)

Royal Shakespeare Company, *The Plantagenets, adapted from William Shakespeare's 'Henry VI, Parts I, II, III' and 'Richard III' as 'Henry VI'; 'The Rise of Edward IV'; 'Richard III, His Death'* (London, 1989)

St Clare Byrne, Muriel, 'Fifty years of Shakespearean production: 1898–1948', *Shakespeare Survey*, 2 (1949), 1–20

Shaughnessy, Robert, *Representing Shakespeare: England, History and the RSC* (Hemel Hempstead, England, 1994)

Sher, Antony, *Year of the King* (London, 1986)

Sinfield, Alan, 'Royal Shakespeare: theatre and the making of ideology', in Jonathan Dollimore and Alan Sinfield (eds), *Political Shakespeare: Essays in Cultural Materialism* (Manchester, 1994), 182–205

Smallwood, Robert, introduction to Russell Jackson and Robert Smallwood (eds), *Players of Shakespeare 3* (Cambridge, 1993), 1–20

Smallwood, Robert, 'Shakespeare at Stratford-upon-Avon, 1992', *Shakespeare Quarterly*, 44 (1993), 343–62

Smallwood, Robert, 'Shakespeare at Stratford-upon-Avon, 1995', *Shakespeare Quarterly*, 47 (1996), 326–9

Smallwood, Robert (ed.), *Players of Shakespeare 4* (Cambridge, 1998)

Smallwood, Robert, 'Shakespeare at Stratford-upon-Avon, 1998', *Shakespeare Quarterly*, 52 (1999), 229–53

Speaight, Robert, 'The Old Vic and Stratford-upon-Avon, 1960-61', *Shakespeare Quarterly*, 12 (1961), 425–41

Speaight, Robert, 'Shakespeare in Britain', *Shakespeare Quarterly*, 15 (1964), 377–89

Speaight, Robert, 'Shakespeare in Britain', *Shakespeare Quarterly*, 21 (1970), 439–49

Thomson, Peter, 'A necessary theatre: the Royal Shakespeare Company season 1970 reviewed', *Shakespeare Survey*, 24 (1971), 117–26

Troughton, David, 'Richard III', in Robert Smallwood (ed.), *Players of Shakespeare 4* (Cambridge, 1998), 71–100

Trussler, Simon, *Cambridge Illustrated History of British Theatre* (Cambridge, 1994)

Warren, Roger, 'Shakespeare at Stratford-upon-Avon', *Shakespeare Quarterly*, 36 (1985), 79–87

FILMS

Richard III, directed by Frank Benson (UK, 1911)

Richard III, directed by M.B. Dudley (USA, 1912, 1913)

Richard III, directed by Laurence Olivier (UK, 1955)

Richard III, directed by Jane Howells, BBC Shakespeare (UK, 1983)

Richard III, directed by Michael Bogdanov, English Shakespeare Company's *The Wars of the Roses* cycle (UK, 1990)

Richard III, directed by Richard Loncraine (UK, 1996)

Looking for Richard, directed by Al Pacino (USA, 1996)

INDEX

This index includes actors, directors, critics and other individuals mentioned in the main text who are connected with a theatre or film production of *Richard III*. It also includes references to other Shakespeare plays. Page numbers in bold refer to illustrations.